The Big Picture

WAR ON SCREEN

Stacy Takacs and Tony Shaw, *Series Editors*

The Big Picture

The Cold War on the Small Screen

JOHN W. LEMZA

 UNIVERSITY PRESS OF KANSAS

Published by the University Press of Kansas (Lawrence, Kansas 66045),
which was organized by the Kansas Board of Regents and is operated and
funded by Emporia State University, Fort Hays State University, Kansas
State University, Pittsburg State University, the University of Kansas, and
Wichita State University.

Library of Congress Cataloging-in-Publication Data

Names: Lemza, John W., 1954– author.
Title: The big picture : the Cold War on the small screen / John W. Lemza.
Description: Lawrence, Kansas : University Press of Kansas, 2021. | Series:
War on screen | Includes bibliographical references and index.
Identifiers: LCCN 2020058635
  ISBN 9780700632527 (cloth)
  ISBN 9780700632534 (paperback)
  ISBN 9780700632541 (epub)
Subjects: LCSH: Big picture. | United States. Army—On television. | Cold
War on television. | National characteristics, American, on television. |
Documentary television programs—United States—History and criticism. |
Propaganda, American.
Classification: LCC UA25 .L46 2021 | DDC 791.45/6581—dc23
LC record available at https://lccn.loc.gov/2020058635.

British Library Cataloguing-in-Publication Data is available.

Printed in the United States of America

10 9 8 7 6 5 4 3 2 1

The paper used in this publication is acid free and meets the minimum
requirements of the American National Standard for Permanence of Paper
for Printed Library Materials Z39.48–1992.

Contents

Series Editor's Foreword,   *vii*

Acknowledgments,   *xi*

List of Acronyms and Abbreviations,   *xiii*

Introduction,   1

1 "Welcome to *The Big Picture*,"   13

2 Making the Army Relevant Again,   72

3 A Big Picture of the Cold War,   98

4 *The Big Picture* through an Exceptionalist Lens,   124

5 A Big Picture of the Army Way of Life,   150

Conclusion,   189

The Big Picture *Catalog,*   *197*

Notes,   *217*

Bibliography,   *253*

Index,   *259*

Series Editor's Foreword

The Big Picture: *The Cold War on the Small Screen,* by John W. Lemza, is the first in a series of books investigating the representation of war, the military, and militarism in screen media. Each book in the series focuses on a particular text or trope common to audiovisual depictions of war and the military and offers a history of the development, distribution, and reception of that text or trope. As the United States and other nations have moved away from conscription and toward the professionalization of their fighting forces, the experience of military life has become relatively mysterious to civilian publics. Films, television programs, and video games are some of the most accessible, and potentially misleading, sites for the construction of public knowledge about the military in the absence of direct experience. Not only do they produce particular, ideologically inflected ideas about life "at war" or "in camp," ideas that may then affect political priorities; they also have been instrumentalized by fighting forces as tools for recruitment, retention, and memorialization, thereby directly participating in the ongoing militarization of civil societies. A critical examination of their modus operandi can provide insight into the institutional discourses that structure and sustain military organizations, as well as the practices that generate popular support for such organizations. It can illuminate the hidden world of military life for civilians and illustrate the influence of mythography on political decision-making processes. Indeed, it can reveal the myth-making process in action.

The argument of the War on Screen series is not that films, TV shows, or video games "document" or "reflect" political processes, at least not in a simple way. It is that cultural texts of this sort shape our ideas about war, the military, and militarism and, in the process, make practices of war—or peace—more or less sustainable. John Lemza's *The Big Picture* is a prime example of the approach. Through meticulous archival research, he explicates the production, distribution, and reception history of this important television series—a series produced by the US Army's Office of the Chief Information Officer with the assistance of the US Army Signal Corps and the Army Pictorial Service. *The Big Picture* was designed as a public relations vehicle to tell the army story to a public skeptical about the need for permanent mobilization post–World War II. With the formation of new national-security state apparatuses in 1947, including the creation of a Defense Department, Joint Chiefs of Staff, and a separate air force, *The Big Picture* became a vehicle through which the Army tried to reshape its identity and sell its relevance to politicians easily distracted by shiny new weapons and modes of warfare (atom bombs, ballistic missiles, air war, maneuver warfare). *The Big Picture* also contributed to public morale-building efforts during the Cold War by explaining the nation's political creeds to soldiers and civilians alike. As Lemza shows, *The Big Picture* offered a primer on American history, political doctrines, and shared value systems and, both implicitly and explicitly, contrasted "our" values to those embraced by the Soviet state. The program didn't just explain "who we (Americans) are," "what we stand for," or "why we must fight." It became a major vector through which to propagate the state's mythic conceptions of national identity and purpose, particularly, as Lemza notes, the exceptionalist canard that Americans are reluctant fighters.

The Big Picture was distributed through syndication to over 300 stations in dozens of markets for over twenty years (1951–1971), making it one of the longest-running TV series in history. Its programs were used into the 1970s for internal army orientation purposes and delivered to a captive audience of millions of military personnel stationed on US bases overseas via the American Forces Network. Multiple generations of future army officers claim it inspired their love of service and helped foster better civil-military relations through partnerships with organizations such as the Boy Scouts and the United Service Organizations (USO). And, of course, it was used as a recruitment and retention vehicle, enticing young Americans into military service with its promises of education, high-tech training, and adventure. Perhaps its most important legacy, however, is the way it humanized the US soldier, inspiring faith in the skill, dedication, and purpose of American service men and women charged with defending the nation. I believe we can see in the series the roots of our current mandate to "support the troops," no matter the cause or their actions.

Because the series charts many of the important shifts in foreign policy and military doctrine from 1951 to 1971, it can be used in college courses or public talks to document those shifts, but, as Lemza argues, strict documentary it ain't. Particularly for college classrooms, this companion to *The Big Picture* can be used alongside the films themselves to inspire critical thinking about the motives behind, and inevitable slant of, the documentary texts. Using it in this way would enable instructors to denaturalize the Cold War consensus and open space for richer discussions of history as a process of negotiation and compromise. As a production history, moreover, *The Big Picture* raises important issues of access (who can speak), power (who can be heard), and impact (what people make of the message) that are central to media literacy, history, and archival studies. For all of these reasons, *The Big Picture* should be a welcome addition to the college curriculum. Military buffs, too, will find much here to cherish, as the book provides the only systematic review of the *Big Picture* catalog—a catalog that stretches to some 600 episodes! As a production of the Department of Defense, *The Big Picture* television series has always been part of the public domain, and you can find many of the episodes on the internet. However, the full body of episodes is available only at the National Archives and Records Administration in College Park, Maryland, which has released only a small sample of *The Big Picture* output. If you want to know more about the episodes that *can't* be found online, this is the book for you!

Certainly, *The Big Picture* is a hallmark of American television history and has influenced the thinking of generations of Americans, both in and out of the service. As a set of expository documentaries, capturing the birth of the modern army and its Cold War–era doctrines, it remains an important tool of military history, and as a glimpse into the bygone past, it traces the nation's changing relationship to war, the military, and militarism. John Lemza's *The Big Picture* provides a big-picture view of the series' historical, social, and cultural relevance, and we hope you will enjoy moving beyond the "worm's eye view" of the series heretofore available.

Stacy Takacs
Professor of American Studies and Screen Studies
Oklahoma State University

Acknowledgments

I want to express my gratitude to those individuals who contributed to shaping and informing this work. Beginning with an invitation to participate in the book series, editor Stacy Takacs has provided valuable guidance and helpful suggestions that have added to the quality and scholarship of the manuscript. I am also particularly appreciative for the assistance provided by archives specialist Suzanne Zoumbaris, whose knowledge and expertise helped navigate the vastness of the holdings at the NARA College Park Campus to discover documents necessary to the completion of this work. Thanks to Rich Zimmermann, who contributed from his vast family collection to share images and valuable information about his father, Carl Zimmermann. I am grateful to Joyce Harrison at the University Press of Kansas who has continued to provide guidance and support through the publishing process, and to the reviewers who provided critical readings and insights that contributed significantly to the improvement of the manuscript. I am ever grateful for the support of my wife, Laura, who is always my rock. I also offer this work in memory of Dr. Marion Deshmukh, mentor, colleague, and friend.

Acronyms and Abbreviations

ABC	American Broadcasting Company
AFI&E	Armed Forces Information and Education Program
AMVETS	American Veterans (nonprofit organization)
APC	Army Pictorial Center
ARC	Archival Research Catalog
ASDPA	assistant secretary of defense, public affairs
CBS	Columbia Broadcasting System
CINFO	chief of information
DOD	Department of Defense
FCC	Federal Communications Commission
HUAC	House Un-American Activities Committee
NATO	North Atlantic Treaty Organization
NARA	National Archives and Records Administration
NATO	North Atlantic Treaty Organization
NBC	National Broadcasting Company
OCINFO	Office of the Chief of Information
OCS	Officer Candidate School
PIO	Public Information Office
POW	prisoner of war
ROTC	Reserve Officer Training Corps
R-T	Radio-Television Branch
SECDEF	secretary of defense
TID	Troop Information Division
USAREUR	United States Army Europe
USNR	United States Naval Reserve
USAF	United States Air Force
USIA	United States Information Agency
WAC	Women's Army Corps

Introduction

It was during one of his many World War II combat tours that the popular, genial, and often exhausted war correspondent Ernie Pyle remarked:

> I haven't written anything about the Big Picture, because I don't know anything about it. I only know what we see from our worm's-eye view, and our segment of this picture consists only of tired and dirty soldiers who are alive and don't want to die; of long darkened convoys in the middle of the night; of shocked, silent men wandering back down the hill from battle; of chow lines and atabrine tablets and foxholes and burning tanks.[1]

Perhaps it was because they understood Pyle's comments about that narrowed perspective that Lieutenants Carl Bruton and David Burkey, together with a small group of US Army officers, conceptualized a film series that offered to widen the lens of understanding for service members, their families, and the general public. While serving in the US Army during the early years of the Korean War, Bruton and Burkey realized that thousands of feet of accumulated combat footage lay unused. Captured by the combat cameramen of the Army Signal Corps, reels of film that included "highly dramatic scenes taken during combat operations" were available to craft into a video narrative of the events occurring during that conflict.[2] Seizing the moment, they began work on the documentary television series that in late 1951 would become *The Big Picture*, "the Department of the Army's first TV project of its kind."[3]

Bruton and Burkey's idea that sparked an innovative project to simply provide an expanded view of the war to the American public caught the energy of emerging contemporary technology. It was at this intersection of need and innovation that they realized opportunity. Although it would take years to fully develop the concept into a popularly recognized television series, *The Big Picture* did evolve into a vehicle whose intention was to help the army tell its story, sell its relevance in the emerging Cold War, connect with the audience, and inform and educate them about American ideals. In doing so, it would also lend a human face to those individuals who wore the uniform. Woven into the narratives of these episodes were messages that emerged and took shape from the energies of the early post-1945 zeitgeist. These served as themes that coursed through the catalog of shows informing productions that reflected a national mood that was anticommunist, steeped in exceptional American foundational principles, and too trusting of elite leadership.

This study reveals, however, that the longer *The Big Picture* maintained those themes the more they began to lose their resonance, especially when the cultural and social environments of the United States began changing in the mid-1960s. In that context, the war in Vietnam served as a turning point for the show as it did for prevailing national attitudes. Under those conditions, some politically progressive elites and members of the public cast the light of criticism on the show, judging the earlier messages as growing faded and stale, disconnected from contemporary interpretations of America's global role and responsibilities. It stands as a critical flaw that the series' producers never sought to adapt to these changes, other than adoption of technological advancements. Instead, they chose to continue to navigate a course that was set during the early Cold War years. As a result, the credibility of the show began to suffer, and it endured some alienation as it remained a public theater for overtly conservative, exceptionalist values.

Throughout the course of its two-decade production run, however, *The Big Picture* cast a big shadow over similar television shows of its time. It outlasted many of the original news and information productions that focused on politics and the military. The *Armed Forces Hour*, *Battle Report*, and *The Facts We Face* preceded it, yet disappeared soon after the *Big Picture* arrived on the scene. Other shows that followed on its heels, such as *On Guard* and *Navy Log*, were born of similar creative energies but lacked the staying power. Within a few years, they also disappeared from television screens, leaving the *Big Picture* as the single, premier military banner carrier from the late 1950s until its termination in the early 1970s. Its primacy was never seriously challenged, and by 1970 the army's *Information Officer's Guide* still considered the show to be the "Army's official documentary television effort."[4] Notching more than 800 episodes to its credit, *The Big Picture* found its way to viewing audiences first through prime-time television slots, then via syndication. This included hundreds of subsidiary stations nationwide and dozens of Armed Forces Network (AFN) affiliates overseas. Several soft estimates vary on the population size of its viewers over the years, but all place it in the millions.

Notably, a large segment of *The Big Picture* audience was composed of military members, their families, and civilian government employees. For them, a portion of their exposure to the show came through the Armed Forces Information and Education Program (AFI&E), broadcast via the AFN, as episodes that provided lessons in American ideals. Overall, a survey of *The Big Picture* catalog shows that it offered a wide variety of episodes to satisfy the curiosity of viewers with an interest in the army and the military, particularly military history buffs, those with an interest in the Cold War and life in the military, and media historians. It also had an appeal for veterans from World War II through Vietnam, whose interest in specific titles flowed from their personal experience and memories or their affiliation with wartime units. Still, there is no source, survey or poll, which provides data specifically on the composition of *The Big Picture*'s audience. The catalog of episodes however, suggests titles that would have an appeal for these various groups both inside and outside the military.

There were dozens of features on military history and heritage, at least a score on emerging technologies, many on the army's roles and missions, numerous on specific units, and a plethora on the army way of life. As this study reveals, all of these were the work of the Army Pictorial Center (APC) producers, who successfully adapted the template set by the popular compilation documentaries of the 1950s, ala *Crusade in Europe* and *Victory at Sea*, to create the *Big Picture*. They engaged emerging video and audio technologies, married with gripping camera work and script writing, to breathe life into the show's narratives and grab the attention of their audience. By the time *The Big Picture* had run its course, it had garnered a number of awards from the Freedoms Foundation, a conservative think tank, as well as several Emmys from the more widely recognized National Academy of Television Arts and Sciences. Some particular episodes garnered special recognition. "The Song of the Soldier" (TV-725) received critical acclaim for the moving artistic performances of the army chorus and band, and John Huston's World War II documentary "Battle of San Pietro" (TV-431) won accolades for its composition and direction under battlefield conditions. Further investigation of these productions, and the hundreds of others, also brings to light the centrality of Hollywood, its actors, directors, and skilled crew members, who contributed significantly to the creative process for the television series.

The Big Picture was the army's effort to harness the energies emanating from Hollywood during the early Cold War decades. As the movie capital began producing films that addressed and exported American ideals, television, the new technological child, followed suit. This study locates *The Big Picture* in that slipstream. It argues that this show, like others produced for television during that time by the armed forces, served as a vehicle for directed propaganda, scripted to send important Cold War messages to those in uniform as well as to the American public. Using *The Big Picture* as the vehicle for this study, the book attempts to show how the producers incorporated specific Cold War themes, such as anticommunism, into episodes, and how the integration of various approaches facilitated those efforts. It also highlights the army's continuing efforts to sell Americanism using *The Big Picture* as a conduit of the military's Information and Education Program. In this context, the book situates *The Big Picture* series, a scion of television's small screen, at the intersection of propaganda and policy during the Cold War period. It offers a perspective from a specific military-themed weekly series where there have been few previous comprehensive scholarly studies of this type. It amplifies existing studies such as Nancy Bernhard's *U.S. Television News and Cold War Propaganda, 1947–1960*, Thomas Doherty's *Cold War, Cool Medium: Television, McCarthyism, and American Culture*, and Anna Froula and Stacy Takacs's *American Militarism on the Small Screen*. It completes the discussions about the influence of military-themed shows begun in single chapter and article pieces such as Jeffrey Crean's "Something to Compete with Gunsmoke: *The Big Picture* Television Series and Selling a Modern, Progressive and Forward Thinking Army," and J. Fred MacDonald's "The Cold War as Entertainment in Fifties Television." In addition, this study complements works such as Tony Shaw's *Hollywood's Cold War* and Lawrence Suid's *Guts and Glory: The Making of the American Military Image in Film*. It accomplishes this by serving as a bridge between the big and small screens, particularly in the discussion of transitioning the military motif through *The Big Picture* into a weekly television series. In a similar manner, this work follows the adaptation of the compilation documentary form from the big ticket productions like *Victory at Sea*, as discussed by A. William Bluem in *Documentary in American Television: Form, Function, Method*, to a suitable weekly television serialization. Just as important, when examined from the perspective of students of media studies, this work offers insights into the development of a television series that was born of a collaboration between corporate networks and the military during the early tense years of the Cold War. In this context, it works through seldom investigated internal and external CINFO correspondence to unpack the struggles producers had in keeping the show relevant, within budget, and accessible to audiences.

Gaining an appreciation for the evolution of *The Big Picture*, its impact and influence on early Cold War American culture and society, and its effectiveness in shaping attitudes toward the army required an examination that plumbed the depths of the extensive number of episodes, located in various collections. Of those, the National Archives and Records Administration at College Park, Maryland, contained more than half. This investigative approach, which incorporated a close review of the films, was logical and essential to this work as being the most effective way to come to terms with the variety of subjects, the composition of the films, and the messages they communicated. It also shed light on the timing of the release of episodes, which this study notes became important to maximize the effectiveness of the delivery of the messages. It was in this that *The Big Picture* had an impact in proving the army's relevancy during the Cold War competition with its sister services. Also important in this approach was the introduction of first-person voices. These appeared in several ways. The first was through interviews by the show's first narrator, Captain Carl Zimmermann, who spoke in the studio with veterans of recent battlefield experience. This technique appeared in several of the early episodes, from "The Turning of the Tide" (TV-170) through "The UN Line Is Stabilized While Truce Talks Continue" (TV-181). Combat camera operators who captured eyewitness accounts on-site while filming also contributed interviews. Producers then wove these into episodes such as "Atrocities in Korea" (TV-242) and "Christmas in Korea" (TV-244) to lend a human voice to the narrative. These recordings, made during tactical operations in Korea, were very effective in adding a certain texture and poignancy to the framed moment, as were the in-studio interviews with veterans. The second manner in which producers incorporated personal impressions was through the accumulated experiences and reflections of service members, the public, and veterans who watched the show, postproduction. Although this provided a slightly altered viewpoint, these voices contributed to an understanding of the show's impact and supported a grassroots perspective. This approach was important in completing a thorough evaluation of the television series in its role as a key representative of the army that sought to inform and educate viewers and offer the broadest range of perspectives from the mud-level through the highest echelons.

Relying on *The Big Picture* films to sketch a full story was, however, not without its challenges. Often, it appeared that other online sites offered many of the episodes missing from the NARA collection. Because this was the case, there was a wide variance in quality, and inconsistencies existed among titles and control numbers. The episodes found in the NARA archives were professionally digitized and complete, and included reference numbers as well as concise textual summaries. Although these were generally of a good quality, they had a certain amount of variation in the video and audio quality based on the limitations of the original films. Most episodes discovered through other online sources however, were of a lesser quality, as second- or third-generation copies, and suffered occasional rough editing that excluded the introduction or conclusion. Additionally, many contained no narrative summary. Often these non-NARA recordings carried no identifying catalog number, and sometimes they displayed titles that did not match the film content. There was also the potential for other-sourced films to disappear from an online site if original sources revoked permissions. Occasionally, when an episode was located both in the NARA archive and at an online source, the titles did not match. One other challenge, not often encountered, was that some films were not available digitally, either through an archive, such as NARA, or any other site. There were nine catalog numbers that did not have any reference or film associated with them. The designation "Not Available" indicates these in the catalog listing of this book. There were also some episode numbers listed in the catalog that research indicates the producers intentionally did not use. The designation "Not Used in the Big Picture Series" indicates those. That is the case for nine episode identifiers, TV-188, TV-195, TV-209, TV-405, and TV-497 through TV-501. The APC may have canceled their production while in progress, or blocked their release after completion for a number of reasons, including cost overrun or appropriateness of content. One example is "Your Army Reports Number 17," which is missing from the catalog with no explanation. It was also nearly the case for the eponymously titled episode "Atrocities in Korea" (TV-242), which this study addresses later. In addition to all of these, the NARA collection included a number of short film pieces that the Signal Corps cameramen made specifically for potential use in *Big Picture* episodes. Often these did not appear in the catalog. Among them were a series of interviews of soldiers on the front lines during the Korean War captured for possible incorporation into episodes about that conflict.[5] Other brief supplemental films included scenes of helicopters, MASH units, and military chapel activities.

Although these proved to be excess, and did not find their way into any production, they serve as examples of the extent that the APC dedicated manpower and resources to the production of the television series. Regardless of the variety, and complications and challenges found in the archives, more than enough episodes were available for this work to complete a comprehensive examination of *The Big Picture* series. This included viewing more than 200 hours of video footage to accomplish the study.

Another shortfall that became apparent while working with materials from the archives and other record repositories is an absence of documentation, such as letters, meeting memos, or notes, that corroborates certain decisions made in the production process for *The Big Picture*. Although there is documentation, cited in this study, to support discussions regarding the planning of some future episodes, reactions to budgetary shortfalls, distribution of films, and general operations, other areas lack this. For example, no documentation reports the development of episodes on race or gender, and no recorded evidence addresses the impact or influence of the Vietnam series of films on the American public. In cases such as this, this study relies on cinematic evidence to develop interpretations of the production process.

Based on the collection of films, the narrative of this study took a form that is both chronological and thematic. Within that structure the work appears into two sections. The first section, which is contained in chapters 1 and 2, investigates the origins of *The Big Picture* series following a chronological trail of its evolution and includes its relationship with emerging technology and early conceptualization. The second section, which includes chapters 3, 4, and 5, divides the film catalog into three general thematic subcategories with the intention of making the investigation more manageable. An initial survey indicated that the majority of episodes could easily be collected under one of these headings based on content and purpose. That approach served to situate each episode into one of the three categories, which are the Cold War, American exceptionalism, and the army way of life. These subcategories then form the framework for each of the three later chapters.

Chapter one of this study, "'Welcome to *The Big Picture*,'" recounts the initial conceptualization of *The Big Picture* and the group of talented army officers that created the show from miles of underutilized combat camera footage of the Korean War. It explores the genesis of the series, describing the early production and directors and the development of a deeper catalog of titles. The chapter also introduces the Army Pictorial Center's close relationship with Hollywood before and during the production of *The Big Picture*. This includes the use of popular actors, personalities, and skilled cinematographers from the film industry, who added their expertise to the creative process. It examines aspects of film form and techniques that production managers incorporated and exploited throughout the process to maximize the full effects of the media as a propaganda vehicle. This incorporates a discussion of the new, mutually beneficial partnership between the military and the television industry and the adoption of evolving video and audio technologies to facilitate a more effective reception of *The Big Picture* messages. It also examines the decision to transition the show from prime-time television slots to syndication as a means of reaching a wider audience and avoiding external commercial control. Overall, the chapter serves as a chronological springboard for those that follow and illuminates the three overarching subcategories.

Chapter 2, "Making the Army Relevant Again," discusses the plethora of challenges the army faced to present itself as a relevant postwar branch of the service. To support that effort, *The Big Picture* offered a number of titles from its catalog that showcased the restructuring of the army to fit the mold of the New Look military and to engage with science and emerging technologies. This chapter presents that effort through an examination of episodes that highlight the service's initiatives, and achievements, in space and north of the Arctic Circle as it competed with its sister branches of the military for recognition and resourcing. Also intrinsic to an examination of the trajectory of *The Big Picture*'s existence is an investigation of the slings and arrows of criticism that the series endured. These came principally from those elites and members of Congress who on occasion perceived the series as overstepping its bounds in attempting to shape and inform public opinion on issues of domestic and foreign policy. This becomes evident in a discussion of the series of episodes produced about the Vietnam War.

Chapter 3, "A Big Picture of the Cold War," addresses the army's central role in the nation's Cold War defensive strategy through the lens of *The Big Picture*. The collection of episodes presented here lend themselves to selling an understanding of the fundamental tensions between the East and the West that formed the crucible of the contemporary geopolitical struggle. The study reveals how *The Big Picture* served as a weapon to deflect propaganda from the East and as a vehicle to explain to service personnel and the American public the concept of the containment strategy, the cornerstone of national defense. It also explains the special relationship between the United States and other nations through alliances that formed mutually supportive defense pacts. Here, it emphasizes that the United States "as leader in the free world has allied itself with other nations dedicated to the preservation of peace and the welfare of Mankind."[6] In addition, the chapter uses the lens of *The Big Picture* to offer explanations and insights to those critical moments in the games of brinksmanship between the superpowers that were typical of that tense period, such as construction of the Berlin Wall and the Cuban Missile Crisis. In developing the Cold War view, the chapter refers to the more than eighty episodes that are collected here that painted a picture of America's commitment to defend the West from an encroaching communist hegemony. The sights and sounds lent to the presentations by the films provide an informative and comprehensive understanding of the Cold War.

Chapter 4, "*The Big Picture* through an Exceptionalist Lens," discusses those foundational ideals that shaped the American identity in the early post-1945 decades. *The Big Picture* took viewers down Main Street, USA, to reveal how Americans inculcated the exceptionalist ideals into their lives and how that influenced the tenets that became one with the American way of life. As an instrumental part of the military's Information and Education Program, *The Big Picture* was key to informing and educating the military and the public on the "fundamental convictions of citizenship."[7] It contributed to this understanding through narratives that showed how these characteristics resonated in the daily lives of the nation's people and soldiers, and reinforced it with images of parades and patriotic celebrations. Coupled to that was the centrality of religious worship, also described by *The Big Picture* as an essential element of the national ethos. As the episode "America on the Move" (TV-549) declared, "The film you are about to see was designed to sharpen the American serviceman's sense of identity with the spirit and purpose of the nation he serves in this moment of historic urgency."[8] It is in this chapter that a fuller understanding of the uniqueness that Americans claim as their own right was an underpinning for the fabric of the national character as much as it was for the esprit of the military.

Chapter 5, "A Big Picture of the Army Way of Life," provides a more grassroots view of the army through a lens that generally focuses on the issues that affected the daily lives of those in uniform and those associated with them. This subcategory of the study includes episodes that illuminate interesting facts about the history of the army and its heritage, subjects that captured the attention of viewers who were interested in that profession of arms. Also included are films that discuss the opportunities available through educational benefits, a path to upward mobility for soldiers, and discussions about army leadership. The latter discussed the various routes for advancement to the officer corps for enlisted personnel and provided background information about the processes, through West Point, ROTC, and OCS. Also very important to the army, and the military in general, was the issue of increasing diversity. This chapter investigates the ways that *The Big Picture* did double duty in that regard. First, the episodes recognize the army's efforts at inclusion, reflecting the changes in contemporary society. This includes the challenges it faced and the reality of its shortcomings. Second, the show served as a recruitment tool for marginalized groups and women. To accomplish this, producers incorporated images and narratives that portrayed scenes of racially integrated units and narratives that spoke of the improved opportunities for women. In both instances, the films depicted minorities and women in positions of leadership. The show's producers offered several episodes that emphasized the importance and contributions of the Army Nurse Corps and the Women's Army Corps (WAC) over the years, featuring the women's training center that was "commanded and staffed exclusively by women."[9]

Chapter 5 also addresses the military's involvement with community service. The APC produced episodes to inform the viewing public of the army's participation at the national level in disaster relief efforts, at the local level to support youth programs, and as an informational platform to endorse special agendas such as President Kennedy's fitness campaign. Above all, they were to underscore the army's understanding of "the importance of being a good neighbor."[10] An additional view of life at the grass-roots level appears in the introduction of episodes about entertainment for the troops. A number of shows discuss Hollywood's commitment to raising the morale of soldiers deployed overseas during wartime and peacetime. Here, the script highlights the contributions made by nonprofit organizations such as the United Service Organizations (USO) and celebrates the role of popular entertainers such as Bob Hope in boosting spirits. Finally, the chapter includes a discussion on the centrality of civilian government employees as critical and necessary members of the army structure. This becomes evident through a number of episodes such as "The Army's Civilians" (TV-726), which highlights their contributions at many levels for the military at home and abroad.

As this study reveals, *The Big Picture* television series was central to the army's effort to tell its story, sell its relevance in the emerging Cold War, connect with the viewing audience, and deliver a message that would inform and educate viewers about American ideals. In that context, it also serves to contribute to the scholarly investigation of military-themed programming on television by offering an examination of "televisual depictions of the military and its operations."[11] During the course of its two-decade production run the service used the series as a conduit to send messages to elites, the public, service members, and civilian government employees and their families that spoke to contemporary themes such as anticommunism and the ideals of American exceptionalism. On more than one occasion, *The Big Picture* became a target for critics who saw the series as exercising too much influence in its ability to shape public opinion, but this never seemed to detract fully from the popularity of the show. In the final analysis, *The Big Picture* was a successful public relations platform for the army that outlasted its contemporaries and provided an accurate depiction of army life and attitudes, while garnering accolades for the quality and variety of its productions. Considering the turbulent times, it also added a human face to those individuals who wore the uniform.

1

"Welcome to *The Big Picture*"

The crew that came together to move this project forward were not unacquainted with mass media communications. One of the first producers of *The Big Picture*, Carl Bruton, had worked for WTVJ radio in Miami prior to his service in Korea. David Burkey had spent time as a television producer, and the first series announcer, Carl Zimmermann, had worked as a writer for the Milwaukee radio station WEMP-AM. He had also seen service as an army broadcast correspondent during World War II.[1] Together with production supervisor William Brown Jr., and director Carl Flint, they would form the initial nucleus of the series production team at the Army Pictorial Center (APC) that worked under the supervision of Colonel Edward M. Kirby.[2] He would function as the first series distributor for the army in his position as head of the Radio-Television Branch, Office of Public Information, for the Department of the Army.[3] With the creative team in place, production of *The Big Picture* could begin in earnest. This chapter explores the genesis of the series, describing its early production and directors and the eventual development of a deeper catalog of titles. It follows the APC's close relationship with Hollywood before and during the production of *The Big Picture* and the new, mutually beneficial partnership between the military and the television industry. Also addressed is the adoption of evolving video and audio production technologies and the transition of the show away from prime-time television slots to syndication as a strategy to reach a wider audience.

The First Thirteen

Expanding on the close focus of battlefield experiences, the first thirteen episodes of *The Big Picture* concentrated exclusively on the Korean conflict. Against a video backdrop of fleeing refugees, columns of foot-weary soldiers, grinding tanks, and raucous artillery explosions, a somber voice-over presented each show to viewers with the explanation that "this is war, war and its masses, war and its men, war and its machines. Together they form *The Big Picture*." After a brief fadeout, a uniformed Carl Zimmermann welcomed viewers with a serious, flat intonation:

> Welcome to *The Big Picture*. I'm Captain Carl Zimmermann. *The Big Picture* is a report to you, from your army, an army committed by you, the people of the United States, to stop communist aggression wherever it may strike. *The Big Picture* during the next thirteen weeks will trace the course of events of the Korean campaign, with firsthand reports from our combat veterans and film taken by combat cameramen of the Army Signal Corps. These are men who daily record on film *The Big Picture* as it happens, where it happens.[4]

That statement regularly introduced each episode just as Zimmermann would conclude every show with a short summary of events and an invitation to viewers to return the following week. In addition, the closing series of images for each of these initial episodes displayed credits noting the documentary was a presentation of the US Army and a production of the Signal Corps Photographic Center. It also noted that Lieutenant Carl Bruton had been the original producer, thus providing a passing nod of recognition to another of the original creators of the series.

The focus of these first twenty-eight-minute-long episodes addressed the American experience in Korea from the first forty days of

Figure 1.1. Captain Carl Zimmermann in the field. As did all of the other early *Big Picture* narrators, he would gain his experience interviewing and broadcasting while serving with the US Army Signal Corps during wartime. (Image Source: Rich Zimmermann)

the conflict, through joint operations with United Nations troops and the ebb and flow of combat, to the final stabilization of a cease-fire line as both sides participated in truce talks.[5] They offered a mud-level GI perspective, complementing it with a broader understanding of events. That provided a revised, elevated view through the context of a bigger picture of intents and purposes for US involvement in Korea. Leading narratives offered to mimic the dog-faced style of Ernie Pyle by claiming, "This story is best told in the language of the soldier who was there."[6] Scriptwriters capitalized on that approach and continually laced the text with on-the-ground expressions such as "Okay, we're here to delay the Reds, let's go!" and homespun comments like "The whole world had seen this [communist aggression] and knew what the score was."[7] Actors portraying typical GIs voiced these comments, and that comfortable, relatable dialogue ensured the attention of the average viewer. To reinforce this approach, Carl Zimmermann often conducted on-camera interviews of soldiers recently returned from the war regarding their experiences.

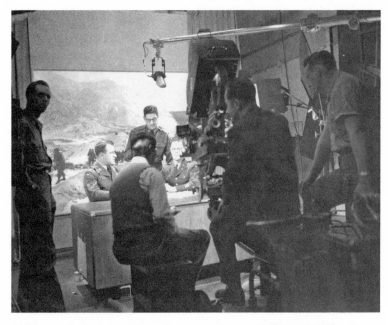

Figure 1.2. Captain Carl Zimmermann on the set of *The Big Picture* at the Signal Corps Pictorial Center in late 1951. He was the first narrator and remained the face of the series through the forty-first episode (TV-210). (Image Source: Rich Zimmermann)

Always aware of their commitment to provide a bigger picture of ongoing events, the show's producers complemented the film scripts with more expansive explanations. For this Korean War series, it would include the use of visual displays, such as graphics depicting operational troop movements on a map of the Korean peninsula. Carl Zimmermann always accompanied these with an explanation describing the larger theater campaign and related actions. Another technique was the production of episodes that described the wider role of the United Nations' involvement as part of the coalition of forces, and the United States' relationship to those nations.[8] The narrative also made frequent reference to the actions and decision-making of higher-ranking officers involved in the peninsular campaign, such as General Douglas MacArthur. Ernie Pyle might have agreed that this short thirteen-episode documentary series had adequately addressed the narrow grassroots focus as well as a broader perspective of the war. The existence of this collection of films contradicts some statements suggesting that the military made little effort to capture the Korean conflict on camera. As the art curator at the Army Center for Military History noted, there had been "no organized effort by either the Army or the private sector, to visually capture the Korean War, so the Army's collection has relatively few images of that war."[9] As *The Big Picture* series proves, this is not the case.

This initial body of episodes, which aired on CBS, set the tone for the show and became a model for the successful *Big Picture* series that would eventually produce more than 800 episodes over the following twenty years. However, more than simply satisfying the curiosity of service members and the American public, these early films also set several important production goals that framed the content of future *Big Picture* episodes.

Coming into Focus

Foremost among the initial goals set for the series was a clear anticommunist assertion. Just as Carl Zimmermann would declare, *The Big Picture* was a report from the army to the American people on the actions taken to check communist aggression "wherever it may strike." That pronouncement came at a time when former wartime allies, particularly the Soviet Union and China, had suddenly transformed into adversaries on the post-1945 global stage. As the United States was engaged in a new game of geopolitical brinksmanship, which included a dangerous nuclear dynamic, it was important that the nation bring to bear all available tools and weapons to deflect the perceived hegemonic intentions of the communists. *The Big Picture* would serve as a Cold War clarion call to shake viewers to wakefulness and action. It would deliver messages of warning about new enemies' evil designs while highlighting America's resoluteness and successes in defending the exceptional American way of life.[10] Although at times dampened, that theme would remain constant throughout the entire series, as this study will show.

After the initial run of thirteen episodes, other goals began to emerge, such as the maintenance of a strong bond between the army and the American public. Telling the "army story" was a key to cultivating that relationship. *The Big Picture* would contain scripted narratives that offered a multidimensional image of the soldier, cast in the light of a contemporary "sentimental militarism."[11] It presented them in heroic form as guardians of American values, defenders against evil, and rescuers of those in need.[12] In addition, it would depict soldiers as ambassadors of goodwill to other nations, and in a more human light show them as citizens, family members, and individuals with basic needs.[13] Episodes would showcase them in the mold of the citizen-soldier of the new army, a product of a greater democratization.[14] One of the techniques used in cementing that bond was the periodic production of army heritage stories that cast the service in a historical light. The series did this by weaving the army's past accomplishments and sacrifices into the broader tapestry of American history. Episodes such as "The History of Cavalry" (TV-382), "Patterns of History" (TV-550), "Old Glory" (TV-625), and "Our Heritage" (TV-684) showcased the army's role in America's past and plucked at a common patriotic chord. Other episodes that focused on the history of particular military units or posts, or on World War II campaigns and battles, played on the same emotion by creating a connection with veterans who may have seen service then. Nicholas Worontsoff Jr., recalls watching the show with his father, a World War II veteran:

It was on TV on Saturday mornings, very early, like 7:00 AM. The show I remember the most was the one I watched with Dad. He somehow learned that an episode was going to be about Fort Monmouth. Dad was stationed at Fort Monmouth I believe after he was first inducted. This was the training center for the Signal Corps of which Dad was in. I remember Dad watching the program and pointing out buildings he remembered, or was in and whether it was used for training, or barracks, etc. Also he recognized some of the men that were shown. I guess he was really interested in seeing whether he was in any of the film footage. Back then we did not have the ability to tape the show, or rewind or watch in slow motion. I don't remember him pointing himself out.[15]

Consequently, *The Big Picture* was a point of contact between the army and the American public, serving as "a mediating point between the

Army's internal image-makers and the wider world of public opinion."[16]

The majority of ideas for these heritage series came from information officers (IO) stationed at various posts who wished to see their particular units or locations recognized for their historical contributions. Another important source were senior military commanders who also felt recognition was due for their particular branch of the service. One example was a recommendation from the chief of the Armored Section of the US Continental Army Command, who requested that the APC produce an episode on the history of the armor branch. This request came after he had viewed "The History of Cavalry" (TV-382).[17] For years the army continued to produce these heritage films seeking to attract a supportive public audience and to celebrate its remarkable past. By 1959, however, Colonel John Weaver, chief of the Troop Information Division, began to view these episodes with a jaundiced eye. In a letter to Colonel W. E. Slisher, Fifth Army chief, Information Section, he opined that these were fast becoming "innocuous" documentaries "that display the Army of the past. A good Army and one with a great history—BUT it is an Army that is not comparable to the Army of today."[18] He thought the series was suffering "excessive dependence on past glories."[19] This concern sprang from worries that the army was failing to achieve an Atomic Age relevance. It was his opinion that the APC needed to shift the focus of its production to *Big Picture* episodes that promoted the army as a modernizing force. Over time, producers gradually set aside development of additional heritage series projects in favor of those that showed the army as more competitive with the other services. For example, this new approach appeared in episodes that featured army operations above the Arctic Circle, such as "Operation Lead Dog" (TV-494), and those that highlighted the collaboration between the army and industry, as in "Partners in Progress" (TV-505). Although the heritage episodes did not disappear completely, they did begin to lose some of their production momentum.

Another purpose the *Big Picture* series served was to act as an advertising platform to gain and maintain the confidence and interest of the elites in power, particularly in Congress. Aside from being informational, these episodes were video appeals that hoped to shape the outcome during interservice wrangling for favorable resource allocations. All of this was important to the army, as well as each of the other services, during the annual round of budgetary and appropriations discussions on Capitol Hill, as each branch attempted to project itself as the most important for national defense, and the neediest. Under such circumstances, the *Big Picture* series could hope to garner support for army programs, technology, and weapons systems. Lawrence Suid, historian of military-related films, alludes to that interservice competition when he notes that the navy, like the army, "maintained that it was trying to have filmmakers present the service, in the best light possible," with the hope "to achieve that aim in time."[20] For the army this was a matter of survival in its competition with the other two services, which were more reliant on costly weapons systems. In this, the army struggled to answer the perennial question, "What role, if any, did conventional force play with respect to the deterrence of Soviet aggression?"[21] The shadow of that challenge appeared in the successive 1953–1956 rounds of Pentagon allocations, which reduced the army's operating budget by half. By 1957, the military's budget was $34 billion—$16 billion to the air force (49 percent), $10 billion to the navy (29 percent), and $7.5 billion to the army (22 percent).[22] This would remain a critical issue for the army until the early 1960s, when funding for operations in Vietnam would demand an increase across the board for all the services. But until then, the *Big Picture* series would serve as the vehicle to communicate the army's relevance through modernization and technological advancement, subjects explored in greater detail later in this study. For example, episodes such as "Meeting Tomorrow's Challenge" (TV-765) and "Pioneering for Tomorrow" (TV-815) were aired to assure the viewer that their modern army was forward thinking while suggesting that support and resourcing were necessary ingredients for future success. Although its purpose was to tout the army, the *Big Picture* nevertheless did with a spirit of bonhomie, and only after global tensions increased, air several episodes that celebrated the other services.[23] While it is difficult to determine the direct influence that the *Big Picture* series had on congressional decision-making, it did leave an impression.

Between 1957 and 1986, congressional hearings referenced *The Big Picture* three times, and the *Congressional Record* referenced it an additional fifteen times. Although those comments were not linked to funding of specific technologies or weapons systems, they did provide opportunities to keep *The Big Picture*, and the army, current in the minds of individual members of both houses and select committees. This was the case with references to the television series during the congressional hearings of 1956 and 1958 regarding allocations of television frequencies for the rapidly expanding national and regional television audiences of America. In each of these hearings, television executives from around the nation included *The Big Picture* when citing examples of educational and informational programming that viewers preferred. In January 1958, John R. Holden, national legislative director, AMVETS, testified to oppose a proposal to make all television viewing subscription based, noting that it would threaten the "destruction of our traditional free method of TV" and levy heavy costs on military veterans who could ill afford them.[24] He further stated that the associated loss of commercial advertising would jeopardize funding of "programs on behalf of public-service organizations," fearing that "national-defense programs would be eliminated" including "Armed Forces programs," in particular "patriotic programs [such] as the *Big Picture*."[25]

The *Congressional Record* contains references to *The Big Picture* beginning in 1957. Representative Charles O. Porter from Oregon inserted that first mention of the show into the record. It was a simple letter from a fourth-grade student to his teacher in support of a recorded version of the "Pledge of Allegiance." The recording grabbed the student's attention when he heard it played in school and he commented, "When our teacher plays that record it makes me think of 'The Big Picture' (it is a television program)."[26] This at the very least was recognition that *The Big Picture* was associated with a patriotic consciousness and was having some impact among a younger American demographic. Still other references followed. In June and September 1968 mention of the *Big Picture* was made by representatives of the National Rifle Association (NRA) who in cooperation with the army produced an episode titled "To Keep and Bear Arms" (TV-557). This was a part of the association's annual "special public service publicity campaign" that raised citizens' awareness about rights and responsibilities regarding the ownership of weapons.[27] At the time, this type of publicity also helped underscore in the minds of some members of Congress *The Big Picture's* place as an educational and informational vehicle. A report in the 5 December 1969 *Congressional Record* gave proof to the widespread distribution of the series, noting that *The Big Picture* "is shown on overseas American Forces Television and in the United States on 313 commercial stations and 53 educational stations."[28] These types of credentials spoke of the popularity and usefulness of the series as a platform for dissemination of information to service members and the American public as it shared episodes from its deep catalog of several hundred titles. But these statistics also attest to the early marriage, and long association, of *The Big Picture* to television and how the rapid explosion in growth of that new cutting-edge mass communications medium propelled the documentary series into homes across the nation and around the globe.

The Arrival of Television

Just three years after World War II, radio still maintained the upper hand as the primary source of news and entertainment in the nation's homes. Still, four regular networks were broadcasting to about one million television sets from twenty-one stations.[29] These reached just as far west as the Mississippi River and linked a simple triad of urban areas, New York City, Philadelphia, and the Washington Capitol District.[30] By some accounts it was still considered a uniquely "urban phenomenon."[31] Almost 50 percent of those television households were in the New York City area alone.[32] But aside from geography, another governor on the spread of television and its technology was a freeze put in place in September 1950 on the issuance of additional station licenses by the Federal Communications Commission (FCC). This was a result of its internal bureaucracy that was overwhelmed by a flood of requests.[33] Aside from the volume of applications, a requirement to negotiate the allocation of signals to issue to the new stations to assure noninterference, as well as equitable coverage, compounded the situation.[34] Exacerbating matters further was the May 1948 FCC standard designating that the distances separating stations on adjacent channels and stations on the same channel could be not be less than 75 miles and 200 miles respectively.[35] The consequences of the freeze, which lasted until May 1952, "left the first 108 VHF stations with the choicest network and advertising affiliations."[36] This provided a greater advantage of coverage to both NBC and CBS over the newcomers, ABC and DuMont.[37] Nevertheless, after several years all these limitations eventually dissipated with the arrival of the Eisenhower administration and the loosening of restrictions.

By 1951, 22 percent of American households had a television, and with the freeze on licensing of stations finally lifted in 1952 that number jumped to nearly 32 percent.[38] That same year the television networks and their affiliates would finally span the continent, reaching eager viewers on the West Coast. Mid-1955 saw the number of households with a TV set increase to 64 percent.[39] It quickly reached 87 percent by the start of the next decade.[40] Certainly, by that time "television had become a living room fixture, ascendant not only over radio but motion pictures and, so it seemed, all of American culture."[41] It is easy to understand why at that time NBC president Sylvester "Pat" Weaver posited it would soon become "the shining center of the home."[42] This sentiment, plus television's phenomenal growth, was the result of two dynamics, a postwar consumerist urge and the exigencies of the Cold War. The first was a happy consequence of a robust economy that saw retooled factories producing goods for consumption by a populace demanding washing machines, vacuums, and cars as they migrated from cities out to suburbia. In this, television provided a golden opportunity for entertainers and commercial enterprises to both construct and sate the needs and desires of millions of ready television viewers. The second dynamic—the Cold War—provided a raison d'être for news organizations and politicians to exploit television's utility and reach into homes to inform and shape Americans' thinking about the state of global affairs.

As historian Jonathan Kahana notes, although television was "the poor cousin of literature, theater or cinema" it was still a "machine that breaches the division between the home and the world by generating emotion" from the viewer.[43] It was that ability to establish a connectedness between the two that was one of its unique characteristics. This in turn, facilitated an easy and intimate connection between the audience and the small screen. Television provided instant access to the world and it "transmitted an alphabet of meaning that required only the senses of sight and sound, not the tedious diligence of book learning."[44] In that context it arrived at a time when the Cold War was heating up and news magnates, elites in Washington, and generals in the Pentagon needed the cathode-ray conduit to reach with authority into Americans' living rooms to offer information that shaped anti-communist impressions, and ensured an exceptional view of America.

Among the first grainy black-and-white reality experiences to reach the post-1945 American television audiences and capture their attention was NBC's coverage of the 1948 Republican and Democratic National Conventions. For this, viewership was small because of the limitation in the number of devices and the scarcity of broadcasting stations. But the connection was significant. The public could now sense the immediacy of events as they occurred. Then, by 1951, with television ownership rapidly expanding, many more Americans became at-home witnesses to the drama that unfolded during the second round of the House Un-American Activities Committee (HUAC) hearings.[45] Here it was, in front of banks of television cameras broadcasting to a national audience, that Senator "Tail Gunner Joe" McCarthy's theatrics and infamous anticommunist diatribes captured attention and stoked hysteria. Building on that energy, television's "combination of mass outreach with the potential for deep individual engagement" and the potential for immediacy made it attractive as a messenger service for Cold War propaganda.[46] As America appeared to be assaulted from within and without, with perceptions of communist infiltration at home and naked aggression abroad on the Korean peninsula, it seemed apparent to television magnates that "every citizen wishes to know as much as possible about the [military] services which will defend" the nation.[47] That was the moment military leaders realized the door was open and opportunity was beckoning.

The transition from the big screen to television was an easy one for the military. Beginning with the golden days of the services' collaboration with the Hollywood studios prior to World War II, the partnership had been long and mutually beneficial. At that time, the film industry had scripted into celluloid form numerous triumphant stories laced with exciting selfless acts of heroism by the army, navy, and marines, men who kept the nation out of harm's way.[48] The studios benefited from the free use of military facilities and equipment, and big returns at the box office. In return, the services were able to demonstrate their patriotic fervor, showcase their arsenals of democracy, gain support of the public and Congress, and lure young men to the recruiting office. In the early postwar years, as the Cold War storm clouds gathered, it seemed a natural and necessary consequence that the union of video producers and military would easily make the transition from large screen to small. Gaining a full appreciation of *The Big Picture*'s appearance on the television screen is possible through an understanding of the emergence of the army's association with that medium.

A New Partnership

Aiding in the military's transition to television was the office of the assistant secretary of defense for public affairs (ASDPA). Formed in 1949, it evolved from the postwar reorganization of the military establishment under the National Security Bill, which brought the services together under one Department of Defense (DOD). The ASDPA in turn created the Office of Public Information (OPI), charging it with serving as a clearinghouse for information shared with the public and various forms of media, including the news outlets. The OPI itself consisted of five internal branches: press, magazine and book, pictorial, public relations, and radio-television. The mission of the last was "to assist radio and television networks and independent stations in keeping the public informed of the activities of the national military establishment."[49] This became important as television executives realized that Cold War informational programs "attained legitimacy when attached to the military," and their association could "promote American military supremacy" while underscoring the need to continue its resourcing.[50] As a result, an apparatus came into existence that would facilitate the continued mutually beneficial relationship between the military and television.

In this symbiosis, the networks and affiliates contributed free air time to the partnership, and the military brought materiel and public trust. One estimate for 1950 was that the networks provided approximately $1.7 million in free airtime to DOD programming.[51] This was significant, considering the approximate cost of producing a typical thirty-minute television show in the early 1950s was $20,000.[52] The importance of that exposure could not be underestimated. As Radio-Television (R-T) Branch chief Charles Dillon noted at the time, the vast radio and television networks spanning the nation combined to reach "100 million Americans daily with information concerning the Defense Department."[53] In return, the military establishment released a variety of films for networks' use, provided clips for newsreels, and supplied production advisors for shows containing military content. Just as important, during the Korean conflict, when civilian camera crews were not on-site in the combat zone, the military worked to provide the networks with live-action film footage for their television affiliates and satisfied their requests for on-the-ground interviews.

One of the first military shows to reach viewers was *Crusade in Europe*. Based on the best-selling wartime memoirs of the former commander of Allied Forces in Europe, Dwight D. Eisenhower, it was the first documentary series produced for television and included combat footage from World War II. Produced by Time, Inc. as part of their *March of Time* series, the program aired on ABC from 5 May to 27 October 1949 and consisted of twenty-six half-hour episodes. *Crusade in Europe* joined the *March of Time* catalog alongside other American exceptionalist Cold War productions intended to shape the public's view with titles such as *The Cold War: Act I, II and III*, as well as *America's New Air Power* and *Answer to Stalin*.[54] Media critics and the public, many of whom were veterans of the overseas conflict, provided the documentary series with a warm reception. Recognized for its excellence as Best Public Service Cultural or Educational Program, *Crusade in Europe* received both the prestigious Peabody Award and an Emmy for Prime Time Television in 1950.[55] For many years critics considered it the gold standard for televised documentaries, and it set expectations for military programming that would follow. It didn't hurt that the central figure, Dwight Eisenhower, would soon gain recognition as an advocate for the new medium.

Although some historians confer the title of "first television President" on John F. Kennedy, because of his on-camera presence and exploitation of the media's capabilities, it was actually Eisenhower who blazed the trail.[56] Early in his presidency Ike became convinced of television's potential to reach the masses, and he staged the first televised fireside chats, the first televised cabinet meetings, and the first TV news conferences. To facilitate this he hired the first presidential TV consultant and had the first White House studio installed.[57] The president also preferred television over Hollywood when telling the military's story because he felt that the "big screen would render history too theatrical."[58] Eisenhower was also the first to "use TV as a bully pulpit," but his audience listened with an open trust because they "believed he had sound judgment, that he would keep them safe."[59] He was "Ike," the war leader who brought them through tough times to final victory. Consequently, it was his "wartime interest in propaganda and psychological warfare [that] carried over into his own Presidential administration."[60] So it was that he understood the potential power of the television and its place in the American home. Eisenhower's popular success with *Crusade in Europe* and his subsequent endorsement of the small screen lent energy to the emerging genre of military documentaries and shows that arrived in the 1950s.

Arriving close on the heels of *Crusade in Europe* was the *Armed Forces Hour*. It aired from 30 October 1949 to 11 June 1950 on twenty-nine NBC affiliate stations on Sundays, then from 5 February 1951 to 6 May 1951 on fifty-six stations of the DuMont network.[61] However, it was not cut from the same cloth as *Crusade in Europe*. The *Armed Forces Hour*, which actually ran in thirty-minute segments once a week, was not a documentary but instead was created specifically as a made-for-television production. It featured episodes with titles such as "Up Periscope" and "Normandy Revisited" cobbled together from millions of feet of existing footage archived by the military. But it also included programmed performances by military bands and occasionally showcased the talents of singing and dancing military members. A creation of DOD, it was hosted by Maj. Robert P. Keim (USAF) and Lt. Benjamin S. Greenberg (USNR) of the PIO.[62] DOD had hoped that the program would serve as a tool to connect with the public while selling the armed forces and putting a human face on the individuals who were serving.

After only two months however, NBC voiced its disappointment over the content of the *Armed Forces Hour*, which left it with failed expectations. According to network executives, the show lacked the immediacy of breaking news as well as the unrehearsed exchanges of a talk show featuring a panel of correspondents. Sensitive to the idea of a potentially spontaneous format, which a DOD program could ill afford, R-T Branch chief Dillon attempted to establish a middle ground with NBC by recommending that any questions posed by journalists on the show be scripted prior to airing, or that a question of the week be posed in advance by commentators, with enough lead time to craft an appropriate answer. In the end, NBC did not warm to that suggestion and did not welcome the show back. After a hiatus of several months, however, DuMont picked it up for a short stint. This experience with the *Armed Forces Hour* was neither a rejection of the military establishment by NBC, nor of its commitment to provide a pulpit for Cold War propaganda. Instead, the network's need to navigate a course between its perceived patriotic duty and the pragmatism of maintaining high prime-time ratings provided the rationale. What the failure of *Armed Forces Hour* did provide, however, was a hard lesson in acceptable formatting and content for DOD and the PIO. This would resonate in the litany of television programs that followed and in the measure of effectiveness they achieved.[63]

Intentional or not, NBC's termination of the *Armed Forces Hour* during the summer of 1950 coincided with the invasion of South Korea by its communist neighbor to the north.[64] Reacting quickly to that event, the network participated in a unique collaboration with the Truman administration to produce *Battle Report—Washington,* a weekly show that featured both commentary on the wartime events transpiring in Korea and a steady diet of hard-edged anticommunist propaganda. This was a format that was absent on the *Armed Forces Hour. Battle Report* would air from 13 August 1950 to 20 April 1952 for a total of eighty-six episodes. For its part in the collaboration, NBC generally provided the technical expertise and airtime, while the administration drafted key personnel from the military establishment and government offices to appear on the show and generated the scripts from their staffs. Produced in the White House office of John R. Steelman, special assistant to the president, *Battle Report* had a purpose in consonance with the prevailing contemporary exceptionalist consensus. It sought to polish the image of the American way of life and provide a rallying point for the American people against an external enemy and conflicting ideologies. In addition, it proposed to give "the people of the United States a firsthand account of what the Federal government is doing in the worldwide battle against Communism."[65]

Unfortunately, as public support for the war began to waver with battlefield reverses in late 1950 early 1951, so did interest in the show. Compounding this was the fact that a number of officials scheduled to appear before the *Battle Report* cameras began canceling due to other commitments. In addition, other networks, together with increasingly vocal Republicans, began leveling charges of political partisanship against NBC. That criticism was hard to dodge considering this was a show produced in a Democratic White House and scripted by Truman's special assistant and staff. That same year, as the Korean conflict ground to a stalemate at the thirty-eighth parallel, production costs continued to mount, and NBC struggled to find support from commercial advertising, generally because of the partisanship charges. Taken together, these challenges became a heavy burden, and by the spring of 1952, NBC made an executive decision to cancel *Battle Report—Washington*.

In the larger context, NBC was not the only network pulled into the media frenzy of the Korean crisis. Both CBS and DuMont launched their own series to chart the unfolding conflict in Asia as well as to highlight the increased Cold War tensions between the East and the West.[66] CBS aired *The Facts We Face* (concurrently with NBC's program, August 1950–April 1952) and *Crisis in Korea* (spring 1951). DuMont followed several months later with *Pentagon* (May 1951–November 1952), which began immediately after the final episode of its version of *The Armed Forces Hour*. CBS's *The Facts We Face* closely mimicked the format of NBC's *Battle Report*, including having its scripts endorsed by the Truman White House. Noted television news anchors Willard F. Shadel and Walter Cronkite were its only two commentators. The format for *Crisis in Korea* was essentially straight documentary filming sans editorializing. This won high praise from *Variety* magazine, which lauded CBS for letting the "documented film speak for itself."[67] DuMont's short-lived *Pentagon* (aka *Pentagon Washington*) had a mixed format of stock film and interviews, but like *The Facts We Face* and *Battle Report* it also fell victim to a variety of challenges, particularly declining public interest and dwindling funding from commercial interests. Still, these shows collectively carried an anticommunist, exceptionalist American charter crafted to both inform and alert the public regarding insidious and dangerous threats from the Soviet-led East. A fuller discussion of how the US Army's production *The Big Picture*, which premiered in December 1951, folded into this mix of shows appears later in this chapter.

During the remainder of the decade, as the energies from the Korean War wound down, the belligerents drew back from a dangerous game of brinksmanship to settle into a brooding Cold War watchfulness. The cut and thrust of East-West diplomacy and proxy actions that followed sculpted a geopolitical landscape that demanded cautious navigation and determined ideologies. This environment served as a functional backdrop to tense times that saw the creation of the 1955 Warsaw Pact as a counterbalance to NATO, the 1956 Hungarian revolution, the 1957 launching of Sputnik I, and the troubling birth of socialist Cuba in January 1959.[68] Americans bore witness to these events through the somber gray eyes of television. Just as they had digested the information served to them by shows such as *Battle Report–Washington* or *The Facts We Face*, they now watched in fitful attentiveness as events unfolded in their living rooms while they sat hunched over their TV dinners. In July 1959, television cameras captured the sharp repartee between Vice President Richard Nixon and Premier Nikita Khrushchev of the Soviet Union as they exchanged ideological ripostes during the now famous Kitchen Debate at the American National Exhibition at Sokolniki Park in Moscow. In a moment of contested symbolism, Nixon advocated for supremacy of American consumer goods while conceding to Khrushchev the superiority of Soviet rocketry.[69] Concerning television, however, Nixon boasted of America's technological edge, while his perplexed counterpart could only respond, unconvincingly, that his nation would eventually match the achievement. It was here, on this international stage, that television had arrived at the important intersection of technology, consumerism, and politics, and came of age in the American century. By 1959, there were approximately forty-four million television sets in the United States, and networks could sense the increased urgency to exploit that technology to deliver their pressing Cold War missives.[70]

It was against that mosaic of Cold War events that the CBS, NBC, and ABC television networks, together with the air force and navy as coproducers, continued to offer shows that centered on the military establishment and endorsed its mission to defend the nation and advocate the tenets of Americanism. Among these were the armed forces documentary series *On Guard* (ABC, April 1952–May 1954), *Navy Log*, a dramatized series (CBS, 1955–1956, then ABC, 1956–1958), *Uncommon Valor*, a documentary series about the US Marine Corps (NBC, 1956–1957), *Adventure Tomorrow*, a series about rocketry and missile research (ABC, 1957–1960), and *Flight*, the history of the US Air Force (US Air Force, 1958–1959).

In parallel with the network offerings, the navy chose to develop two additional documentary series that were popular successes. The first mirrored Eisenhower's *Crusade in Europe*. Titled *Crusade in the Pacific*, it was a production of Time, Inc. as part of their *March of Time* series. It aired from 1951 to 1952 for twenty-six episodes on ABC and included, with a broad view, film and commentary on the Allies' victorious campaign against Japan in the Pacific during World War II, as well as the ongoing Korean conflict. The final episode addressed future relations between the United States and Asia, and unsurprisingly, the need to curtail the spread of communism there. The second series focused on the US Navy's triumphal island-hopping advance across the Pacific to defeat the Japanese and carried the title *Victory at Sea*. Produced for NBC by Henry "Pete" Salomon, it ran from October 1952 to May 1953 on the network that edited, wrote, and coproduced it with the navy.[71] Critically acclaimed for its well-scripted narrative, its integration of combat film footage, and an impressive musical score written by Richard Rodgers and conducted by Robert Russell Bennett, *Victory at Sea* won a Peabody Award in 1952, an Emmy in 1954 as Best Public Affairs Program, and the George Washington Medal from the conservative, patriotic Freedoms Foundation.[72] It was an epic work that celebrated an artistic "blend of military splendor and moral righteousness."[73] The opening credits, in bold lettering with Rodgers's symphonic melody rising behind it, heralded NBC's connection with the service in a way that could only have made the network proud of the association and the praise it garnered: "A Production of the National Broadcasting Company in Cooperation with the United States Navy."

Title of Show	Air Dates	Awards and Notes
Crusade in Europe	5 May 1949–27 Oct 1949 (ABC) 26 episodes	1949 Peabody Award and Emmy Award (Best Public Service Cultural or Educational Program) Sponsor *Time* Magazine Produced by *March of Time*
Armed Forces Hour	30 Oct 1949–11 Jun 1950 (NBC)	
Battle Report— Washington	13 Aug 1950–20 Apr 1952 (NBC)	
The Facts We Face	Aug 1950–1952 (CBS)	
Armed Forces Hour	4 Feb 1951–6 May 1951 (DuMont)	
Pentagon	6 May 1951–24 Nov 1952 (DuMont)	
The Big Picture	December 1951-December 1971 (CBS, ABC, and DuMont) 828 episodes	1960–1970 George Washington Honor Medal 1967 International Film Festival Award 1968 Emmy (Special Award)
Crusade in the Pacific 2	1951–1952 (ABC) (*March of Time*) 6 episodes	Sponsor *Time* Magazine Produced by *March of Time*
On Guard	28 Apr 1952–29 May 1954 (ABC)	
Victory at Sea	26 Oct 1952–3 May Apr 1953 (NBC)	1952 Peabody Award (Special Award)
Navy Log	1955–1956 (CBS) 1956–1958 (ABC) 103 episodes	Dramatized series
Uncommon Valor	1956–1957 (NBC) (Syndicated) 26 episodes	
Adventure Tomorrow	Apr 1957-Jul 1960 (ABC)	
Flight	1958–1959 (US Air Force) (Syndicated) 39 episodes	

Table 1.1. Military television shows that aired during the period 1949–1959. Included are documentaries as well as anthologies. Although *The Big Picture* did not premiere until December 1951, it was the longest lasting. The final episode was broadcast in December 1971. Sources: Nancy Bernhard, *U.S. Television News and Cold War Propaganda, 1947–1960* and Alex McNeil, *Total Television*.

Trailing three years behind *Victory at Sea* came *Air Power*, a CBS documentary series coproduced with the US Air Force.[74] The network cooperated with the service in developing scripts and weaving "some 300 million feet of film" from the air force archives into twenty-six episodes in the hope of creating a show to rival the navy's earlier success.[75] Its purpose was to portray the story of air power in the United States and around the world, from the earliest beginnings to modern times. In favorable comparison to its predecessor, the television audiences most appreciated the exciting moments in *Air Power* that portrayed the "drama of men and machines at war."[76] Producers again enlisted the well-recognized voice of newscaster Walter Cronkite as narrator for the show, and several active-duty air force generals portrayed themselves during dramatized versions of actual events. Unfortunately for the show, it drew criticisms throughout its run. Perry Wolff, the CBS producer, eschewed the inherent "special pleading from military interests" as well as the perceived projection of air force power as the ultimate means to American world domination.[77] This he made quite clear during an interview years later when he stated that the show was "pure propaganda" and that the Air Force had guys telling me what to do."[78] He also groused when told he needed "official sanction for the series outline."[79] Another well-known newscaster, Edward R. Murrow, claimed that some episodes distorted history, and General Scott, former director of the Air Force Office of Information Service, charged that the same episodes were too anti-American in tone. *Air Power* did however, attract a large viewing audience and did turn profits for CBS, but it never achieved the same level of popular acclaim as *Victory at Sea* and would always remain in its shadow.

Alone, *Victory at Sea* stood as "a landmark in documentary film-making technique," but more important, coupled with the trio of *Crusade in Europe*, *Crusade in the Pacific*, and *Air Power*, their influence established the military documentary as a popular, viable television genre.[80] These compilation documentaries, created from existing archives files, integrated with dramatic stories and an evocative musical score, were the new version of authenticity born from the style of World War II productions. As historian A. William Bluem notes in his study of the documentary in American television, these compilation series were born of the tradition of works such as Frank Capra's

Why We Fight. They "showed men a different method of presenting reality" in which "the artists—director, film editor, writer, narrator, and composer—could seek, each within his own craft, common and purposeful thematic expression."[81] This dynamic resonated through those *March of Time* productions and the documentary television series that would follow.

The Big Picture on a Small Screen

Although it was not among the earlier *Big Picture* episodes produced by the Army Pictorial Center, the story of "TV in the Army" (TV-265), which aired in 1954, was a timely description of how the service recruited that new technology to serve its needs. It was seen then as "one of the most unique and versatile devices now being used by your Army" to educate, train, and inform the soldier.[82] Always aware that the investigation and application of new technology was a necessary pursuit, the film discussed the army's experimentation with television to determine how to best maximize its use. In this process, it quickly came to understand that when aired over commercial networks, televised military shows would "bring the Army closer to the American people."[83] So it was, as the narrator explained, that "by combining technical knowhow and human imagination with the electronic magic of television the Army is employing one of the most direct and effective methods devised for keeping the soldier and civilian well-informed."[84] Accordingly, the episode observed, "that is the big picture, the picture of your army looking forward to the future security of the nation through the eyes of television."[85] A follow-on episode, titled "Pictorial Report No. 23" (TV-342), expanded on this theme by heralding the army's new lightweight portable television camera, which made it easier to capture training events and activities. As the narrator proudly announced, "This camera is an example of just one more step forward in your army's technological search for new equipment to do a better job in less time."[86] In that regard, the army realized what a keen advantage television offered in maintaining its reputation and relevancy in the Cold War and how the *Big Picture* could figure prominently in that effort.

The first thirteen episodes of *The Big Picture*, as conceived by Carl

Figure 1.3. Image of scaffolding and cameras filming army
training at a field location. Technological advances made it
possible to move television crews to where the action was with
cameras that were more portable. Note the mobile van parked
nearby. See the *Big Picture* episode "Pictorial Report No. 23"
(TV-342). (Image Source: *In Focus*, September 1959)

Figure 1.4. APC camera crew in the Peruvian Andes filming the episode "U.S. Army in the Andes" (TV-686). Another example of how evolving technologies made it possible for crews to move out of the studios to various locations around the globe to capture action footage for episodes. (Image Source: *In Focus*, December 1963)

Zimmerman and Carl Bruton, were a dedicated effort to weave together thousands of feet of unused Army Signal Corps film of the war in Korea into a visual narrative of the action. They wanted to tell the story, and share the experiences as Ernie Pyle might have wished, from the grassroots perspective to the wider-angled bigger picture, as historian Lawrence Suid explained, to "capture the ambience of battle."[87] This would be the essence of "translating Pyle's words into visual drama."[88] Caught up in the same rush of frenzied energy as the television networks to exploit the immediacy of the new media, the Zimmermann-Bruton team went to work in earnest, and as expeditiously as possible, using existing resources. By the time this initial project had run its course in December 1952, with the last episode highlighting the continuing truce talks ("The UN Line Is Stabilized

While Truce Talks Continue," TV-181), *The Big Picture* had established a presence, and the US Army producers realized they were onto something special and necessary. While that final episode was a coda to the first thirteen weeks, it also served as the start point for the longest run of a televised military documentary series and what was "probably the most widely televised public service program in history."[89]

Focusing initially on the three suggested goals: promoting anticommunism, connecting with the public, and gaining elite support, the *Big Picture* crew, under the auspices of the Public Information Office, began to develop a strategy. While it was simple enough to weave anticommunist rhetoric into the narrative of each show, the producers needed to maximize the potential of the television media to sell the army. Following that line, they began to develop scripts that told the army's story. The very first of these, sporting the title "The Mission of the Army" (TV-182), described how the army fit into the national defense structure. It was followed in quick succession by "The Army Combat Team" (TV-183), then "The Citizen Soldier" (TV-184), "The Combat Soldier" (TV-185), and "Duty, Honor, Country" (TV-186) a presentation about the United States Military Academy at West Point. The APC designed each of these for general interest and scripted them as informational productions to educate the public about their soldiers—active duty, reservist, or officer in training—and build the essential military-civilian rapport that the army feared was missing.

As *The Big Picture* continued to develop its early television presence, it incorporated one project that was already in development: a collection of thirteen episodes that the production catalog listed as Series IV, the "Blue Badge Series." Its creator and chief narrator was Colonel William Quinn, who at the time was serving as the chief of staff of the Pentagon. The short series focused on the lives of the army's battle-tested foot soldier, who wore the distinctive Combat Infantryman Badge (CIB) with its unique blue background. As Quinn noted during the first episode, as he peered into the camera, "This series is a tribute to those of you who served as a rifleman."[90] It was a nod to veterans in the viewing audience. Each episode focused on a different infantry division or unit, and Quinn provided details of their unit history and most recent combat actions, including short descriptions of the equipment and weapons they carried. The genesis of this thirteen-part series was Quinn's own experiences as an infantry officer during World War II and Korea. Although it was not originally a part of the *Big Picture* series, producers managed to fold it in. Also, coupled to the start of each *Blue Badge* segment was the standard boilerplate introduction for *The Big Picture*, well-recognized by the viewing public. Although sometimes mistaken as the predecessor to the *Big Picture* series, the *Blue Badge* developed in parallel, and later the APC adopted it into the series. As this study will later show, Quinn would assume a key role in the development of information management for the army.

Inside this cycle of twinning of the two series, the *Big Picture* producers often returned to the subject of Korea. It is possible that this emerged from a feeling of an incomplete mission since the original thirteen episodes ended while peace negotiations were still ongoing and did not describe the eventual outcome of the Korean police action. Or it might have arisen from an understanding that the last opportunity the army had to prove that it was battle tested was the Korean conflict, and a program about that war might attract the interest of the public, including many recent veterans watching at home. Regardless of the reasoning, the APC produced a number of *Big Picture* episodes postbellum that focused on the events in that struggle. "A Day in Korea" (TV-196) was the first of these, and writers scripted it in a poignant manner to maintain a personal connection between the soldier and the American at home. It began with an introduction by Carl Zimmermann who announced that the show would revisit the war in Korea: "In terms of the solder on the front lines, the individual who fights the battles, who lives in a bunker and washes his socks in a steel helmet. He's enduring a way of life remote from the daily living he once shared at home with you. Do you remember how you began this day?"[91] The episode continued by telling the story of a soldier's day via a first-person account. This was followed by "Civil Assistance, Korea" (TV-201), which spoke about humanitarian operations of relief and supply for the civilian populace; "Third Korean Winter" (TV-223), which described the harsh winter conditions of 1952–1953 endured by soldiers; and "Korean Wind-Up" (TV-235), an effort to provide closure to the war through a visual narrative. Using a patriotic overtone, the narrator informed the viewers that "the guns are quiet again in Korea," before going on to proudly proclaim: "The Armed Forces of the United States together with our Allies in the UN stopped the march of armed Communism cold in Korea. They did it against tremendous odds in manpower and in a land half way around the Earth from their own. This is a report from the now silent front."[92]

Perhaps the greatest appeal to a human connection in the Korean *Big Picture* series was in the episode "Christmas in Korea" (TV-244).[93] Crafted to tug at the heartstrings of viewers, it offered scenes of soldiers singing holiday carols and sharing gifts from home. Tucked between those images were a number of on-the-spot interviews with soldiers, noncommissioned officers, and the commanding general of the Seventh Infantry Division as they all shared a holiday meal. In concert with these types of episodes, the *Big Picture* APC producers aired periodic "Pictorial Reports" that addressed worldwide army operations, but during the 1950s always included short segments about Korea. Some of the subjects covered were mobile army surgical hospital operations, postarmistice aid to the Korean people, and celebration of the fifth anniversary of South Korea's independence.[94] Finally, *The Big Picture* visited Korea with a retrospective titled "Korea Today" (TV-451), which reflected the rebuilding efforts in that postwar nation. It featured the army's focused efforts to construct new housing and roads, piece together an infrastructure, train the South Korean Army, and bring normalcy to the lives of the people. Altogether, the US Army produced a total of twenty-four episodes covering Korea, including fourteen in 1952 alone and five in 1953.

Each of these episodes on Korea, including the original thirteen, relied to some degree on camera and sound techniques and the cinematographic skills of the APC studios to enhance the effectiveness of their messages. Central to the first series (TV-169 to TV-181) were the reels of combat camera footage that provided a visual frame for the scripted narrative. Overlaying these battle images were sound tracks of brooding, ominous music broken by the staccato sounds of machine-gun fire and thunderous artillery. Producers edited scenes of Korean refugees lining the muddy roads into the combat reels to create the gray feelings of despair and hopelessness of war. The message seemed clear: America was in a desperate fight to save the West and its ideals against communism wherever that fight might take it. These images that described the high stakes in the Cold War would appear sharpened and defined in greater detail as the series continued to press that theme of the East-West struggle. By the second and subsequent series the *Big Picture* included episodes on Korea that incorporated many of the same cinematographic techniques, but the messaging strategy was more refined. Scripted narratives provided explicit messages, and film craft offered more nuanced, implicit messages. As the narrator spoke of defending against communist aggression, video footage showed images of fleeing families laden with all their possessions, American GIs feeding and caring for small children, and the unloading of shipments of rice to nourish the people. Cameras showed the Koreans as a defeated, paupered people, picking through the ruins of their cities, voiceless on film, hollow-eyed and struggling to survive. The faces of hungry children pressed in toward the camera, breaking into smiles when an American would show them a kindness. The message communicated spoke of the superiority of the United States and the West, come to rescue the blighted and submissive Koreans, just as it had come to Asia a decade earlier in another war to save another people. These techniques and cinematographic themes appeared with regularity as a thread through the Korean episodes and later, in a similar way, in those about other nations such as Germany and Vietnam. It was an effort to sell the nation, and in particular, the US Army.

Hollywood and the APC

It was with a measure of satisfaction, and some relief, that New York City's Mayor Fiorello H. La Guardia stood at the site of the new Signal Corps Photographic Center (SCPC) on 22 September 1942 and announced to the assembled press and VIPs, "I've been trying to get moving pictures back in this shack for a long time."[95] The large studio complex was at the time nicknamed "The Big House."[96] La Guardia's dedication followed the movement of the Army Signal Corps' Training Film Production Laboratory from its previous location at Fort Monmouth, New Jersey, to its new home on Long Island, New

Figure 1.5. An aerial view of the APC complex at Astoria. Over time it grew to encompass several buildings that surrounded the main studio in the center. These housed facilities for film development and editing and storage of equipment, scenery, and wardrobes, as well as a barracks for the soldiers. (Image Source: NARA photo 111-SC-367347)

York, after a short but focused search that began in January 1942. At that time, just a month after the attack on Pearl Harbor, the War Department made the decision to invest resources in the production of training and informational films to support the war effort. Surveying possible sites on the East Coast, it eventually identified two possibilities, the Warner Brothers' Flatbush Brooklyn Studio or Paramount's Eastern Services Studios at Astoria, in Queens, Long Island. Both film studios had suffered during the hard economic times of the Depression years, but it was the Paramount facility that stood completely dormant. This, plus the greater availability of necessary floor space, influenced the War Department's decision to offer Paramount $500,000 for its 5.14-acre workspace at Thirty-Fifth Avenue and Thirty-Fifth Street in Astoria.[97] Although Paramount was at first hesitant, because of a fear that concentrating all its production capacity

Figure 1.6. Scene of a typical training film production at the APC during World War Two. By the early 1950s the center used the same soundstages, and a mixture of civilian and military production crews and actors, to create the *Big Picture* series. (Image Source: NARA photo 111-SC-148806)

on the West Coast might make it susceptible to a Japanese attack, in the end it relented and agreed to the sale.

Initially, because of concerns for wartime security, the government held information about the move from New Jersey close. As the *New York Times* reported, "The Signal Corps has requested that the name of the studio and its location be treated as a military secret."[98] But by the time that article had gone to press *Variety* had already trumped the *Times* by running an article several weeks earlier that shouted "Army Taking Over Astoria Plant as Lab."[99] The sudden influx of military personnel, vehicles, and equipment to the quiet neighborhood erased any lingering doubts. Ultimately, espionage did strike the APC, when Nazi operative Simon Emil Koedel was able to infiltrate the facility during the war. Investigators suspected he made off with numerous copies of films showing training and the latest weapons.[100] The complex, which encompassed a "full city block," included sound studios, laboratories for film development processes, a carpentry shop, maintenance and repair shops, and administrative offices, plus a barracks

Figure 1.7. The US Army's Building 4489, Redstone Arsenal, Huntsville, Alabama, housed the last studio and laboratory that served in production of *The Big Picture*. (Image Source: US Army)

to house enlisted soldiers.[101] The center would remain at that location until 1970, when the army disbanded it. Many of the personnel would move on to Redstone Arsenal, Alabama, where they would continue to work on the series as members of the US Army Motion Picture/ Television Production Division, a government-owned, contractor-operated facility, until its end in June 1971. All subsequent military audiovisual activities were then concentrated at Norton Air Force Base in San Bernardino, California.

By the time the initial facility was set up and functional in 1942, it had become the workplace for approximately 250 soldiers and 35 officers.[102] That number eventually swelled to a combined 3,000.[103] During the course of the war it would also become a magnet for "many draftees from the motion picture industry" who found themselves reassigned there for the convenience of the government, especially to take advantage of their various production skills.[104] As former production crew member Lester Binger recalls, "Fancy Hollywood people got themselves into the Signal Corps. All of a sudden, you had people arriving in limousines for the morning reveille."[105] Most of the soldiers assigned to the SCPC would remain for the duration of the war, then afterward return to their civilian lives and careers. Over the ensuing years hundreds of military personnel, officers, noncommissioned officers, and enlisted soldiers rotated through the facilities, performing various functions as photographers, working in the labs or on the cameras and sound equipment, writing scripts, directing productions, constructing props and scenery, or providing makeup and wardrobe services. In addition, those who were in uniform were subject to the sometimes mundane demands of army life that included guard duty, in-ranks uniform inspections, kitchen police (KP), physical training, and small arms weapons qualification. On the lighter side, Arthur Laurents, a former writer at the APC, recalls that on one occasion the entire military unit was "ticketed by the police for obstructing traffic" while conducting marching drills in the street outside the facility.[106] The studio subsequently relocated the activities to a nearby National Guard training site.

Among those who served at the APC during World War II were a number of Hollywood notables who brought their skills to the studios. One example was famed director John Huston, whom the army had posted there during the war. Wearing the rank of captain, he produced and directed three films for the Army Signal Corps: *Report from the Aleutians* (1943), *The Battle of San Pietro* (1945), and *Let There Be Light* (1946). Unfortunately, censors delayed the release of the last two films because of concerns for public sensitivities to scenes of combat deaths and the potential of psychological damage to veterans. Those concerns aside, the *New York Times* recognized *The Battle of San Pietro* as "one of the greatest American documentaries ever made."[107] Nevertheless, before his discharge, Huston attained the rank of major and received the Legion of Merit for his work under combat conditions during the filming of scenes for that production.[108] A truncated version of this story, which does include footage extracted from Huston's documentary, did appear later as the *Big Picture* episode "US Sixth Corps" (TV-219). Another contributor to military film production was director Frank Capra, who as a colonel created and directed the wartime propaganda series *Why We Fight*. Although Capra rarely worked at the APC, his staff did, and he remained in charge of film production there in support of his series. A third noted director, who was familiar with the Astoria studios, where he worked for Paramount prior to the war, was George Cukor. He also directed information and training films at the Astoria location and after his discharge went on to receive acclaim for his other work.[109] Still, there were other individuals who grew into their reputations after the war but passed through the APC and shared their talents while on duty in Astoria. This was the case for William Franklin Beedle Jr. who as a US Army Air Corps captain acted in several APC wartime productions. He would later gain stardom as the famed actor William Holden. Another figure was Arthur Laurents, who wrote scripts for training and informational films. He would go on to become an award-winning playwright, stage director, and screenwriter. Laurents later received credit for such productions as *West Side Story* and *Gypsy*.

Generally, interactions between those soldiers who were members of the regular army and those who came into the service directly from Hollywood went smoothly. However, the one noted wrinkle was in the area of promotions and rank. According to one soldier's sardonic recollection, "Those from Hollywood got all the rank, New York guys got nothing," and "If you were from Hollywood, whatever you told the Army, they believed it. There were guys running around with all kinds of rank, but they didn't know anything."[110] Eventually, as the postwar years arrived, those individuals who had emigrated from Hollywood migrated back to the West Coast, and the mix of military and civilian workers began to change with the integration of an increasing number of nonuniformed personnel. By the late 1950s and mid-1960s it was not unusual to see familiar faces around the studio complex dressed in civilian attire who had previously worn military khaki.[111] Many of them returned to perform the same functions, others to assume new roles. But this collection of various talents that passed through the APC, whether by attraction or contingency, left in its wake a unique culture of creativity within the military and established a commitment of engagement with emerging technologies and audiovisual professionalism for years to come.

Part of the enduring legacy was the continuing association between the APC and Hollywood that lasted long after the coming of peace in 1945. This resonated in the *Big Picture* series that began production in Astoria in 1951 with the Bruton-Burkey-Zimmermann collaboration on the original thirteen episodes about the Korean War. From that time, a steady parade of familiar faces—actors, news announcers, and directors—lent their names and expertise to the *Big Picture* productions. Among the very first was the popular singer and comedian Al Jolson, who appeared visiting the American troops in Korea during "The United Nations Offensive" (TV-171), just the third episode of the *Big Picture* series. Another early presence of a personality was that of World War II hero, and actor, Audie Murphy, who first appeared as a guest narrator in "Third Division in Korea" (TV-302), an episode that told the story of the actions of his old unit in that conflict.[112] Murphy would again appear before the APC cameras together with his two young sons in the 1962 episode "Broken Bridge" (TV-508). Scripted to be a sales pitch for the modernizing army, it featured vignettes of several new missile weapons systems and included visits with NATO partners in Norway and Turkey. It aired at a crucial moment, as the army was in steep competition with its sister services to prove its relevancy, and technological edge, in the dangerous Cold War world. In this context, Murphy was once again in the service of the army, and his presence was an essential ingredient to the success of the episode. He was a recognized war hero and actor, his children were in the film, he carried a curiosity about the new weapons that most Americans shared, and he exhibited pride and patriotism toward the army's latest accomplishments. In this one episode, the APC ensured all the key elements were in place to establish and maintain strong connections with the public and, with hope, Congress.

A diverse number of personalities contributed their names to the *Big Picture* series over the course of its production run, some for personal gain through popular exposure and some for patriotic sentiments. Regardless of their reasoning, their presence lent a certain gravity that attracted both military and civilian viewers and added credibility to the series and its messages. While one can only sense the motivation of personal gain, participation in *The Big Picture* as a patriotic pulpit became evident through their in-person narratives delivered before the lights and cameras of the APC. This was the case with "Challenge of Ideas" (TV-512), which aired in 1961. It offered a biased contrast of political philosophies between the democracy of the West and the communism of the East, elevating the first and casting the second in a dark light. The narrator, celebrated news correspon-

Figure 1.8. Image of John Wayne in the APC studios for filming of the episode "Challenge of Ideas" (TV-512). Wayne joined other notable performers from Hollywood, as well as contemporary news personalities, in this patriotic, exceptionalist view of the ideals of Americanism. (Image Source: Army Pictorial Center)

dent, and at this time the new director of the USIA, Edward R. Murrow, introduced the episode by offering to review with the audience "the great conflict of our time," and later, peering through a wreath of cigarette smoke with his signature stare, he added that the "Communist bloc would like to see the entire world under communist domination."[113] Other than Murrow, the episode featured appearances by

John Wayne, Hanson Baldwin, Helen Hayes, Lowell Thomas, and Frank McGee. Each of these individuals was a well-known, popular film, stage, or television figure, particularly John Wayne and Edward R. Murrow.[114] The contribution of their professional reputations to a *Big Picture* episode was evidence of their commitment to the contemporary patriotic, exceptionalist ideals of America but was also evidence of the deliberate, careful packaging of the messages transmitted via the *Big Picture* series during that time of Cold War geopolitical competition.

A number of other celebrities also participated in the symbiotic relationship between Hollywood and the APC. Some notable newsmen and actors, including Mike Wallace, Lorne Greene, Walter Matthau, Raymond Massey, and Ronald Reagan, lent their talents to a series of *Big Picture* biopic episodes of famous military leaders. Walter Matthau alone narrated at least four during the 1963 season, on Generals Pershing, Eisenhower, Bradley, and Patton. Award winning newsman Walter Cronkite contributed his narrative talents to several episodes, two that were biopics about Generals Marshall and MacArthur, and two historical pieces on the Anzio beachhead and the Battle of the Bulge. Other personalities of stage and screen, such as comedians Bob Hope and Jerry Colonna, also brought their talents to *The Big Picture*. The 1963 episode "Shape of the Nation" (TV-582) provided a vehicle for their humorous quips as they reported on the physical shape of the nation in support of President John F. Kennedy's program to improve the health and fitness of the United States. It featured visits to rugged outdoor army training and sporting events and encouraged widespread popular participation by focusing on the lethargy of the average American, a result of a too comfortable lifestyle. The episode concluded with a lengthy voice-over by President Kennedy, challenging all Americans to become involved in practicing a more active way of life. Much more than another simple petition for support of army programs or weapons systems, "Shape of the Nation" brought together Hollywood, the army, and the executive branch in a collaborative, informational presentation, another innovative use of the small screen to show how the army was an active participant in public service.

As the political atmosphere of the nation began to change with

Figure 1.9. Popular actor Walter Matthau on the set of *The Big Picture* during filming of a historical episode. Matthau contributed his skills as a narrator for a number of biographical episodes of famous generals. (Image Source: *In Focus*, July 1963)

America's increasing involvement in the Vietnam conflict, some Hollywood figures continued to contribute to the *Big Picture* series, although the number decreased dramatically. Among those who did continue were James Arness, Robert Mitchum, Bob Hope, and John Wayne. After 1965, Hope actually "doubled down on his patriotism and began to espouse an active support of the war effort."[115] Arness narrated "Hidden War in Vietnam" (TV-562) about Special Forces operations there. In a later appearance, Robert Mitchum appeared on film touring the battlefield in Vietnam with the troops of the 101st Airborne Division in the episode "Screaming Eagles in Vietnam" (TV-714), which aired in 1967. A year after this, Hope served as narrator for an episode titled "When the Chips are Down" (TV-723) about the

National Guard. Sporting a beret and fatigue shirt, and character-istically swinging a golf club, he provided a review of the mission and responsibilities of the National Guard, including segments on the Army Guard participating in flood relief, providing protection during rioting in Detroit, and flying transport missions to and from Vietnam. One scene also included Phyllis Diller, a popular female comedian, who appeared in a cameo as a nurse. Although there is no supporting record of APC production board guidance, the production of this episode may suggest that its intended purpose was as a foil to deflect criticism of the army by providing some distance from the conflict in Vietnam by exhibiting activities that were not directly war related, such as flood relief. Still, for some entertainers such as Hope, it signaled an enduring connection with the military, while also offer-ing another perspective of the contemporary army.

Known widely as a "living symbol of American patriotism," John Wayne participated as host narrator for "A Nation Builds under Fire" (TV-695).[116] In this episode, he drew comparisons of South Vietnam's struggle for freedom and independence with that of the American colonies in the late 1700s. Standing before the camera, dressed in military battle fatigues, Wayne admitted that Saigon was the "capital city of a nation at war, the strangest war in which Americans have ever been involved."[117] He then added, "It is also the capital of a nation in the throes of a social revolution, and America's participation in that revolution is just as urgent as its involvement in the war."[118] During his narrative delivery Wayne also disclosed that his presence in the ep-isode was at the invitation of the Department of Defense. This served as a full disclosure that the military had enlisted the assistance of a Hollywood figure in preparing this video message to support its pres-ence in Southeast Asia. Noteworthy also was the appearance of then vice president Hubert H. Humphrey, who presented the introduction to the episode and spoke of the nobility of the Vietnamese people and the urgency of aiding them in their quest for independence and liberty.[119] He noted that "they are also proving their faith in us, be-cause we have taken our stand beside them."[120] Further endorsing America's involvement, Humphrey added, "We are making possible the conditions under which they can build their nation."[121] Episodes such as this contributed to the ire that eventually emerged among some members of Congress, such as Senator J. William Fulbright and his progressive colleagues, whose protests against the perceived politicization of the *Big Picture* series became a matter of record. Still, the marriage of Hollywood and *The Big Picture* through the APC was long lasting, and to a degree, it remained mutually beneficial.

Putting the Pieces Together

The talent and craftsmanship brought to the APC through its association with Hollywood and the blossoming television industry helped establish the standard for production of the *Big Picture* series. Although the earliest episodes, such as the original thirteen or the *Blue Badge* series, appeared as hastily cobbled together efforts from available film footage, changes in film and television techniques and practices, as well as the evolution of video technology, had an impact on the development of APC productions, improving the level of professionalism and the quality of the product. This was important as the producers of the *Big Picture* series worked to keep pace with the industry to maintain the interest of their viewers and to ensure that the messages they were transmitting would be clear and acceptable. The trajectory of these changes is evident in the evolution of the quality of the *Big Picture* films from the first muted gray images to the colorful, orchestrated stories of later episodes.

Much of this developmental success of *The Big Picture* is attributable to the triumph of early television's compilation documentaries. Award-winning series such as *Crusade in Europe*, and a few years later *Crusade in the Pacific* and *Victory at Sea*, encouraged emulation by APC producers, directors, and staff, whose work suggests they chose to mimic the successful formula of these shows. Although the goal was not always attainable, these documentaries offered inspiration for the creative teams inside the army's Astoria studios. It was the particular "blending of music, poetic narration, and visual flow" of the documentaries that captivated audiences.[122] So it was the "fusion of each element within a balanced and harmonious whole" that APC directors and writers understood was essential to breathing life into the video presentations.[123] This would evoke a response from and connection with the viewer. After the first few years of production the *Big*

Picture episodes began to exhibit some of the key characteristics of the successful documentaries.

Foremost, and easiest of the key essentials, was the integration of actual combat footage. This added a dimension of realism that most viewers appreciated. It riveted attention and lent credibility to the narrative story. Producers of *Victory at Sea* admitted to sifting through approximately 60 million feet of film, derived mostly from the navy's archives, finally using 60,000 feet.[124] Similarly, combat footage and films of in-progress training events or associated army activities were central to each *Big Picture* episode, from the fighting in Korea to historical biopics and operations north of the Arctic Circle. With the arrival of the portable television camera the series producers were further able to embrace the emerging technologies that were available and complement dated combat films by capturing current events as they unfolded. As Lieutenant Colonel William Ellington, chief of the Radio-Television Office, commented during the filming of "Hidden War in Vietnam" in 1962, "shooting these films on location can be hazardous and, sometimes fatal," but he added with a measure of pride, "The *Big Picture* goes to the world's trouble spots to film the Army in action."[125] This added an immediacy, and relevancy, to the *Big Picture* episodes that was missing early in the series when archived footage was the only recourse. Substitution of newer, relevant footage also satisfied an existing criticism of the sometimes awkward insertion of an archived video sequence, which historian Lawrence H. Suid notes was a distraction in earlier documentaries such as *Victory at Sea*. During those moments, Suid writes, "rather than becoming absorbed in the action, some viewers undoubtedly spent their time recalling where they had previously seen the sequence."[126] Over time, the use of newer camera technologies lessened the frequency of this occurrence for *The Big Picture*.

But as much as this type of film added to the composition of any episode, at times the APC needed actors to supplement existing stock film. In these cases the studios at Astoria, or on-site locations, came alive with full crews of actors, writers, directors, and sound personnel working to create a scene. One example was "Military Police Town Patrol" (TV-325), which featured a combination of actors and soldiers staging the activities of military police patrols on city streets. Another was "Military Justice" (TV-331), which offered vignettes of the military justice system. A related example appears in the episode "Hidden War in Vietnam" (TV-562), which included in its opening sequence a notice that "portions of this film have been recreated to portray typical events in Vietnam."[127] It involved soldiers staging mock tactical operations in a jungle environment. Although the integration of actors and staged sequences did fill gaps where archived footage did not exist, it is evident that it was infrequently used, and *The Big Picture* relied less on the docudrama format, as was the case in the *Navy Log* series, and more on films with a higher impact that recorded events as they were unfolding. This was consistent with some concerns such as those earlier voiced by President Eisenhower, who felt dramatizing a military documentary would create a theatrical production, which lacked a necessary authenticity.

Integration of musical scores was also important to the *Big Picture* series. In the early 1950s, the soundtrack for the Peabody Award–winning *Victory at Sea* enthralled television viewing audiences. The background music, which followed the events of each scene, rising and falling with the action, was an essential element that contributed to the success of that production. As A. William Bluem noted in his study of documentaries, together with the right words and film, the music "could reflect the predetermined point of view throughout" the episode and the entire series, and so set the mood.[128] This understanding set the standard for compilation series that followed, including *The Big Picture*. Throughout its production its episodes incorporated sound tracks that followed and reflected the on-screen activities, often offering typical orchestral background music. As Bluem observes regarding television theme documentaries, the "suggestive power of the musical score" shaped the presentation of the content.[129] But also with the passage of time, the soundtracks for the *Big Picture* episodes did reflect some popular trends. Dramatic orchestrations, and a military drum and bugle prelude that became iconic, accompanied introductions to the earliest episodes. Later, by the mid-1960s, a contemporary jazz bass and drum had replaced the previous set. Over time as audio technologies improved, so did the quality of the sound. As the equipment became available, the APC Sound Branch converted from optical film to magnetic tape. This accommodated live sound recordings from the field locations that were "adding the realism" to video footage.[130] It also permitted the creation of music and effects tracks that accommodated the recording of music and sound independently of narration or dialogue, and allowed the revision of voice tracks as needed. Still, throughout the twenty-year course of the series, music remained an integral piece of *The Big Picture's* successful documentary-like formula.

Closely linked to the audio improvements were video advancements. One of the most noticeable transitions that followed the trajectory of technological change was the introduction of color. By 1966 the APC switched away from 35 mm and began relying on 16 mm color negative for field production of *Big Picture* episodes.[131] This coincided with the increase in sales of color television sets in the United States. This was a cause for celebration by network sponsors, who foresaw the benefit in product sales through color commercials. The networks also realized a potential advantage in the annual ratings wars that followed in the wake of the growing television fad in America. Shows produced in color attracted wider audiences. By one estimate 9.5 million households owned a color television set in 1965, and by 1969 that number had risen to 19.2 million.[132] Keeping pace with the popular trend was important to APC producers, who were determined to remain at the cutting edge of technology and prevent their programs from lagging too far behind contemporary commercial programming. The advantage to *The Big Picture* was apparent in the visual impact that episodes carried. Stories such as "Science Moves the Army" (TV-668), which featured advancements in mobility and weapons systems, appeared more aesthetically pleasing to viewers and possessed more energy compared to the mundane newsreel appearance of dated black-and-white footage. By the time producers were airing *Big Picture* episodes about Vietnam, color television ownership in the United States was widespread. So to keep pace with prime-time network news shows and documentary series, color became the norm at the APC. This remained the case through the final episodes in 1971.

One documentary trend *The Big Picture* did not generally follow was the epic multiepisode concept that wove together a lengthy narrative over an extended period.[133] Instead, the series maintained a format of unique short feature films no longer than twenty-eight minutes. This provided creative flexibility while maintaining audience interest. Although *The Big Picture* did carry a few story lines through for several episodes, such as the ten-part series "Army in Action" (TV-634 through TV-643), they tended to remain with the single-episode format. This worked well for the *Big Picture* producers because as Bluem notes, by the 1958 season after the succession of triumphant compilation documentaries, *Victory at Sea*, *Crusade in the Pacific*, and *Air Power*, American television audiences were quite sated, having "already seen many impressive demonstrations" of the method.[134] To remedy this situation, Bluem posits, newer shows such as *The Twentieth Century*, as well as *The Big Picture*, began focusing on the "back of the book," those events that in many cases told a smaller, yet still significant, story.[135] That solution worked, and these shorter features were able to maintain viewer attention by keeping interest piqued with new offerings each week. This was the model already employed by the *Big Picture* writers and directors, who hewed closely to the concept of short interest pieces that changed week by week. It worked to "promote regular, habituated viewing," which also encouraged "robust sales in the syndication markets (where producers make most of their money)."[136] This avoided the potentially dulling repetitiveness of a lengthy twenty-six episode series. The one unifying theme for *The Big Picture* was telling the army's story, but through a variety of perspectives and approaches. That combination of the documentary-style blending of storytelling with music and video, together with the episodic format, contributed to the series' longevity. The APC gambled that it could maintain audience interest and deliver the *Big Picture* message in a manner that was both informational and palatable.

Just as the audio and visual dimensions of the *The Big Picture* had changed over time, so too did the opening sequences. This reflected the changing political and cultural times as much as the changing artistic format of the program. The introductory sequence for the original thirteen episodes featured video footage of artillery explosions, fleeing refugees, dusty marching troops, and armored columns. Carl Zimmermann, the narrator, introduced each of those initial episodes as a view of an army committed to "stop communist aggression wherever it may strike."[137] This set the purpose of the series in terms framed by an early Cold War geopolitical struggle that set East against West in the arena of the Korean War. But even before the end of the first year, the tone of the show's introduction began to change. The black-and-white newsreel-style images of the battlefield were gone, replaced by video segments of the army training in the various reaches of the globe. The introductory narrative no longer fixed on a communist threat, but instead in a broader sense proclaimed, "From Korea to Germany, from Alaska to Puerto Rico, all over the world, the men and women of your army are on the alert to defend our nation, you the American people, against aggression. This is *The Big Picture*."[138] The initiation of truce talks between the United Nations forces and those of North Korea, which began in July of 1951 and carried through to the armistice, suggests that a toning down of any rhetoric perceived to be provocative was in order, although there is no recorded evidence of a discussion of this among producers. Even with the airing of "Atrocities in Korea" (TV-242) in 1953, which focused on the mass executions of South Korean civilians by the North, the tone of the introduction remained moderated. This also suggests deference for the "Terms of Reference" discussions regulating prisoner-of-war-repatriation between the belligerents that began that year with the signing of the armistice agreement on 27 July 1953.[139]

By 1955, the producers had again altered the show's introduction and logo. Capturing the current mood of the military, it announced, "Today the latest weapons, coupled with the fighting skill of the American soldier, stand ready, on the alert all over the world to defend this country, you the American people, against aggression. This is *The Big Picture*."[140] This was that desperate time when the army found itself in sharp competition with its sister services to prove both that it deserved its place along the bulwarks in the defense of Western freedoms and that it was not lacking in technological know-how. All this was against a backdrop of shrinking resources. In conjunction with the updated narrative, the introductory video included segments showing an army television camera recording the launch of a tactical missile, the detonation of an Honest John atomic artillery round, and an airmobile assault.[141] It was during this period that *The Big Picture* was airing episodes of army adventures north of the Arctic Circle, such as "Exercise Arctic Night" (TV-337) and "Operation Lead Dog"

(TV-494), and its place on the modern frontline in the "Atomic Battle-field" (TV-396), all to justify its relevancy.

With the approach of the end of the decade the opening would again pass through several modifications, reflecting the producer's efforts to keep pace with contemporary television shows and to engage viewer interest. These included the frequent deletion of any introductory narrative and any standard video lead-in as the 1960s progressed. Instead, episodes would often open with thirty seconds of video relevant to the theme of the upcoming show. The 1962 episode "Special Forces" (TV-547) for example, began with special operations forces engaged in a tactical training exercise. Many other episodes followed suit, continuing into the late 1960s and early 1970s. The 1971 episode "There Is a Way" (TV-806) about the US Military Academy Preparatory School followed this format by opening directly into a scene of cadets marching on the grassy plain of West Point. Missing from *The Big Picture* was the staid, often overstated mission statement of the army. Following that trend, somber, direct references to any Cold War narrative also disappeared from each episode's prolog, replaced instead by filmed action sequences or a simple rotating globe circled by a beeping satellite. Eventually, even the recognizable three-dimensional rotating globe found replacement in a series of artist's cartoonish renderings of tanks, missiles, and soldiers in training, accompanied by a colorful two-dimensional image of the iconic *Big Picture* globe. It was an aesthetic change that offered a contemporary feel to attract viewers. With these cosmetic changes, it seems as if the series producers were reflecting a desperate gamble by the army to reinvent itself as something different, in a modern, upbeat, and popular sense, and not mired in dated, and often controversial, geopolitical struggles. With the end of conscription just around the corner in January 1973, the need to sell itself in a more attractive light to bolster future recruitment would have made sense.[142]

Other changes to the introductions involved the individual narrators and opening credits. The first narrator and cocreator, Captain Carl Zimmermann, opened each episode of the original thirteen and served as the face of *The Big Picture* through two dozen more, until the APC found a replacement. His departure from the show coincided with his return to a successful civilian life after a three-year

Figure 1.10. An image of the original *Big Picture* opening logo as it appeared in the earliest shows in the 1950s. Simple, in black and white, to reflect the sobriety of the programming, it would change over the ensuing years to reflect technological advancement as well the army's efforts to maintain audience appeal.

call-up to serve during the Korean conflict. Unfortunately, he never had a chance to enjoy presenting the final episodes about the Korean campaign, which concluded with "Korean Wind-Up" (TV-235). A different combat veteran who had served in the Signal Corps, Master Sergeant James Mansfield, replaced Zimmermann. His tenure began with the "Big Red One" (TV-210), which was coincidentally the first episode of Colonel Quinn's *Blue Badge* series. Mansfield remained for only a short while, until "Soldier in Berlin" (TV-232) aired in 1953. Master Sergeant Stuart Queen, another combat veteran, was his replacement. Queen remained the face of *The Big Picture* for the longest period, until the mid-1960s, when APC producers modified the introductory sequences to eliminate the need for any on-screen narrator.

Concurrent with the elimination of a narrator, the army studio also modified the opening of each episode. They accomplished this by

Figure 1.11. By the late 1950s a modified version of the original show logo included an orbiting satellite, a reference to the army's commitment to technological advancement.

bringing the credits forward from the conclusion. Instead of stating that the film was either "Produced by the Signal Corps" or "Produced by the Army Pictorial Center" and was "Presented by the United States Army," the official imprimatur simply claimed that it was "Produced for the Office of the Chief of Information by the Army Pictorial Center."[143] This change might suggest it was a move to relocate the responsibility for the production of *The Big Picture* away from an individual branch or activity to a single coordinating office for the dissemination of all information in the army. This would assign greater agency to the series as an official organ of the OCINFO, but it also suggests greater centralization of management and control over its production. However, there is no archived documentation indicating that the OCINFO issued any guidance in this regard. It was during this time also that the *Big Picture* series producers began introducing an increasing number of episodes that addressed military activities in Vietnam. That was central to the criticism from some members of

Congress, such as Senator William Fulbright, who voiced concerns of impropriety and charged that the CINFO was intentionally shaping the messages of these episodes to influence national foreign policy. Nevertheless, those format revisions would remain until the last episode in 1971.

Prime Time to Syndication

From its debut in December 1951 through the 1953 season, *The Big Picture* aired in the Washington, DC, area on the CBS television affiliate, *Washington Post*–owned WTOP. Just prior to the final fade-out for each of the early episodes, the last frame announced, "This program was originally produced for the Military District of Washington by Lieutenant Carl Bruton." After this original thirteen-week stint the show reappeared on ABC, filling prime-time slots until 1956. During the 1953–1954 season it appeared on Monday evenings at 9:30 p.m. opposite the popular *Red Buttons Show*, which maintained a ranking in the top twenty. The next season, 1954–1955, ABC moved it to Sunday at 8:30 p.m., but the competition for viewer percentage was stiffer against Ed Sullivan's *Toast of the Town* variety show, which ranked in the top ten. Finally, during its last year with ABC, 1955–1956, the network moved *The Big Picture* back to Mondays at 10:00 p.m. There, the series faced little competition, but the later night hour did not promise a wide audience. During these three seasons, a typical American family watching at home would have witnessed, among others, a plethora of *Big Picture* episodes detailing events on the Korean peninsula, including the "Korean Wind-Up" (TV-235); the army's early efforts to remain on the cutting edge of emerging technology, "Tools for a Modern Army" (TV-208); and its efforts to build its reputation north of the Arctic Circle in "Operation Blue Jay" (TV-227) and "Ice Cap" (TV-273). If the show had remained on the prime-time television carousel, through the late 1950s and into the 1960s, audiences would have seen the army's continuing efforts to sell itself as a relevant, modern force through its experimentation with guided missiles and satellites, or its further exploration along the polar ice cap. But this was not to be. Decision-makers within the Office of the Chief of Information and the APC seemed determined to break the army's relationship with the major television networks. This seems to have been predicated on three factors. The first was a dislike for the idea of associating the show with a prime-time sponsor who might possibly attempt to leverage control of episode content. In this context, the army chief of information made it clear that "the Army must maintain strict creative control" of its programs, with a complete understanding that if it maintained a strict oversight it "could inhibit the Army's ability to have a presence on prime-time television."[144] The second concern was apprehension that networks might drop *The Big Picture* or relegate it to a disadvantageous time slot if ratings lagged. Finally, there was APC producers' belief that switching to a distribution model that reached more viewers was possible through off-network broadcast syndication. This would make it possible to ship episodes of the show to as many television stations within as many markets as possible. That concept gained support from senior military leaders such as the commanding general of the US Sixth Army. In a March 1959 letter to the CINFO he encouraged taking steps to distribute *The Big Picture* more widely through his area, in the American southwest. The show, he noted, was "a valuable tool for winning public support for the Army" while "holding the line against increasing competition from other Government agencies for public-service air time."[145] These positions—avoiding external leverage, managing time slots, and reaching a wider audience—helped frame a new distribution model.

Distribution

Prior to July 1959, the Office of the R-T Section of the PID was the central authority for distribution of the *Big Picture* series. This made dissemination of episodes cumbersome by creating a bureaucratic bottleneck at the national level. When responsibility for production of the show passed from the PID to the TID in that year, the distribution system changed. The chief of the TID, Col. John O. Weaver, pushed the responsibility out to the Central Film and Equipment Exchange Office within each of the six army headquarters in the United States. This located a distribution authority within six geographical regions instead of one overarching agency. With this change, accessibility to area television stations increased. The result streamlined the distribution of *The Big Picture*, which then occurred through coordination between television stations and the command information officer (IO) within the Audio-Visual Support Center (AVSC) at each army installation. The IO prepared and scheduled the appearance of each film. The AVSC would then package and deliver the film to the television station according to the agreed schedule. The IO was responsible for coordinating a rotation of *Big Picture* episodes among the stations in their area to ensure adequate distribution. Groups or individuals could also request specific episodes in parallel to this procedure to satisfy their additional needs. To obtain episodes of *The Big Picture*, civilian requestors first reviewed the Department of the Army's Pamphlet 108-1, *Index of Army Motion Pictures and Related Audio-Visual Aids*, which contained a listing and description of available *Big Picture* episodes.[146] After deciding on a particular title, the organization or television station then had to follow the guidelines outlined in Department of the Army Field Manual (FM) 11-41, *Audio-Visual Support Center Operations*.[147] The instructions were straightforward and required that contact be made with the IO or Audio-Visual Support Center (AVSO) on the nearest military installation. Depending on the need, the IO would either approve or disapprove the request. There were some episodes that the army did not consider appropriate for release to the public; these generally involved informational or training films about new weapons systems.

By taking advantage of the new distribution model, regional army headquarters were in closer contact with local television stations. A 1959 memo from the chief of information for the Fifth Army to the army CINFO notes that fifty new regional stations requested the *Big Picture* series, with regular scheduling planned for each day of the week including prime time.[148] In this particular case, the coverage included viewers in a swath of eleven states in the north central region of the United States. The bounds were from the greater metropolitan area of Chicago in the east to Colorado in the west, and from North Dakota south to Missouri and the St. Louis area.[149] This increased distribution of the show continued through to the 1968–1969 season, when it aired on 313 commercial and 53 educational television stations nationwide.[150] The army offered episodes free to stations, but supplied them only on request, and stations generally showed them

Figure 1.12. Cover of the *Big Picture* catalog listing the title and description of each episode in the first nine series of the show (1951–1956). The army made this publication available to stations, the media, and any organization inquiring about the films. (Image Source: Rich Zimmermann)

as part of their public service time. Catalogs of the episodes were available also on request, and promotional materials were available at broadcasters' conventions.

In contrast to the prime-time slots offered by the major networks, *The Big Picture* began appearing at less traditional times that offered the possibility of access to a wider demographic cross-section across multiple geographic markets. For example, it aired on WPIX-TV in New York City at 12:30 p.m. on Saturday; WATR-TV in Waterbury, Connecticut, at 5:00 p.m. on Tuesday; WLWC-TV in Columbus, Ohio, at 1:00 p.m. on Thursday; and KLXA-TV in Hollywood, California, at 2:30 p.m. on Sunday. In addition, viewers could find the show in US possessions on channels such as WSVI-TV in the US Virgin Islands at 6:30 p.m. on Saturday.[151]

An additional survey of distribution and viewership reveals that *The Big Picture* increasingly appeared in intermediate-sized standard metropolitan statistical area (SMSA), such as Richmond, Virginia. Between January 1959 and May 1971, the series appeared regularly on one of three major network affiliates in Richmond (ABC, CBS, and NBC) and WCVE-TV, an independent educational channel.[152] For example, from 11 January 1969 to 28 December 1969 *The Big Picture* aired consistently on Saturdays and Sundays, at 7:00 a.m. and 8:00 a.m. respectively, alternating between WXEX-TV (ABC) and WTVR-TV (CBS), for at least two viewings weekly. During this time it also appeared periodically on WCVE-TV 23. This pattern spanned twelve years and occasionally included WRVA-TV, the NBC affiliate. After 1959, the series had moved to syndication, and those Richmond stations that procured copies of its films adjusted the time slots as necessary to fit their needs. Thus, prior to 1969, *The Big Picture* also occasionally filled 2:00 p.m. time slots on Saturdays and 1:00 p.m. slots on Sundays. The stations broadcast the show to a Richmond SMSA covering an area that included 436,044 potential viewers in 1960, which grew to 518,319 by 1970.[153] The size of the population together with the frequency of appearance of *The Big Picture* suggests that the show enjoyed wide exposure in this geographical region. There is the suggestion that *The Big Picture* also enjoyed comparable viewership in similar intermediate-sized SMSAs. Another such area was Des Moines, Iowa, within the Fifth Army area mentioned earlier

City	Time	Channel	Call Sign
	Sunday, 8 Jan 1967		
Des Moines	10:00 a.m.	8	WHO-TV
Rochester	11:30 a.m.	10	KROC-TV
Cedar Rapids	2:00 p.m.	9	KCRG-TV
	Monday, 9 Jan 1967		
Des Moines	8:00 p.m.	11	KDPS-TV
	Friday, 13 Jan 1967		
Mason City	3:30 p.m.	3	KGLO-TV
	Saturday, 14 Jan 1967		
Rock Island	2:00 p.m.	8	WQAD-TV
Omaha	3:30 p.m.	3	KMTV-TV
Fort Dodge	5:00 p.m.	21	KVFD-TV

Table 1.2. From 8 January through 14 January 1967, the *Big Picture* series aired across the greater Des Moines, Iowa, metropolitan statistical area. It appeared in eight time slots on various days and times across the region, on eight separate television channels. Outside of Des Moines viewers could also see the show in locations as far away as Cedar Rapids and Omaha. *Source*: "TV Magazine," *Des Moines Iowa Register*, 8 January 1967, TV-4, TV-6, TV-10, TV-11.

in this chapter. With a population size that was just under that of Richmond, it also had the potential to reach an increased number of viewers.[154] Coincidentally, that region includes the town of Ottumwa, the subject of a *Big Picture* episode titled "Ottumwa, U.S.A." (TV-387). An example of one week's airing of *The Big Picture* in the Des Moines area in January 1967 appears in Table 1.2.

Although the move from prime time to syndication did remove any leverage major broadcasting networks or sponsors may have had on the series and its messaging, further analysis reveals that the move did come with certain costs. The new distribution model was effective in sending the series into a broader base of outlets, through more independent stations and intermediate-sized markets, but in doing this the army sacrificed the advantage of prime-time viewership in larger, more densely populated markets, such as New York. Also, most independent stations slotted *The Big Picture* where they needed a filler:

early morning, afternoon doldrums, or late night. As such, it some-times aired in less frequented weekend time slots, or on less popular television channels. As the "TV-Films Reviews" columnist of *Billboard* acknowledged, "The Army distributes the show free, and practically every station in the country carries it, tho [*sic*] not always in the best time slot."[155] Still, the move to syndication did eliminate unwanted external influence and promised a measure of longevity, since major networks may have eventually dropped the program if ratings were lagging.

Understanding the show's impact through the lens of distribution, however, offers other insights. For example, it suggests that Senator Fulbright's 1969 congressional diatribe against army propaganda lacked authority when he singled out *The Big Picture* as a leading culprit. By the late 1960s, the television series had been navigating the vagaries of syndication scheduling. Although Fulbright argued against the show's messages, its distribution in secondary and smaller markets would have reduced its impact as a vehicle of unwanted pro-paganda. Even as the army continued to celebrate increased distribu-tion of the *Big Picture* series, throughout the span of its production, it lacked a presence in larger SMSAs and prime-time markets. As a result, claims by critics that it possessed great influence in shaping audience opinions are difficult to credential. A dearth of supporting data in records or archives of polls, ratings, or audience numbers con-tributes to undermining claims made by *Big Picture* critics.

The few available ratings of *The Big Picture* that do exist are those provided by Ziv-TV and the American Research Bureau (ARB) in the *Billboard* newsletter for the years 1952 through 1955.[156] On 14 June 1952, the Ziv annual ratings listed *The Big Picture* as #8 out of the top ten Non-Network TV Shows. In that same issue the Public Service Di-vision of *Billboard*'s first quarterly station survey of TV-films listed *The Big Picture* as #1 out of twenty-six public service films "as mentioned by stations."[157] The series had garnered 196 points in station votes, besting the second-ranked show, *Industry on Parade*, by over one hun-dred points.[158] By that September, the *Big Picture* only gained honorable mention in the next quarterly rating survey for Non-Network TV shows falling out of the top ten behind #8-ranked *Crusade in the Pacific*, and #10 ranked *Crusade in Europe*.[159] In February 1953, in the *Billboard* First

Annual TV-Film Show Awards the *Big Picture* rated #5, behind #1 *Victory at Sea*, #2 *Crusade in Europe*, and #4 *Crusade in the Pacific*.[160] The last rating that included the *Big Picture* appeared in the 31 July 1954 issue of *Billboard*. At that time, the Second Annual TV-Film Awards listed *The Big Picture* as #9 of ten. Here, it at last bested *Crusade in the Pacific* at #10, but fell far behind in points awarded (1657 to 5) to the very successful *Victory at Sea* ranked at #1.[161] Several media reviews substantiate the success of *The Big Picture* in the early years of production. One reviewer noted that the series "is far better than many of its friendly competitors . . . because it tells a public service story in an interesting manner, without the flag-waving monotony so often associated with films of this type."[162] He concluded with the comment, "This is one public service show that certainly encourages the viewer to tune in, week after week."[163] *Variety* magazine concurred, noting the show had "a realistic quality that lifts it above the routine documentary."[164] These were heady words, considering the competition included *Victory at Sea*.

The *Billboard* ARB ratings for *The Big Picture* during the same window of time, are less reliable and show great variance. For example, on 4 October 1952 the ARB rated the series at 6.0 points on WBZ-TV (Boston), and on 25 October at 4.3 points on KLAC (Los Angeles).[165] By 14 March 1953 it was at 0.6 points on WTTG (Washington, DC) and a month later, on 18 April 1953, it was at 2.1 points on the same station. ARB ratings for the show in 1954 do not appear in *Billboard*. But by 26 March 1955 *The Big Picture* secured a rating of 2.0 on KGO (San Francisco), and on 30 July 1955 a 13.2 on KEDD (Wichita). These were the last ARB ratings for the show in *Billboard*. Altogether, these sparse ratings provide little basis for an accurate or consistent evaluation of the series during the first few years of *The Big Picture's* production. Nevertheless, the evidence of actions suggests the army producers took a risk, choosing a secondary-tier distribution plan to ensure the possibility of longevity, maintaining production control, and reaching a wider demographic, over the prospect of shorter term, prime-time viewership in larger markets. These considerations all suggest that regardless of how the military celebrated the move to syndication, or how critics evaluate the show's impact, the efficacy of the new distribution model remains difficult to judge. *The Big Picture* did, however, outlast its television competition.

Substantial evidence discloses certain enticements that the army offered to the secondary markets for airing *The Big Picture*. Other than letters of thanks to station managers and producers from the OCINFO, that office also forwarded plaques of appreciation to the stations. Among several of the archived communications is an October 1958 memo directing the purchase of 400 plaques from the OCINFO chief, Liaison Division, to the commander of the Army Exhibit Unit. These would serve as awards to certain stations for regularly broadcasting *Big Picture* episodes and would be "an excellent publicity gimmick for the Army."[166] Similarly, a December 1958 communication from the deputy chief, Troop Information Division, to the chief of the Army Exhibit Unit contained a request for the acquisition of an additional 350 award plaques. As the note instructs, affixed to each plaque would be a metal plate embossed with the words, "To the Management and Staff of Station ___ for outstanding public service in programming the Department of the Army weekly TV series—The Big Picture—and for continued interest and cooperation during the ___ season."[167] The same memo requested the production of two large panels to use as advertisements about *The Big Picture* at the 1959 National Association of Broadcasters' Convention in Chicago. It also ordered the distribution of ten of the plaques to each of the six army military regions in the United States prior to the convention. This was to generate interest prior to the gathering. Another such memo dated 18 March 1959, from the CINFO to the commander, US Army in Alaska, notes the recognition of several local television stations there and mentions the forwarding of plaques of appreciation to those station managers. For a number of years the army worked diligently to sell *The Big Picture* to stations across the nation, offering devices such as certificates and plaques as enticements.

Aside from the *Big Picture* series appearing on television in the United States, the Armed Forces Network Television (AFN-TV) channels overseas also regularly broadcast it. There, it was available to American service members, government civilians, and their families, wherever they could receive the broadcast signal. This included established military communities as well as many isolated locations. Over the years, as the AFN signal spread in Europe through the placement of additional signal towers, so did the television viewing audience. Beginning in West Germany, this grew to include Italy, France, Belgium, and England. Typical AFN-TV schedules, conveniently printed in the ubiquitous, popular *Stars and Stripes* newspaper, reveal that *The Big Picture* enjoyed prime viewing slots. For example, in 1963, AFN-TV channels also aired it on Saturdays at 3:30 p.m. and 5:30 p.m. This accommodated children after school and families during the dinner hour. By 1969, it remained on the two available channels with broadcasts at 6:01 p.m. and 6:00 p.m. Again, this was an accommodating time to capture the attention of entire families. An additional effect of the wide array of signal towers broadcasting AFN-TV signals was the collateral sharing of programming with local civilians, who could intercept the transmissions with their televisions. In this manner, AFN-TV often shared shows, including *The Big Picture*, with host-nation citizens and had an opportunity to shape and influence understandings of American culture and society.

The Pacific edition of the *Stars and Stripes* reveals that *The Big Picture* enjoyed a similar experience in that theater. A July 1962 printing carried an AFKN (American Forces Korea Network) television schedule that listed the show in 7:00 p.m. and 7:05 p.m. time slots on the two available channels. Through the mid-1960s the US military's Far East Network (FEN) TV channels in Japan offered the military communities there showings of *The Big Picture* on Wednesdays at 7:00 p.m. A survey of television listings for AFKN, FEN, and AFN shows that those networks continued to air episodes, although at a lesser frequency, through the 1970s and into the 1980s, at least until 1983. As American involvement in Vietnam deepened, so too did the availability of television entertainment for service members stationed throughout the country. By early 1967, the American Forces Vietnam Television (AFVN-TV) began airing episodes of *The Big Picture* from their signal tower in Saigon. From there, it continued to spread. For example, a 1970 edition of the Pacific *Stars and Stripes* reveals that *The Big Picture* was airing at Nha Trang on Tuesdays at 6:00 p.m. and Thursdays at 8:00 p.m., at Pleiku on Tuesdays at 4:30 p.m., and at Da Nang on Tuesdays at 4:30 p.m. On the schedule for Da Nang, it was nestled between Johnny Carson's *Tonight Show* and the sitcom

Get Smart, both very popular back in the States. Given the situation in Vietnam however, the *Big Picture* was not in competition with these two shows so it could enjoy a certain privilege that was absent when it jousted for prime-time slotting on the major networks back home a decade earlier. During the years that *The Big Picture* appeared on television sets overseas, in homes and barracks, millions of service members and civilian government employees and their families who rotated through these assignments watched the APC production and gained exposure to the narratives and messages of the well-crafted series. It provided information, training, and, through a number of episodes, a touch of home.

Ideas for episodes came from a variety of sources. Occasionally, regional IOs would forward their own thoughts, or suggestions submitted to them by various units or individuals stationed abroad or in the United States. In one instance, a set of "story topics concerning United States Army Europe" arrived in a letter from the deputy chief, Information Division, USAREUR, to the chief of public information, OCINFO, with a note that "these story ideas are for your consideration for *Big Picture* or other outlets."[168] An additional comment that "USAREUR is providing a lion's share of 'Big Picture' footage [to the APC] but we feel we have only scratched the surface" hinted at some level of competition among units and commands to gain exposure and recognition in *Big Picture* productions.[169] Several months later, another recommendation arrived from the USAREUR Information Division suggesting the creation of an episode titled "Pentomic Seventh Army." An archived memo reflects the eager acceptance by the chief, PID, and production began after some preliminary script work.[170] It eventually aired as episode TV-421, under the same title. Suggestions also included historical subjects. After viewing the episode on "The History of Cavalry" (TV-382), the chief of the Armor Section, US Continental Army, recommended the development of a show on the "History of the Armor."[171] Reacting quickly, the APC produced it as "Armored Combat Power" (TV-389). The archives reveal a large number of letters and memos proposing topics for episodes from a variety of sources. This suggests an interesting relationship between service personnel and units, who saw in the television series an opportunity to feel as if they were participants in telling a story or crafting a narrative about the army or an aspect of military history, and the production itself. In this context, a link of common purpose emerged between the soldier and *The Big Picture*.

The *Big Picture* series developed from a need to tell a story about the American army's involvement in the Korean War. With the rapid evolution of communications technology, the military leadership realized the advantage television provided as a platform to deliver a variety of messages. For two decades *The Big Picture* would serve as a vessel to reach into American homes, as well as public and political spaces, to make important connections and shape thinking about the role of the army in the early Cold War period, its modernization trends, its history, and the lives of service members.

2

Making the Army Relevant Again

The US Army understood that all its efforts at propaganda were critically important as it was losing the battle of public relations compared to the other services in the early postwar decades. The collection of compilation documentaries, particularly *Victory at Sea*, *Crusade in the Pacific*, and *Air Power*, attracted the public's attention and surrendered a public relations primacy to the US Navy and US Air Force that the US Army could only envy. This became more evident over time as the other services also began producing their own self-serving series such as *Navy Log* and *Uncommon Valor*. In this context, the presence of *The Big Picture* "served as a mediating force between the Army's internal image-makers and the wider world of public opinion."[1] The army hierarchy understood this imperative and were sensitive to an environment where "in many instances the Army has been poorly portrayed by the other services in their television series."[2]

This chapter follows the army's efforts to present itself as a relevant postwar branch of the service as it restructured to fit the mold of the New Look military. This includes initiatives to engage with science and emerging technologies that brought the army to the edge of new frontiers.

The Army's New Look

Informational episodes crafted to pique the public interest followed the early *Big Picture* run. They included stories about "Army Aviation" (TV-188), "The Army Medical Corps" (TV-189), and "The Eyes and Ears of the Army" (TV-192), an overview of the US Army Signal Corps and how it assists the US Navy and US Air Force with their communications needs. In the words of narrator Carl Zimmermann, the signal corps "provides the intricate communications and other facilities without which modern warfare would be impossible."[3] This statement was significant for the army, which continued to feel marginalized by the other services and a Congress that began to question "its relevance to the larger project of Soviet deterrence."[4] It was during this decade that the size of the military began to shrink, with the army reduced from 1.6 million personnel in 1952 to approximately 860,000 by 1959.[5] Although all the services felt the impact of the post-Korea drawdown in manpower, the army felt it the most keenly. Both the air force and the navy traditionally carried less personnel on their rosters and were systems oriented, while the army relied primarily on the ground soldier—easy to train, easy to equip, and easy to replace.

As American forces in NATO transitioned from a conventional ground war strategy to one more reliant on tactical nuclear deterrence during the late 1950s, the shift away from the army to the more technocentric services was more apparent. This was part of the military establishment's "New Look" restructuring program, which placed the concept of "massive retaliation" at its core. Inspired by President Eisenhower, it emphasized advancements and funding for weapons with a quick-strike capability, such as nuclear-equipped Polaris missiles for the navy and Minuteman missiles for the air force.[6] One reaction from the army, in 1957, was a directed restructuring of all of its infantry and airborne divisions into a "Pentomic" configuration of five battle groups, each with augmentation by an artillery rocket regiment armed with Honest John tactical nuclear missiles. The army chief of staff, General Maxwell Taylor, thought this would provide a modern feel that showcased the marriage of deterrence and technology and serve as a foil to a further diminishing of resources.[7] It was featured in at least four *Big Picture* episodes: "Pentomic 101st" (TV-351), "Pentomic Army" (TV-394), "Pentomic Seventh Army" (TV-421), and "A Sharper Sword and Stronger Shield" (TV-449). Each described an army that melded structural flexibility with the latest nuclear and conventional weapons systems. But this concerted sales pitch was only a minor salve to remedy the struggle against perceived obsolescence. Still feeling the pressure to adjust to changing times, the army's desperate hope to maintain relevancy rested in continued public relations, and *The Big Picture* remained one of the best weapons at hand.

To offer proof of the army's relevance, the APC began its work in earnest, producing one new episode of *The Big Picture* approximately every ten days.[8] The episodes that spilled out of its Long Island studios as part of this initiative to continue to bolster the army's image followed two parallel approaches. The first continued to present contemporary achievements and portrayals of army life to the American public, while the second focused on proving that it was keeping pace with the other services in technology and modernization—the latter being more essential in attracting congressional support and grabbing a bigger slice of the funding pie.

One of the earliest episodes to address a new focus was "Tools for a Modern Army" (TV-208) in 1951, which featured segments on such systems as atomic artillery, jet helicopters, and increased mobility via multi-airdrops. This was a new and important direction that *The Big Picture* was taking, as noted during the introduction by Carl Zimmermann, the narrator: "In the past we've talked to you about the soldier and his weapons. Today *The Big Picture* concerns itself with the research and development necessary to provide those weapons. The tools for a modern army. The tools that ensure our freedom."[9] The episode was quite clear about the connection between technological innovation and American survival, and scripted into the closing narrative was the following rather bald solicitation:

There is no frontier of human knowledge left unexplored by the scouts of military research and development. From their trail blazing there will emerge a more secure America, a nation as nearly invulnerable to aggression as a strong military establishment armed by technological superiority can make it. Only, we must not rest on the accomplishments of the past. Time and money are needed to produce the best tools and equipment possible. The price of liberty, a great American once said, is eternal vigilance. We must be watchful, we must be alert, we must be stronger than any potential foe.[10]

Another early episode that addressed the "New Look" focus was "Guided Missiles" (TV-245) in 1954. A narrator introduced it with the claim, "Today we bring you the story of America's newest weapon in her arsenal of defense, the guided missile." Then, leaning in toward the camera with a conspiratorial smile, he added, "Portions of this story have been filmed in secrecy and now have been declassified in order that you the American people might know the progress that is being made in the field of guided missile development." The episode featured an exercise showing the destruction of a fake enemy bomber by an army guided missile, a weapon that was "developed after years of research by army ordnance."[11] Following that thread were other episodes that expounded this theme of technology and the new army. They addressed the orchestrated effort to demonstrate the integration of army missile units, radar technology, and communications networks in protecting the American homeland from a surprise Soviet nuclear attack.[12] That also included the testing of weapons and training of a Pentomic division in the Nevada desert under conditions of an atomic bomb detonation. Characteristic of these mini techno-tele-films was the 1958 production "Army Satellites" (TV-397). It focused on the successful launching of the army's Explorer I satellite earlier that year as a national response to the Soviet launching of Sputnik I in October 1957. This was a matter of importance for the army, and the narrator's voice swelled with pride as he proclaimed: "Today's *Big Picture* will reveal the dramatic, suspenseful story of how the army, when the prestige of the United States throughout the world had been shaken by events beyond its control, stirred the hearts and emotions of the American people with an epic display of scientific and technical teamwork."[13] As a summary, the narration reminded that audience that it was all possible "by the close cooperation of the army with some of the best technical and scientific minds in the land."[14]

Each of these films revealed the army's new obsession with technology. Unlike other episodes listed in the APC catalog, which highlighted the service's wide range of achievements, missions, and heritage, these featured scientific advancement as a central character. Almost as an East Coast version of the air force's Lookout Mountain facility, the APC drew from its talented pool of writers, camera crews, and producers to bring together this collection to make clear the army's contribution in meeting America's future needs.[15] Typical of these was "Army Satellites," which introduced scenes that brought together men and machines in a synergistic relationship resulting in the army's successful launching of Explorer I. The film showed army scientists and technicians sitting at consoles active with dials and switches, hunched over drafting tables, monitoring rocket engine test sites, and watching hopefully at launch pads. In those moments, the cinematic record stripped the soldiers of their familiar olive-drab field uniforms and cloaked them in technicians' lab coats, the new warrior's robes. Again and again, the camera captured the rockets standing at attention, the focal point in the frame, ready at Man's command to do his bidding. The music that followed the images was serious and driving, hurrying and pressing the scientists and technicians along in their need to respond to the Soviets' challenge and in their competition with the other services to gain the pole position in the race to be at the technological vanguard for the military. As the film unfolds, it eventually brings the viewer into the control room on the day of the scheduled launch—the atmosphere electric with excitement—to witness the climax of the operation, the satisfactory completion of America's "first attempt to fire a manmade moon into orbit."[16] The viewer is on hand to witness the ringing success of the mission, the camera bearing record of the achievement. Bringing "Army Satellites" full circle, the film comes to an end with the renowned rocketeer Dr. Wernher von Braun, who speaks at length celebrating the military's latest scientific effort and achievement.[17] Like a harbinger in each film, the *Big Picture* narrator constantly reminds us that the impetus driving the technological imperative is the threat of foreign aggression. Although this collection of productions paled in comparison to some of the efforts of the air force studios on the West coast, for the moment, they made a strong argument for the army's engagement with emerging technologies.

For these efforts, *The Big Picture* served as a strong, and available, sales platform to maintain a connection with the public and curry favor with congressional elites by demonstrating the army's key role in national defense, alongside the air force and navy, through contributions in research and development. Unfortunately for the army, then the air force, the creation of the National Aeronautics and Space Administration (NASA) in 1958 obviated the military's role in space exploration. For the army it was already a losing proposition, as only a year later the crew selection of the first astronauts for participation in the Mercury 7 manned-flight program included three navy candidates, three from the air force, and one from the marine corps. No army pilots met the requirements.[18] In 1962 the next group of nine space candidates also did not include a representative from the army. Under those circumstances, the army understood that it needed to establish a new initiative and public relations angle.

Sensitive to the need for a retooled image, the APC followed the lead set forth by the Association of the United States Army (AUSA), the service's premier lobbying organization, during its annual convention in 1959. Proclaiming a theme of "The Modern Army," the AUSA hoped to influence change in the coming years. This shaped the APC's decision to continue to reformat the *Big Picture* series to "tell the Army's story in the fields of research and development, education of the individual soldier, and his responsibilities to the Free World at home and overseas."[19] For the APC producers this was a commitment to a "Changing Picture" in which "television audiences will see the 'modern Army,' what it is accomplishing and what its mission for tomorrow is expected to be."[20] In that context, *The Big Picture*'s role would be to promote the "vast change which has taken place in the Army since the end of hostilities in Korea."[21]

New Frontiers

One new possibility that appeared was the army's investment in Arctic operations. It provided a fresh theater that, like space, showcased another bold initiative undertaken by the army to prove that it could operate on the edge of science and technology. Although the air force was also moving in that direction with its own operations, between 1952 and 1965 the army produced at least eleven *Big Picture* episodes that featured its efforts to explore, exploit, and inhabit, for national defense purposes, the hostile spaces of the severe north. It was in that place, a cold, rugged desert, devoid of human presence, that the army advanced, pushing to the extreme the front line of America's defense. That was the narrative this Arctic series conveyed to its audiences. In taking on that challenge, the army was engaging with those "new frontiers," technological and geophysical, that appeared consistent with President Kennedy's challenge to the nation to discover its full potential and its future. Aside from space, the uninhabited region north of the Arctic Circle provided those possibilities. That was the story the APC wanted to sell by evidence of films in its catalog; although corresponding documentary evidence of office memos, letters, and notes in the archives is not present, the cinematic record provides proof. This saga began with "Operation Blue Jay" (TV-227), "one of the great military secrets of our time."[22] *The Big Picture* told the story of the newly declassified joint civil-military project to construct a military facility in Thule, Greenland. This was in response to a growing global communist threat as perceived by then president Harry S Truman, who had "proclaimed a national emergency."[23] Conceived as the "greatest feat of military construction since World War II," the goal was to establish an airbase for American airpower in a hostile environment.[24] Through the lens of *The Big Picture* the project it served to distinguish the army's unique capabilities from those of the other services.

"Operation Blue Jay" set the tone for the other episodes that followed. Its storyline traced the blending of a joint venture between the American military and modern industrial might to plan and prepare for a grand adventure. Scenes showed the gathering of assets, mountains of supplies and squadrons of machines collected for the task at hand. Cameras framed crews of workers laboring at loading trains and ships, busy hands securing loads, and feverish supervisors checking and rechecking plans. As with all these episodes, the narration described the efforts as concentrated and focused, bent to a purpose. At last, the Blue Jay expedition was ready, and in a spirit reminiscent of early colonists, an armada of almost one hundred ships left port at Norfolk, Virginia, bound for their new world. The film shared with viewers the hazards of travel at sea, ice fields that blocked the path and rain squalls that hampered the ships' journey. As the drama increased, the story at last brought the modern pioneers to the shores of their new station. But as the narrator cautioned, the work was just to begin. Teams of men hastily erected shelters, machines carved out a landing strip, and basic facilities became operational. The tempo was swift and efforts were in haste, as the narrator reminded viewers that time was of the essence with the fast approach of the harsh winter season. Throughout the entire episode there was a pervasive sense of urgency encouraged by images of men and machines hard at their tasks, accompanied by an integrated musical score that helped create a serious, determined atmosphere. So it was, as the cinematic story unfolded and the outpost on the barren shores emerged, that an admixture of harmonies, including the faint strains of "Ode to Joy," ushered the effort to completion. For the time, it appeared that the army had planted its public relations flag 900 miles north of the Arctic Circle.

Through the remainder of the 1950s, *The Big Picture* continued to capture army operations as they unfolded in the cold north. A plethora of episodes followed the example set in "Operation Blue Jay," carrying the message that the army could perform its mission even in the most extreme conditions. More important, it "did not miss the opportunity to demonstrate that it was undertaking its own exploration of geophysical extremes,"[25] underscoring the army's participation in the International Geophysical Year (IGY) for 1957–1958 intended to compile "data to contribute to Man's understanding of the world in which he lives."[26] Subsequent episodes in the 1960s carried the theme of army adventures in the northern tier forward. They recounted efforts to construct Camp Century, a city of tunnels under Greenland's snow and ice, complete with a functioning nuclear reactor. Other *Big*

Picture productions stressed the necessity of pushing the envelope of scientific exploration without straying far from the contemporary geopolitical reality that "it is imperative that we push the outpost line of defense of the Free World far to the north into the very shadow of the pole itself," to forestall further communist expansion.[27] As part of that initiative, several of the episodes included a screenshot of the Danish flag during the introduction that read, "This film is the story of a research and development project, filmed in Greenland, a part of Denmark. The cooperation of Denmark in making this project possible, as one of her contributions to the North Atlantic Treaty Organization is gratefully acknowledged."[28] This served a dual purpose, both as notice of the army's scientific achievement and a passing nod to the staunch unity of NATO against possible communist aggression.

The most innovative of the Greenland-themed *Big Picture* films was the "U.S. Army and the Boy Scouts" (TV-520). Innocuous title aside, it spoke of more than just the army's long-standing mutually beneficial relationship with the Scouts. Central to the story was the offering of a unique invitation to the Boy Scouts of both the United States and Denmark to send one scout each to spend a six-month winter as a guest at Camp Century. Against images of the scouts performing various tasks, the narrator commented that they had "earned their keep as junior scientific aides in one of the world's most unusual communities," adding that their behavior in the severe climate was a "complete credit to the army and the scout movement."[29] This *Big Picture* film was a clever and well-conceived public relations ploy that at once celebrated the army's scientific achievements and its relationship with the other NATO member nations, as well as the Boy Scouts. Through this, the army could hope to gain the necessary recognition and support from the American political elites.

During the years that spanned the 1950s through the early 1970s, the *Big Picture* catalog listed episodes, beside rocketry or the Arctic, that served as continued reminders of the army's efforts to blaze a trail into the technological future. For example, "Science Moves the Army" (TV-668) was one of a series produced by the APC that focused attention on specialized army centers of technological excellence such as the Army Tank Automotive Center, a place where "military and civilian personnel are facing Space Age problems and producing sophisticated machines of war."[30] Also featured were the Army Combat Developments Command, whose motto was "Today's Vision, Tomorrow's Victory," and the Army Materiel Command. These were unique organizations within the army that addressed the contemporary challenges of procuring and maintaining the latest equipment and weapons systems. Complementing these were other episodes that offered to pull back the curtain for a look into the army's future. They carried titles that left little doubt as to the message contained in each, such as "Meeting Tomorrow's Challenge" (TV-765) and "Pioneering for Tomorrow" (TV-815), which proudly proclaimed, "Fluid logic, lasers, semiconductor technology, total instrumentation—these diverse areas of investigation are only a small part of the research and development program being called on by scientists and engineers of the United States Army Materiel Command laboratories."[31] Up until the end of its production run *The Big Picture* continued to stress the army's technological prowess. In this regard, one of its last episodes in 1971, "The U.S. Army in Space and under the Sea" (TV-819), heralded the service's accomplishments: "Americans are justly proud of their nation's achievements in space exploration—achievements in which the United States Army played an important early role."[32] Here, it also introduced yet another possible frontier for the service by adding that "beneath the sea, men of the army move in another alien environment as army divers go underwater to repair military facilities and salvage costly equipment."[33] The spirit of the film was that it was an army prepared to meet the nation's needs anytime and anywhere, and hopefully through the *Big Picture* series the congressional appropriations committees would recognize that.

Unlike the cinematographic approach used for the Korean War episodes and others in the catalog, the APC changed the mood of the theme of the scientific and technological films by varying its techniques. Setting the tone, the episode "Science Moves the Army" appeared in color. This switch to the new format allowed *The Big Picture* to keep pace with the newer generation of televisions in American homes and to send a signal that the army was also following technology's lead. Scenes from "Top of the World" (TV-543) and "Icecap" (TV-664) showed Camp Century in Greenland, where audiences witnessed military scientists sliding control rods into an atomic reactor to support a "nuclear powered city under the ice."[34] The visual record replaced narration to tell the story of an army that was multifaceted, ready to fight aggression but also ready to face new scientific challenges. Light, energetic musical scores accompanied scenes of Sno-Cat and Sno-Scout vehicles sprinting across open white expanses and helicopters delivering supplies to northern reaches amid swirling snows. Gone were the gray-toned scenes of struggling military columns wending their way across a ruined landscape alongside desperate refugees. Gentler leitmotifs replaced the heavy-toned musical dirges of war. This was new and exciting, this was the future. Cameras revealed the military working side by side with civilians in boardrooms and laboratories, handling complex equipment and monitoring complicated gauges. Still images of futuristic weapons and vehicles delivered the message as well as any scripted dialog—the army could, and was keeping pace with the other services to build a brighter tomorrow. The APC production crews applied all their skills to show the army in this light.

Big Picture Out of Focus

During its twenty-year run (1951–1971), the *Big Picture* series encountered certain periods of time that offered challenges to its production. Some were minor, others were significant. Among the minor was a potential boycott threatened by the New York branch of the Screen Actors Guild (SAG), which disputed the rate of pay of civilian actors and crews at the APC in October 1967.[35] That was quickly resolved without any disruption to operations at the studios. However, more significant challenges arose, which had the potential to bring production to a complete standstill. These came in the form of competition from other shows, funding shortfalls, and objections to the contents of the *Big Picture* message. In each case except the last, the *Big Picture* was able to weather the tempest and continue its course. Of these challenges, the first was a consequence of a national zeitgeist and required the least response.

As a military-themed show, *The Big Picture* never appeared alone during its production run in the 1950s. Aside from the popular but shorter-duration documentaries such as *Victory at Sea* and *Air Power*, some other anthology or series that offered *The Big Picture* competition for audience share always existed. Shows such as *Battle Report—Pentagon* or *The Facts We Face* premiered a year sooner than *The Big Picture*, then aired concurrently on other television networks. Other shows such as *Navy Log* launched later but also aired for several concurrent years. Among these others, the only program that ran for more than 100 episodes besides *The Big Picture* was *Navy Log*, which listed 103 stories. Although the army show exhibited greater longevity with over 800 episodes, by comparison the *Navy Log* tales, which contained dramatic reenactments by professional actors, seemed to garner greater popular appeal during its television lifespan. As historian Lisa Mundey notes, the anthology, which only ran from 1955 to 1958, "presented positive images of the sea service," while showcasing its role in the Cold War and projecting the navy as "family friendly as well."[36] It offered mixed story lines of interpersonal relationships together with individual successes and disappointments. Contemporary polls offered positive comments about the series from a younger male demographic, who opined that the show helped to "show the Navy as a good builder of men" and "that it's tough, but it makes you admire them."[37] This set a challenge for the army, which eschewed drama and was concomitantly focusing a great deal of its effort through *The Big Picture* on selling itself as a modern, technologically savvy service. Against this, the army was also competing for a larger share of age-eligible recruits, finding it difficult to meet its post-1947 goal of 30,000 volunteers a month, but gaining only 12,000 through enlistments.[38] As a partial solution, the army concluded many of its contemporary *Big Picture* episodes with this upbeat on-screen pitch, "You can be an important part of *The Big Picture*. You can proudly serve with the best equipped, the best trained, the best fighting team in the world today, the United States Army."[39] Faced with stiff competition from shows like *Navy Log*, recruitment became a difficult task when compounded by a growing spirit of antimilitarism in the nation driven by war weariness from both World War II and the Korean conflict, a pervasive wariness from Cold War fears of nuclear destruction, and an unpopular draft.[40] While some historians may consider that *Navy Log* "was the programme [sic] the *Big Picture* would vainly aspire to become," this aspiration seems hardly likely, considering that its army producers did little to adjust either the format or content to achieve its competitor's popularity.[41]

Another on-screen television challenge was posed by situational comedies that appeared opposite *The Big Picture*, such as the *Phil Silvers Show* (1955–1959). Its fictionalized main character, Sergeant Bilko, was a consummate con man, always out to make money through gambling and get-rich-quick schemes while flouting army regulations. In the process he made fools of officers, the military hierarchy, and any authority figure. As a sitcom it drew rave reviews from critics and the public as it "lampooned much of contemporary active duty military life."[42] But this did not always sit well with the army, particularly the Public Information Division, which protested that several episodes of the show had gone too far in lampooning the military. They considered the many exploits of Bilko and his gang as poor representations of army life. As Colonel Robert Shinn of the Public Information Division protested to the assistant secretary of defense for public affairs: "While it is appreciated that the program is a comedy and therefore must necessarily deal in exaggerated and often implausible situations, we have found from experience that some viewers take quite seriously those aspects of Bilko's portrayal bordering on criminal acts."[43] Shinn also noted that the show went beyond criticizing the military and on at least one occasion lampooned President Eisenhower and President Charles de Gaulle of France, and "made snide remarks about the Democrats."[44] The PID forwarded an appeal to the show's producers to modify the scripts to remove the offending segments, but they ignored it. In the end, the episodes aired in their original form. Although the show may have ruffled the feathers of army leadership, as well as some veterans and members of the public, it still garnered a host of accolades. In 1955 alone it won Emmy awards for Best Comedy series, Best Actor, Best Comedian, Best Comedy Writing, Best Producer, and Best Director. Subsequently, it won three Emmys each of the following years through 1958. As much as the *Phil Silvers Show* may have smudged the army image, it remained widely popular and stood in contrast to the more sober army portrayals by *The Big Picture*, which remained fact based and relied heavily on its use of a documentary-style format of narrator voice-overs and archived film footage. This might suggest that it was an understanding that "anti-militarist sitcoms" with an irreverent cast of characters like Bilko "eased fears associated with the move to a permanently mobilized military force" after 1945.[45] Nevertheless, it was hard for the army to accept that type of image.

In addition to television, Hollywood provided some challenges to the army image. These transpired as film producers worked to convert popular postwar novels such as Norman Mailer's *The Naked and the Dead* (1948), Herman Wouk's *The Caine Mutiny* (1951), and James Jones's *From Here to Eternity* (1951) from print to the silver screen. As historian Lawrence H. Suid notes, in his work *Guts and Glory: The Making of the American Military Image in Film*, the effort threatened to sour the previously strong relationship between the studios and the military. The difficulty was in the novels, which the military establishment considered "essentially unflattering portrayals of the military."[46] As a result, the army balked when Columbia studios approached them to establish a cooperative arrangement for the production of *From Here to Eternity*, a story of pre–World War II military life in Hawaii. The studio expected to once again take advantage of Hollywood's earlier "long-standing reliance on military men, equipment, and locales to provide accurate ambience."[47] But this time it was not to be unless the studios made significant changes to the story line. That included rectifying negative portrayals of incompetent, weak officers, illicit extramarital affairs, and explicit brutality and punishment. The army was concerned that "the portrayal of a situation that no longer existed would mislead the millions of mothers, wives, and sweethearts of men currently in the service."[48]

Although the army made a number of suggestions for adjustments to the proposed scripts, the film's producers, who were determined to remain as true to the original story as possible, subsequently rejected most of them. Speaking on behalf of the Army Pictorial Center, Clair Towne, a representative of the Defense Department's Public Affairs Office, commented, "The treatment [of the story] portrays situations which, even if they ever did exist, were certainly not typical of the Army that most of us know, and could serve only to reflect discredit on the entire service."[49] Concurring with Towne, Donald Baruch, chief, Motion Picture Production of the DOD Public Affairs Office, added that the film was "never going to be a good story for the Army."[50]

Upon its release in 1953, *From Here to Eternity* received critical acclaim and several Academy Awards. Against these types of films and television shows, fraught with negative depictions, the army continued to produce and rely on its *Big Picture* series to cultivate a positive public image and portray a contemporary branch of the service that was professional, modernized, and technically competent.

Another challenge for *The Big Picture* during this period was funding. Between 1952 and 1957 the army budget decreased by half, falling from $15.7 billion to $7.5 billion.[51] Within those allocations the service had to determine how to best resource all of its major program areas, which included training, maintenance, operations, research and development, and personnel support. Folded into this was the army's public relations mandate to continue to sell the service's story and maintain its recruiting goals. Central to that effort was *The Big Picture*. With an internal goal set to produce thirty-nine episodes a year, the Army Pictorial Center was sensitive to any constriction of the funding pipeline.[52] The ASDPA budget shrank from $14 million at the height of the Korean conflict to $3.2 million in 1956.[53] Correspondingly, the OPI budget shrank from $971,445 in 1952 to $500,000 in 1954.[54] During the 1956–1957 season, when the army budget was reaching a six-year low, the chief of information, Maj. Gen. G. S. Meloy, petitioned the army's deputy chief of staff for operations to increase the existing APC budget from $223,000 to $248,600 to cover rising production costs for a projected schedule of thirty-five films.[55] These tight conditions continued through 1958, with the cost estimate of a typical episode placed at $11,600 and Col. John Weaver, troop information chief, declaring "the Financing problem to be basic and in greatest need for attention."[56] By late 1959, the approximate cost of writing and producing a single episode had risen to $14,000.[57]

During those thin budget years, however, the Office of the Chief of Information never eschewed the offer of a helping hand when it appeared. A number of archived letters and memos reveal the appearance of unsolicited sources of financial aid and resources during the late 1950s. A May 1957 letter from the CINFO to the president of KOATV-Radio in Denver, Colorado, gratefully acknowledged the studio's cooperation and support in the production of the *Big Picture* episode "Mister Army" (TV-371). This included the use of floor space, lighting, technicians, and "union members of KOA," all at great cost savings to the APC.[58] In December 1958, a letter from the new CINFO, Maj. Gen. H. P. Storke, conveyed appreciation to the army's chief of engineers for that office's contribution of $15,000 toward the completion of the episode titled "Thayer of West Point" (TV-432), which featured the army's "first engineer," Sylvanus Thayer.[59] These funds helped bridge a production shortfall of approximately $20,000. A different unsolicited offer of $10,000 came from the USO toward the completion of "United Service Organization (USO): Wherever They Go" (TV-467), an episode that celebrated that organization's long history of entertainment and support of service members deployed overseas.[60] As welcome as they were, these unexpected bonuses provided little salve for the wounded budget. This situation would continue until the overall military funding began to rebound with the advent of the nation's involvement in Southeast Asia in the early 1960s.

The army's *Big Picture* resourcing situation was, however, never improved by the service's refusal to surrender creative control of the series' production to a commercial backer. Although there was earlier consideration to develop *The Big Picture* as a commercially produced army television series, this concept never gained traction, because the army wanted complete creative control. As attractive as commercial resourcing might have been as a solution to alleviate funding shortfalls, it could have opened the door to unwanted external shaping of the army's message, or endorsement of a corporation, system, or particular product. Although there is no evidence to claim that commercial support had an influence on *Navy Log*, *The Big Picture*'s 1955–1958 competitor, its relationship with first CBS then ABC might suggest that the navy remained sensitive to the expectations of those networks. In return, *Navy Log* enjoyed prime-time television slots, granting it a larger share of viewership than the syndicated *Big Picture* series.[61] Regardless of the funding challenges, *The Big Picture* still possessed a lifespan that far exceeded that of any comparable military television series of the time.

Some of the greatest of the challenges that *The Big Picture* faced were objections to the contents of its episodes. A contentious situation first arose when the producers attempted to release a 1954 episode titled "Atrocities in Korea" (TV-242). The APC developed the

piece as a "documented report of the crimes and atrocities committed against Americans and other United Nations prisoners of war by
their Communist captors," and it was replete with footage of bodies in ditches and the pallid faces and sunken eyes of survivors.[62]
The narrator described the images as "shocking" and "not pleasant,"
and added a dramatic edge by disclosing that "some of them are revealed for the first time" to provide the "stark truth that every American should know."[63] Firsthand accounts gained from interviews
with former prisoners of war, several of them still in hospital gowns
during their recovery, laced the episode. The narrator was also keen
to establish a sentimental connection with viewers by having each of
them state their name and hometown, ala Ernie Pyle. Among those
interviewed was Maj. Gen. William Dean, former commander of the
Twenty-Fourth Infantry Division, whom the enemy had captured and
held as prisoner for thirty-seven months. In all these cases the stories
told of harsh conditions, physical brutality, lack of adequate food and
medical care, and repeated attempts by the North Koreans to indoctrinate the POWs.

Just prior to the episode's airing, however, the deputy secretary of
defense, Roger M. Kyes, and the under secretary of state, Gen. Walter
Bedell Smith, jointly moved to deny its release. The approach of a
Big Four Conference, scheduled for 25 January 1954 in Berlin, drove
their fear that it might cause some difficulty by irritating the Soviet
delegates.[64] Other notes of caution they expressed were for the impact
it might have on the sensitivities of the American public, as well as
the possible negative effect on the ongoing diplomatic efforts at Pan-
munjom.[65] Several Republican members of Congress criticized any
restrictions on its release, claiming that the State Department was
"following the line of appeasement" and calling for a congressional
investigation of the reasons cited.[66] Senator Charles E. Potter (R-MI)
earlier that month had submitted for the record a lengthy request
for a United Nations committee to investigate the communist atrocities.[67] This was an initiative he and other members of Congress had
been pursuing since June of 1950. In this context, the appearance of
the *Big Picture* episode became an additional weapon in their fight
to uncover the facts and sell them to the public. It was again referenced in February of 1954 by Congressman R. Thurmond Chatham

(D-NC), who stated for the *Congressional Record* that "no one should be surprised at the United States Army's report on the horrible Communist atrocities in Korea," adding that "official documentary films show thousands of mutilated civilians' and prisoners' hands tied behind their backs."[68] Eventually, "Atrocities in Korea" aired that February even though the APC had already shipped ten copies of the films to several television stations in the greater New York area.[69] Although the contents of this one episode received challenges in what at first appeared to be a tempest in a teapot, its importance grew as it emerged as a key piece of propaganda through its exposure of communist misdeeds during the tense anticommunist atmosphere of the 1950s. Though the series managed to survive this storm, that was not to be the case with the next greater challenge, when *The Big Picture* would find itself an unwitting pawn in a larger political game.

In December 1969, Senator J. William Fulbright (D-AK), chair of the Senate Foreign Relations Committee, submitted evidence into the *Congressional Record* that suggested the military establishment was using television improperly as a means to manipulate the thinking of the American public. In this context, he cited the army and *The Big Picture* as a prime example. Fulbright claimed that "the manner in which this program [*The Big Picture*] operates illustrates how the military services can quietly develop their extensive public relations capability with little public or Congressional knowledge or interference."[70] Central to his complaint was concern that the army was crafting *Big Picture* segments on military operations in Vietnam with the intent to cultivate public support for the war. Evidence of the existence of these concerns resides in the tone of some comments revealed in an earlier internal office memo to Maj. Gen. Harry Storke, the army chief of information. Its content advised caution in the production of the *Big Picture* episode, "Your Defense" (TV-399), because "certain dialogue introduces a distinctly political flavor to THE BIG PICTURE and raises many questions such as using THE BIG PICTURE for political purposes."[71] Phrases such as "defense is costly to be sure, but it is cheaper than war," and "we cannot afford to relax now. An adequate national and international defense is necessary to our peaceful way of life" were just some of those woven throughout the narrative, and these do appear scripted to shape public and political opinion toward supporting a more expansive military.[72] Visual evidence such as this fueled Fulbright's quest, together with that of other politicians, to begin to question the military's motivations and its use of the *Big Picture* series.

In parallel to this concern, Fulbright also exhibited worry regarding the excessive amount of funding the series required to remain operational. He felt there was a need to curb the spending, which reached a cost of $902,529.34 for that year.[73] In November of 1970, Congressman Charles E. Bennett (D-FL) added his voice to the *Congressional Record*, endorsing Fulbright's position regarding costs with a proposal to cap Pentagon public relations spending among all the services at $10 million. Referring to Fulbright's earlier criticisms, he made the claim that "millions of dollars are being spent by the Department of Defense for public relations purposes" adding, "this is an unconscionable waste . . . we are dangerously skimping on vital projects necessary for survival."[74] This was accompanied by the insertion of an article from the *Wall Street Journal* that quoted Representative Henry Reuss (D-WI), who claimed that the Pentagon's public relations program was nothing more than "propaganda, hucksterism and flackery at public expense."[75]

The pages of the *Congressional Record* reveal that Senator Fulbright had continued his criticism of *The Big Picture* and the military public relations apparatus on into December of 1970. That month he claimed, "I have here an illustration of just how far the Defense Department goes in brainwashing the American people in the guise of an information program . . . this is a film catalog of the Army's 'Big Picture' series."[76] As chair of the Foreign Relations Committee he felt sure that the military designed its effort to "persuade the people of the United States to certain points of view, especially about foreign policy."[77] He continued his criticism, emphasizing that "the films are made with government money, paid for by the taxpayers, for the purpose of what they [the military] call informing, but I would call it brainwashing of the American people."[78] In parallel to these accusations, which became a matter of record, Fulbright penned *The Pentagon Propaganda Machine*, which appeared in publication that same year. Intended as an exposé, it charged that one of the arms of the Defense Department monster bureaucracy is the military public relations apparatus that today is selling the Administration's Southeast Asia policy, just as it sold the Vietnam policy of the previous Administration, with increasing emphasis on patriotic militarism and activity directed against its critics. The enthusiasm and dedication of the purveyors of the hard military line are such that their present course could easily be changed so as to direct attention to the removal of those in the Congress who question actions of the executive branch and the growth of military influence.[79]

In evidence, a review of The Big Picture's film catalog does reveal that between 1962 and 1971 there were 41 episodes out of 240 that addressed army operations in Vietnam. Of these, 31 were specifically about Vietnam, and another 10, under the title "Your Army Reports," incorporated five- to seven-minute segments on a topic relating to the conflict there. The preponderance of all these, 34, were released during the shorter period 1966—1971, and of those, five specifically addressed policy making by sharing with their audiences the motivations for American intervention in Southeast Asia. The reasoning, offered by Gen. Paul D. Harkins, commander of the Military Assistance Command in Vietnam during the 1962 episode "Hidden War in Vietnam" (TV-562), was simply that "we have helped and are helping all free people who seek to defend themselves from the Communist scourge."[80] This was at a time when only American military advisory groups were in the country. But by 1966, a year after the first combat units came ashore at Da Nang, another episode, "Why Vietnam?" (TV-674) took a different approach and used historical film clips to make its case. Beginning with the 1938 appeasement of the Nazis at the Munich Conference, followed by combat footage of the seemingly unprovoked North Korean invasion of its southern neighbor in 1950, the episode traced the trajectory of events and emphasized that it was the responsibility of all free people to check aggression wherever it appeared. Included in the narration was the admonition "peace in our time—a shortcut to disaster."[81] So the buildup in Vietnam was justified as a means to stem the spread of the communist stain. Any documentary proof, however, that the OCINFO or the APC was pur-

Date	Episode Number	Title
1962	562	Hidden War in Vietnam
1963	574	The Fight for Vietnam
	605	U.S. Army Advisor in Vietnam
1964	607	Operation Montagnard
1965	654	Action Vietnam
	672	Your Army Reports: Number 1
	674	Why Vietnam?
1966	677	Your Army Reports: Number 2
	678	Your Army Reports: Number 3
	680	The Unique War
	683	Lifeline of Logistics
	685	Your Army Reports: Number 4
	692	Your Army Reports: Number 6
1967	695	A Nation Builds under Fire
	700	Your Army Reports: Number 8
	703	Probe and Pursue
	704	The Army and Vietnam
	705	Vietnam Village Reborn
	707	Your Army Reports: Number 9
	708	Stay Alert, Stay Alive
	713	Your Army Reports: Number 10
	714	Screaming Eagles in Vietnam
	716	The Big Red One in Vietnam
	718	Your Army Reports: Number 11
1968	720	The Sky Soldiers
	724	Ready to Strike
	729	Your Army Reports: Number 13
	732	The Role of U.S. Combat Engineers in Vietnam
	735	Fight for Life
	736	Vietnam Crucible
	746	The Ninth Infantry Division
	748	The First Air Cavalry Division
	749	Logistics in Vietnam
1969	752	The Army Air Mobility Team
	764	The Fourth Infantry Division
	768	The Americal Division
	770	The 11th Armored Cav Regiment
1970	772	82nd Airborne Division
1971	792	Progress to Peace
	807	The 1st Infantry Division in Vietnam (1965–1970)
	809	Mission in Action

Table 2.1. A total of forty-one episodes addressed American military involvement in Vietnam. Those under the "Your Army Reports" title provided short segments about operations there. An example is "Your Army Reports: Number 8," which contained a story about the South Vietnamese Women's Army Corps. (Data Source: NARA, College Park)

posely shaping the development of episodes to deliver a message regarding American involvement in Vietnam is lacking. Investigation of available archival materials did not reveal any memo, letter, or prescribed guidance outlining production plans for these films.

Military intents and purposes aside, these *Big Picture* episodes were still interpreted by Senator Fulbright and his political allies as much more than simple informational or patriotic films created to educate the public and military members about the army's worldwide operations. They interpreted them as being intentionally manipulative. In that regard the senator noted, "It is belaboring obvious, but they understandably glorify the army's role in that war."[82] He went further by claiming that these *Big Picture* films "take an approach to the complexities of today's world that is oversimplified and one-dimensional."[83] To Fulbright, the military—and in this case the army—had overstepped its bounds by taking on a role that was the province of other government offices, such as the State Department. It had in that course attempted to shape Americans' opinions with films that "hardly can give the viewing public an objective and considered explanation of our overseas military involvements."[84] Tarring both radio and television outlets with the brush of collusion, Fulbright charged that they were "heavy users of the military's propaganda and public relations output" and that "some of their executives should devote more attention to filling their public service time examining the grave domestic problems besetting the country instead of using 'V-films' and the Army's 'Big Picture.'"[85]

What also appears evidential, if not coincidental, was the fact that some of the army chiefs of information between the mid-1950s and the early 1960s had histories of work in the information and intelligence fields while in the service. While not necessarily surprising, or condemning, that fact does lend itself to the argument that the *Big Picture* series, along with radio productions such as *The Army Hour* and other media vehicles, served to shape the thinking of viewers and listeners. Such was the case of Lt. Gen. William W. "Buffalo Bill" Quinn, who served as the army's chief of information (CINFO) from 1959 to 1961. Earlier, as the chief of staff of the Pentagon, he had become familiar with the power of the video during his experiences producing the *Blue Badge* series through *The Big Picture*. Sev-

Figure 2.1. Lieutenant General William Wilson "Buffalo Bill" Quinn. He served as the army chief of information 1959–1961 during a period of tight resourcing. Typical of most chiefs, he regarded the *Big Picture* series as key to selling the army as a modern, progressive force. In the latter half of his military career Quinn was involved in intelligence work, and after retirement served as chief of operations of the CIA. (Image Source: US Army)

eral years afterward, he became the army's deputy chief of staff for intelligence (G2), subsequently filling the positions of deputy director of the Defense Intelligence Agency (DIA) and chief of operations of the Central Intelligence Agency (CIA).[86] This résumé suggests that Quinn was always cognizant of the effect of information flow and management and its persuasive power among audiences. He was in position to influence the development of the post-Korea *Big Picture* episodes that the APC scripted to sell the army in a better light: "Our established information objective [is] to depict the Army as a modern, progressive and forward thinking force."[87] Quinn was also on hand to influence the development of the episodes celebrating the polar ice cap expeditions and early Vietnam episodes such as "Hidden War in Vietnam" (TV- 562), which cast the mold for others to follow.

Major General Charles G. Dodge succeeded Quinn in 1961. He maintained the philosophy of casting the army in a positive light and notably provided a lecture at the Army War College (AWC) in April

1962 titled "Public Understanding and the Army Information Program." In it he emphasized that a key goal of the Army Information Program (AIP) was to continue changing public attitudes "towards a favorable view of the Army."[88] Filling the chair as CINFO after Dodge in February 1963 was Maj. Gen. George V. Underwood, who had served as his deputy since January 1961. He remained in the position as CINFO until 1966, and like Dodge, he emphasized the importance of maintaining a strong public image for the army. As his predecessor had done, Underwood also lectured on the subject to an audience of senior military leaders at the AWC, in 1963. Together, both Dodge and Underwood understood that an affirming image was imperative for the army, but both also emphasized in their lectures "candor is an indispensable ingredient in the Army's public relations formula."[89] This attitude, offered with candor by men who believed they were doing the right thing, was a commitment to sell a prescribed catalog of defined American values and actions through the military.[90] When that is taken together with the content of the *Big Picture* messages, there is little surprise that the army public relations apparatus drew the charges leveled by Senator Fulbright and other progressive politicians who no longer accepted the exceptionalist consensus endorsed by the military, seeing it as an outmoded lens through which to view the world. The political winds were shifting, it seems, and the United States military establishment was feeling the increasing heat of criticism from Congress, the American public, and foreign allies concerning its operations in Southeast Asia.

Within a year of Fulbright's last congressional diatribe, the army position became untenable and, acceding to external pressures, it decided to terminate the production of *The Big Picture*. A short article on page 3 of the 16 July 1971 *Stars and Stripes* Pacific edition announced the decision. Titled "Army's Famed Series Signs Off, 'The Big Picture' Fades from TV Screen," the news account listed the reasons for the termination. These included a need to develop a more relevant contemporary television series, a large production price tag of $727,000 per year, and declining audience interest. However, no mention was made of the accusations of propaganda or content manipulation. The final episode, "Drill Sergeant" (TV-823), aired in late 1971. It signed off without any recognition that it was the last in a series that stretched

Figure 2.2. Image of Maj. Gen. William Quinn, chief of army information (second from left), receiving several awards from the conservative Freedoms Foundation, including one honoring *The Big Picture* (March 1960). (Image Source: *In Focus*, March 1960)

back two decades. Only a notation that it was "Presented by the Office of the Chief of Information" brought it to a close. In the end, as the screen went blank on *The Big Picture*, officially a victim of changing times and the budget axe, the show still possessed a wide audience on "428 commercial, educational and cable television stations, including 51 of the American Forces Radio and Television Service in Europe and the Far East."[91]

During the course of its twenty-year production cycle *The Big Picture* received a number of accolades in recognition of its accomplishments as a television series. For a period of ten years from 1960 to 1970 the show won the conservative Christian Freedoms Foundation's George Washington Honor Medal for the best military documentary of the year.[92] In 1960 alone, three *Big Picture* episodes gained recognition with the award.[93] Another honor came in 1967 with the episode "The Red Diamond" (TV-693). Developed as a history of the Fifth Infantry Division (Mechanized), it featured training of individuals and units at its station in Fort Carson, Colorado, and was "selected as the best of its kind" at the annual International Film Festival in Versailles, France.[94] Still, the highest honor came in 1968 when *The Big Picture* won an Emmy, the first for a DOD production. The National Academy of Television Arts and Sciences presented the award for the episode "The Song of the Soldier" (TV-725), which focused on the talents of the US Army band and chorus. The film, which differed in format from other *Big Picture* episodes, sans the usual sober introductory narrative, contained vignettes of America's martial past set to song and music. Viewers appreciated it for its moving renditions and innovative style that bridged the past from the Revolutionary War to the ongoing Vietnam conflict and seemed a fitting coda for a series that in a few short years would fade away.

To more fully understand those messages that the *Big Picture* broadcast, and the influence they had, this study continues by examining the catalog of *Big Picture* films by separating them into three categories according to overarching subjects: the Cold War, American exceptionalism, and the army way of life. Each of the following chapters takes one of the themes and collects the relevant episodes to unpack and examine them in the context of the messages they delivered.

3

A Big Picture of the Cold War

Even as narrator M.Sgt. Stuart Queen declared, "The guns are quiet again in Korea," to open the final *Big Picture* episode depicting active combat on the Korean peninsula in 1953, the series producers had already developed and aired a new film to explain the importance of facing down the ever-present global communist threat.[1] "Soldier in Berlin" (TV-232), released that same year, reminded the American public of the Western military presence in that city located one hundred miles deep within East Germany and its significance as a symbol of democratic freedom. As Queen noted, the American soldier was there to defend "the prestige and interests of democracy. While in the East sector of the city the Russians and their puppet government plot and propagandize against us."[2] This episode was one of many that described the tense geopolitical confrontation between the East and West that evolved in the post–World War II period that would become the Cold War. In that conflict, *The Big Picture* would find utility as a claxon to raise the alarm alerting Americans to communist hegemonic designs and to neutralize propaganda from the East through its own well-crafted messages about the West. It is not possible to understate the impact of the series—the "Cold War of the 1950s became America's first 'television war.'"[3]

Including key hotspots such as Korea and Vietnam, the Cold War evolved into a series of proxy wars mixed with the cut and thrust of diplomatic negotiating and moments of suspenseful brinksmanship between the opposing global superpowers. This all unfolded beneath the clouds of potential worldwide nuclear devastation that hung heavy and low for the first score of years after World War II. Although that danger would eventually lift, the tense conditions between the East and West remained through the time of the Eisenhower administration. It was then that the president assumed the strategic reasoning of his predecessor Harry S Truman, which had been shaped in large by a succession of National Security Council (NSC) documents generated between December 1947 and April 1950. These laid out the designs for appraising the threat to national security and developing a means to confront the communist East.[4] Through these assessments the administration eventually determined that American leadership and dominance in the postwar world depended on two things: the skillful application of psychological warfare and a commitment to the theory of containment. Toward the first, the president understood that it was a battle for the hearts and minds of people at home and in other nations and that among all the "soft power" weapons at hand, including diplomacy, economic assistance, cultural exchange programs, and trade, telling the story of the West's superiority was paramount.[5] Eisenhower set it as a goal for the United States to prove its "peaceful intentions, and to persuade others of the ideological and cultural superiority of the American way of life."[6]

Toward the second objective, the president, as well as most political and military elites, adhered to the doctrine espoused by the American diplomat and historian George F. Kennan. In a lengthy, strongly worded telegram dispatched from his post in Moscow in February 1946, Kennan encouraged an approach to check Soviet hegemonic ambitions through a global containment strategy.[7] This would incorporate the stationing of American military power at strategic points around the world joined with the establishment of a supporting network of cooperative alliances of like-minded nations to counter communist expansion. Inspired by both the need and the possibility of success, the American leadership wove together the concepts of propaganda and containment into a grand strategy to combat communism in the first decades of the Cold War. In this, *The Big Picture* was instrumental in telling the American public and service members the dangers they faced from the insidious communists as well as describing the actions the American government was taking to forestall those threats.

Selling the Ideology

The original thirteen episodes of *The Big Picture*, together with a number of others that the APC produced over the ensuing years, painted a clear picture of the confrontation between America with its coalition of allies and the communists on the Korean peninsula. The narrative was clear as the introduction of the early episodes described the need to "stop Communist aggression wherever it may strike." As episode followed episode, the message remained unchanged: it was a battle against tyranny and oppression born of the East's corrupt ideologies. Even deeper into the *Big Picture* catalog, episodes born of the Korean conflict returned to that message. The 1954 story "Armed Forces Assistance to Korea" (TV-271) spoke of the army's efforts to "rehabilitate certain areas of civilian life" as a "living monument of friendship between peoples" and to continue to safeguard their hard-won freedoms.[8] In that same context, "Korea and You" (TV-519), produced in 1961, eight years after the armistice, described the American soldier's continuing role in Korea as part of the "bulwark against Communist aggression."[9] In each of these cases, APC producers scripted the *Big Picture* episodes to communicate a strong anticommunist narrative and deliver a message espousing the superiority of Western freedoms. This remained consistent with the administration's grand scheme, but within that design darker dangers began appearing.

As the energies of the war in Korea began to subside, disturbing reports of American POWs' behavior emerged. A burst of articles by various media outlets, including the military's own *Stars and Stripes*, described American soldiers' susceptibility to the pressures of enemy interrogation. One contemporary military psychiatrist claimed that the behavior of "many of our soldiers in [North Korean] prisons fell far short of the historical American standards of honor, character, loyalty, courage and personal integrity."[10] More disconcerting were some media reports that alleged that unlike in previous wars, American GIs had become soft and quickly collaborated, sometimes refusing to escape, and died at an alarming rate from "a morale malady called 'give-up-itis.'"[11] According to one army report, the responsibility rested squarely on the American home, because "parental training failed to provide them [the soldiers] with moral values and Yankee resourcefulness."[12]

Afraid that service personnel no longer understood the foundational principles of American freedoms or why they were fighting, the Eisenhower administration quickly took action. The president charged Secretary of Defense (SECDEF) Charles Wilson to develop a code of conduct for service personnel, which when complete consisted of six articles. They would serve as a declaration of American ideals to recommit the serviceman to "the principles which made [our] country free" and would encourage them to "trust in [our] God and in the United States of America."[13] Each of the service branches adopted the new credo, which the president signed in August 1955, and *The Big Picture* reflected that effort to reinculcate the army personnel with the fundamental patriotic values and to make the American public aware of the situation.[14]

Among the first episodes to deal with the issue was "Escape from a Prisoner of War Camp" (TV-320). Released in 1955, it reviewed the tenets of the new code of conduct and offered re-creations of actual escape attempts made by American soldiers who were once prisoners. It did importantly note that occasionally "our men do get captured through no fault of their own," perhaps as a salve to former American POWs from the Korean conflict.[15] Another episode was "Defense against Enemy Propaganda" (TV-360). Broadcast in 1957, it served as a response to the early concerns regarding the effectiveness of communist propaganda. Initially created as a troop information film for use exclusively by the army, its purpose was "to alert the American soldier against a hidden enemy, an enemy that can destroy morale, rob the soldier of the will to fight, and even trick him into surrendering."[16] Realizing its utility, however, the APC soon released the episode for wider dissemination. As narrator MSG Queen soberly declared, "We think you the American public will also find it pertinent and enlightening."[17] Throughout the film, examples of communist propaganda appeared as proof of the East's duplicity and at times desperate measures to undermine the morale of American service members. Riding this wave of concern, the APC continued to produce episodes that showcased a retooling of the soldier's defense against enemy propaganda.

In 1958, the episode "Code of the Fighting Man" (TV-428) appeared as a direct endorsement of the six-article code of conduct published by the SECDEF just a few years earlier. Its purpose was to inform and train both the soldier and the public by explaining that the code "outlines the soldier's moral obligation to his country."[18] Created as one of the few docudramas produced for *The Big Picture*, it used a fictionalized situation of an army unit surrounded and cut off from retreat by an enemy. A sequence of scenarios showed the capture of small groups of soldiers, whom the enemy then subjected to harsh interrogation. But ultimately the soldiers were successful in deflecting the enemy's determined attempts, and they did not break under the pressure. As the narrator reminded the viewer, this was due to the "kind of training which the army is giving its soldiers to prepare them for every eventuality on the battlefield."[19] Hard on the heels of this episode the APC produced the next, which continued with the concept of shaping the individual soldier's core values. Following the unwritten mandate of the administration and the Department of Defense, the episode "Character Guidance" (TV-429) focused on the US Army's monthly character guidance training program that centered on openended scenarios that posed ethical and moral questions to soldiers. As the script emphasized, "The character of the American soldier is representative of the character of his country, and the strength of character of any country may well be its most precious possession."[20] The meaning of these collected episodes was as a palliative to remedy any perceived lack of moral fiber or resoluteness of purpose within the soldier. As such, they were ingredients in the administration's strategy to win the ideological war with the East by bolstering the psychological resiliency of Americans so that they could better withstand the onslaught of enemy Cold War propaganda. But this was only part of that equation.

This collection of episodes, particularly "Escape from a Prisoner of War Camp" and "Code of the Fighting Man," were informational in tone. Although both were docudramas, each began with a serious, descriptive introduction by the narrator and a member of the Judge Advocate General's Corps (JAG) to add a certain gravitas to the message. The camera captured scenes in standard gray halftones, and the music was slow and matched the forlorn aspect of the soldiers, especially when showing lines of American POWS being marched to a prison camp. The enemy in the former episode was a hybrid European figure who spoke a composite gibberish of German and Eastern European dialects. In the latter episode, the environment was Asian, with the enemy interrogators dressed as North Koreans. The films left little to the imagination regarding who the enemy was in either case. Scenes of dirty GIs with dirty, bruised faces, sweating under intense interrogation, appeared in each film, a clear message that the experience of the American POW was not going to be an easy one. But the camera also showed that those who escaped did receive a hero's welcome back to their own units with smiles and glad-handing all around. As "Code of the Fighting Man" came to a close, with its lesson of abiding faith in American ideals complete, the American flag appeared on-screen, snapping smartly in the breeze. This type of production existed as a foil against propaganda from the East. Each side was competing with the other through specific messaging shaped to deflect the other's efforts to influence thinking. Films such as "Code of the Fighting Man" were examples of the psychological warfare efforts that flowed from the APC and that producers did not consider in any way hypocritical. They were necessary and useful weapons for the Cold War.[21]

The other factor in the ideological formula was reeducating the American military and public in the nation's foundational ideals. The 1961 *Big Picture* episode "Challenge of Ideas" (TV-512) served that purpose. Although the opening narration offered a Cold War reminder that "the entire globe . . . is today the site of a momentous conflict as each side attempts to prove to the world the superiority of its position," it was the parade of notables who appeared on screen that provided the substance of the message.[22] The first was Edward R. Murrow, the noted journalist, who somberly addressed the viewer: "I would like to review with you the great conflict of our time, one which demands and must get the attention and the involvement of each one of us."[23] Following his overview of the Cold War was John Wayne's lengthy description of a wide array of freedoms that Americans enjoyed. The story line coupled this with an additional litany of those rights of the individual that were available in the West, specifically to NATO member nations. These were rights such as the "freedom of speech, of conscience and religion, or opinion and belief," and the "right of every man to work and receive his just reward."[24] The episode made it clear that these inalienable rights were those that the East coveted and was determined to rob from Americans and anyone living in the West. As a vehicle of directed propaganda, "Challenge of Ideas" more than satisfied its role as an ideological touchstone for the military and the public.

Explaining Containment

Just as the skillful application of psychological forces was important to America's Cold War strategy, so was a solid commitment to the concept of physical containment of the communist threat. In this regard, the catalog of *Big Picture* episodes provided a wide selection of titles. Many of the earliest episodes that addressed this piece of the grand strategy focused on the American and allied presence in Europe. Shortly after the production of "Soldier in Berlin," *The Big Picture* aired "Soldier in Europe" (TV-238). As a follow-on episode it stressed that ongoing world tensions generated a need for "American servicemen to serve on another continent during peacetime" to fulfill a "complex role in the defense of the Western World."[25] It traced the trajectory of the American military presence in Europe from occupying force, helping to revitalize a devastated postwar landscape, to shielding those nations living under the shadow of communist threat. Other episodes shared a similar narrative, emphasizing the American commitment to that continent. The videos "Division in Europe" (TV-326), "8th Infantry Division" (TV-787), "The 3rd Armored Division—Spearhead" (TV- 795), and the double episode "USAREUR Story, Parts I and II" (TV-541 and TV 542) also contributed to the explanation of the requirement for forward-based units on that soil as part of the containment barrier.[26] This was not a difficult sell to an American public whose suspicions of Soviet intentions were already at a heightened state during the 1950s, driven by propaganda that inspired fears of communist infiltration of American society, an emergent Communist China, a Castro-led Cuba, a nuclear-ready Soviet Union, and the ever-present Red Menace.[27]

Other than Korea, another country that received a great amount of attention during this period from APC producers was West Germany. It was the keystone to containment in Europe. Besides the obvious reason that it shared a geographical boundary with communist Eastern bloc nations and held a central place in early Cold War negotiations, it was home to the largest concentration of American troops and family members stationed overseas. Between 1950 and 1960, the number of service members in Germany grew from 97,820 to 232,256, and the number of dependents expanded from 58,000 to 170,000.[28] The *Big Picture* listing reveals that the nation was the subject of at least ten separate episodes from the mid-1950s until the early 1960s. These told the story not only of America's serious military commitment there through episodes such as "USMAAG Germany" (TV-424) and the double episode "U.S. Army in Berlin: Timetable for Crisis (Part One)" (TV-530) and "U.S. Army in Berlin: Checkpoint Charlie (Part Two)" (TV-536), but also of the growing personal bonds between the occupier and the local populace.[29] By featuring this human face, the United States made great gains in the psychological battle against the East. Those personal connections, which were always unique to the *Big Picture* film series, provided a grassroots perspective to the stories that was reminiscent of Ernie Pyle's style employed during the Korean War episodes.

Among the stories that featured such a special personal touch in West Germany were "German Youth Activities" (TV- 243), "Operation Friendly Hand" (TV-336), and "People to People" (TV-430). The first episode addressed the desperate situation in postwar Germany that left thousands of young Germans without adult supervision or structure to their lives. Into this vacuum came the American GI, always ready to play the role of caregiver and big brother to the needy. The film records how soldiers organized and participated in youth sports programs, clubs, theatrics, and other activities to engage adolescent Germans. High postwar participation figures attest to the success of the GYA initiatives. Wrapped within this organizational spirit of

Gemütlichkeit, however, were opportunities for the Americans to also tutor their young charges on the benefits of democracy.[30] As the film noted, it began with GIs' "spontaneous gestures" of friendliness and through the GYA grew into a "reorganizing and democratizing of the youth of Germany."[31] The episode itself afforded a double-edged endorsement of the overarching American postwar strategy: first, by depicting the overseas stationing of military power to block Soviet expansion, and second, by offering a view into the exercise of psychological manipulation to spread beneficial information about Western ideologies. Camera angles, staged scenes, and accompanying music helped shape the story. In "German Youth Activities," opening sequences showed uniformed Hitler Youth marching in tight formations to dark musical overtones and the deep pounding of kettledrums. Gradually, as the script described the postwar efforts of the American servicemen to reshape the lives of the destitute youth of Germany, the music lightened, with sweet symphonic strings. Bright images appeared to show soldiers handing out candy and feeding long lines of hungry but smiling scarecrow-thin children. As the narrator noted, this was all done through "friendship and understanding."[32] The imagery of soldiers coaxing German children out of the shadows of the rubble of their homes, and dark pasts, into the bright daylight of their future alongside the Americans adequately substituted for any scripting that was absent.

The other episodes, "Operation Friendly Hand" and "People to People," followed similar formats, with some differences. The producers of "Operation Friendly Hand" scripted the story to tug at heartstrings and encourage an emotional tie with the German people. It featured an American sergeant and his family sponsoring a poor German girl for a month's vacation with a typical military family stationed in Kaiserslautern, Germany. Although it was framed as an intercultural exchange, a perceptive viewer could see that the German girl was more the beneficiary of American largesse and consumer wealth as she benefited from plenty to eat, gifts of new clothing and bubble gum, a bubble bath, Saturday afternoon movies, and a new hairdo and cosmetics. While the obvious message to audiences was the strengthening of the bonds of friendship through kindness, the subtext highlighted American economic superiority and beneficence.[33] A press release accompanying the film noted: "Time after time, American GIs would make it their business to make friends with German youngsters--some of them family men themselves, even going so far as inviting German kids into their homes, inviting them to spend time learning *about* Americans *from* Americans."[34] Here, producers and crews applied the same artistic techniques that they did for all stories regarding Germany. They had to be light and engaging. Moving from scenes of wartime bombing and smoking devastation, the young girl in this episode arrives in the care of a smiling, happy American family. The cameras show them all relaxed and enjoying the bounty of American life. The brooding background music carries the viewer away from the carnage of war and melts into lighthearted strains that follow German and American children together in play. It was a time when the United States was working diligently to rebuild a West Germany that could serve as a partner against the communist East. The APC was bringing all its professional talent to bear to cultivate the necessary bond between the nations to make this possible and to cultivate feelings of Gemütlichkeit. In doing this the series also brought into stark contrast the living conditions that existed on the opposite sides of the border: revitalization, a thriving economy, and optimism in the West, and repression of liberties and a struggling existence in the East. This theme ran through these productions.

Produced in 1956, "Operation Friendly Hand" was, however, a bit of a subterfuge. Although the story line reflected an actual event, producers recrafted the narrative to take better advantage of the situation. They decided to change the rank of the soldier from a captain, who was the actual participant, to that of a sergeant, possibly believing that would provide greater grass-roots appeal "through further humanization of the documentary."[35] Also, in conjunction with the release of the film, the Department of Defense brought the young German girl, Gudrun Paskarbis, who starred in the original episode, to the United States to live with the captain and his family for one year at Fort Huachuca, Arizona. Along the way the government feted her, and civil and military elites in New York and Washington, DC, received her. Any benefit accrued was purely for public relations purposes. As was noted in a memo originally proposing the plan to the deputy assistant secretary of defense for public affairs, "The Department of the Army considers that much favorable publicity will be generated, in Germany and the U.S.A., if the child can be brought to this country."[36] To fend off any possible media criticisms or questions of credibility, the Office of Information and Education prepared a statement that readily admitted that the *Big Picture* producers were departing from the "usual documentary format," concerning the rank adjustment of the soldier, just for this one episode, believing again that the "human aspects of the story will appeal to the Public in such a way that nothing but favorable comment is expected."[37] This was hardly a typical scenario for *The Big Picture*, but the episode showed that the DOD and the Department of the Army considered the television series an important propaganda tool to gain public approval and to continue to polish America's global image. The episode "People to People" followed suit and also told the story of American military personnel working closely and harmoniously with the local host-nation populace no matter where stationing brought them. The episode brought to light the Eisenhower administration–sponsored People-to-People program, which called on every American to be an ambassador. Although its effectiveness as an ideological tool was never widely evaluated, the president "took pains to stress that People-to-People was not propaganda."[38]

Several others films that the APC produced through to 1970 also focused specifically on Germany. Among the titles were "Germany Today" (TV-455), "The West Berlin Struggle" (TV-628), and "The Border Watchers" (TV-789). Each served its purpose as a record of America's commitment to "hold back the tide of Communism in Germany and the free world" and to show the "face of West Germany today re-carved in the image of freedom."[39] Central to the second film was a discussion of the West's efforts to save Berlin during the desperate days of the airlift and the city's "place as a symbol of the West's freedom."[40] The last film, "The Border Watchers" stressed the necessity of military vigilance along the "frontier of freedom" between West Germany and the countries of the Eastern bloc.[41] Like the other contemporary *Big Picture* productions, it appears that the Department of the Army, through the APC, produced these episodes to underscore America's unity with Germany as a bulwark against communism, to sell American ideals to the world, and to serve as a vehicle to further imprint those ideals on service members, their families, and the public. The evidence for this exists in the cinematic record and not in the existence of recorded documentation such as office memos or guidance from the OCINFO.

Other *Big Picture* episodes helped complete an understanding of the stationing of the American military around the globe as part of the Cold War containment strategy. These included a story about the "Soldier in Austria" (TV-269), stationed there "to prevent that partitioned country from being drawn into the Red orbit."[42] Other episodes followed suit, such as "Soldier in Panama" (TV-283), "Defense of Japan" (TV-285), "Soldier in France" (TV-328), and "Assignment Iran" (TV-655).[43] Perhaps the most declaratory among this group however, was "Ready around the World" (TV-717). Produced in 1968, it pronounced the US Army as an ever-vigilant guardian in the "complex international world of the 1960s."[44] It was, as the script noted, the soldiers' service "at freedom's outermost perimeter" that mattered.[45] Accompanying this narrative was video footage of the army conducting patrols along the East German border, training with artillery, rockets, and radar, and participating in joint exercises with NATO allies. This episode served as much as a public relations piece for the American viewer as it was a cautionary warning to the communist East, lest it had any aggressive designs while events in Southeast Asia were diverting American attention and resources.

Special Alliances

Throughout the Cold War, key alliances with allied nations became essential pieces of the strategic containment barrier. These generally served either to augment American military forces on the ground with those of a host nation or to fill a void when American military power was geographically absent. Consequently, *The Big Picture* was instrumental in informing and educating the American military and public about these critical special relationships, especially the North Atlantic Treaty Organization (NATO) and the Southeast Asia Treaty Organization (SEATO).

The premier strategic alliance of the two, featured in *Big Picture* episodes, was NATO.[46] *The Big Picture* first addressed the organization in "NATO: Partners in Peace" (TV-267). The film explained to viewers the creation of the association that focused on mutual defense against post-1945 Soviet aggression in Europe. For the United States, it was a key strategic move, which was a "new and revolutionary development in American History."[47] A second episode, "NATO Maneuvers" (TV-291), which also aired in 1954, summarized the combined air, sea, and land military exercises that took place that year between the fourteen member nations. As the narrator boasted, "Since the formation of the North Atlantic Treaty Organization the Communists have gained not one foot of new territory in Europe."[48] The episode, which the APC crafted as informational as well as ideological, served several purposes. First, it was a vehicle to educate the service members and their families living abroad about their mission and role in the defense of Western Europe. Whether viewed in military movie theaters prior to the main feature or in unit classrooms, the film worked to inculcate an anticommunist, pro-West, pro-NATO mindset in the audience, very much in line with the information and education mission. Second, the episode, as well as those that would follow, stressed the "alliance's contribution to collective security" and the point that the "related network of U.S. military facilities were not there for American benefit, but to protect Europe."[49] This was particularly important to organizations such as the US Information Agency (USIA), which at the time was peddling the idea of an "Atlantic community" of common needs and concerns. This would essentially make the United States appear to be a part of a larger whole and mask any appearance of shaping and steering Western European attitudes and thinking, "to minimize the psychological disadvantages generated by . . . impressions of U.S. hegemony in Western Europe."[50] Follow-on episodes, "Why NATO?" (TV-402) in 1958, "Decade of NATO" (TV-491) in 1959, and "NATO: The Changed Face of Europe" (TV-632) in 1964, all continued to transmit that message. As guest narrator for the first, the noted news analyst Edward R. Murrow answered the question "Why NATO?" for the audience by reiterating that the organization's key mission was to prevent the nations of Western Europe from falling to the same fate as those of the East, which had succumbed to Soviet occupation. Consequently, it would make possible through NATO a "bond welding the

Old World and the New."[51] Chilling proof of that missive came with the crushing of the incipient Hungarian Revolution of 1956 by Warsaw Pact forces under control of the Kremlin. As a result, Western Europeans and Americans alike understood the aggressive nature of the communist bloc. The last episode, "NATO: The Changed Face of Europe" followed suit, reminding viewers of NATO's mission and their responsibility to support it at the risk of losing their own freedoms, adding with a hint of braggadocio that the face of Europe "has been transformed to one of despair among the Communist satellites and of unprecedented prosperity among the free nations."[52]

The timing of this collection of *Big Picture* episodes was not coincidental. They appeared in the mid-1950s as the army found itself locked in a desperate competition with the other services to prove its relevancy in the Cold War. The APC produced other contemporary episodes. such as "Research and Development in the Arctic" in 1957 and "Army Satellites" in 1958, to give a boost to the army's image as a technologically savvy service, but the NATO episodes told a different, yet more compelling, story. Intentionally scripted, they underscored the key role the army was playing in the defense of Western Europe. Certainly the US Air Force and US Navy had a presence there, but it was the army that was manning the borders and physically occupying the ground that the East was coveting. As the black-and-white images of *The Big Picture* flashed across television screens in America, it was evident that the army's ground forces were playing a key role in the defense of Western Europe.

On occasion the army used *The Big Picture* to single out certain NATO partners for special recognition. Such was the case with the episode titled "U.S. Army and the Boy Scouts" (TV-520). The story line described the close relationship and joint mission training between the United States and Denmark, a key NATO partner. This was an essential relationship, which established a presence of Western powers at the top of the globe, a short distance from the Soviet threat. Similarly, an earlier episode, "Salute to the Canadian Army" (TV-414), produced in 1958, recounted the close relationship and history shared between the United States military and the Canadian armed forces. Highlighting the fact that they were "partners in the defense of two free nations" and that they were "serving the common purpose of free nations everywhere," it contained footage of Canadians fighting alongside Americans during World War II and in Korea.[53] Crews from the APC filmed the episode on location at several sites in Canada under the guidance of a Canadian military advisor. Subsequently, stations of the Canadian Broadcast Network telecast the show and included a special French narration for the predominantly French speaking areas. The APC was well pleased with the results. These appeared in a letter from the director of public relations (Canadian Army) to Maj. Gen. Harry P. Storke, CINFO. Among the assorted accolades, it noted that "the picture was an unqualified success in Canada" and that "it certainly has been of benefit to the Canadian Army."[54] Aside from cementing a special relationship between the two nations, the episode's warm reception in Canada contributed to the continued cultivation of an interested *Big Picture* audience north of the border.

The *Big Picture* episode on SEATO served the same purpose as those focusing on NATO, to inform and excite. As the narrator in that film proclaimed, it was created as a counterbalance to Chinese communist influence in the region and was "a force defending liberty and the independence of free nations," not very different from those describing the mutual defense of Western Europe.[55] Black-and-white images played out in footage showing columns of well-drilled multi-national forces marching past cheering crowds, and a bank of member-nation flags snapping in the breeze. In parallel to these episodes were others that addressed the American resolve in Asia. "Japan—Our Far East Partner" (TV-254) and "Aid to Nationalist China" (TV-293) described the bolstering of relationships with those nations in the common cause of defense against aggression in that region of the globe. But scripted into all these episodes about special alliances and relationships was the hope that political elites in the United States would take notice and not threaten to slash the army budget or mandate lower manpower levels.

Another purpose these episodes served was to describe to the viewer the United States' application of the "soft power" approach in cementing the important Cold War relationships and cultivating new ones. It was through specially designated civil affairs programs that the army ingratiated itself with nations in need. One such episode, "You in Japan" (TV-354), served to instruct service members and their families about the culture and traditions of their host nation. Its intention was to foster strong relations between the people of both countries. Another, "The Army's Helping Hand" (TV-790), which aired in 1970, addressed the teams of American military engineers, medical personnel, construction crews, and scientists who applied their skills in a wide variety of humanitarian projects around the globe. Footage of servicemen building schools and bridges or offering vaccines to villagers helped to reinforce the idea of a beneficent United States, not necessarily out for hegemonic gain, but simply acting as a good neighbor. This was a view into America's application of a "soft power" approach to convince other nations of the good intentions of the United States and to encourage them to accept the ideologies of the West.

Games of Brinksmanship

The Big Picture also played a role in providing a view into those critical moments of brinksmanship that played out during the Cold War. On 12 August 1961, as communists began construction on the fence line that would eventually grow into the infamous wall separating East from West in Berlin, tensions between the two superpowers reached a dangerous high. Thousands of West Berliners immediately began protesting the action that would restrict their movement into the Soviet-controlled zone of the city and that would prevent the exodus of thousands of East Berliners to the West. At the same time, NATO forces in West Germany went on high alert and the United States began moving an army mechanized battle group to the city to reinforce the brigade already there. The front page of the European *Stars and Stripes* headlines raised the alarm: "1,500 U.S. Troops Sent to Bolster Berlin Force: Johnson Says U.S. Pledges Lives for Berlin."[56] It was a dangerous gambit made by the Soviets to put pressure on the Americans to leverage concessions in diplomatic discussions involving the future of West Germany and to stem the flood of lost labor from the East. But it also provided fodder for Western propagandists, who saw the move as yet another opportunity to inform and educate by citing the aggressions of the East and the necessity of maintaining a strong anticommunist Western alliance.

The Big Picture brought this story to its television viewers in three specially crafted episodes: "U.S. Army in Berlin: Timetable for Crisis" (TV-530) in 1961, "U.S. Army in Berlin: Checkpoint Charlie" (TV-536) in 1962, and "Road to the Wall" (TV-560) also in 1962. The first pair provided some historical background leading up to the crisis, but focused on the impact on the lives of West Berliners and the reaction of American forces stationed in West Germany and Berlin. The last episode offered a view into the historical progression of communism from early conceptualization by Karl Marx, through the Russian Revolution in 1917, to the end of World War II and the construction of the Berlin Wall. As the account unfolded, the film emphasized the aggressive nature of communism, how its precepts robbed millions of their individual liberties, and how "they [communists] intend to put the world on their road."[57] The intent of the film was not only to inform and frighten viewers, but to offer them assurance that the West was there to protect them: "We intend that the world shall be free."[58] This was communicated with a fierce resolve that "each new threat must be met, force with force as in Korea," and the knowledge that "the choice is not Red or dead, the choice lies between ignorance and wisdom, cowardice and bravery, slavery or freedom."[59] Subsequently, the government released a version of the film through the Directorate of Armed Forces Information and Education (AFIE) in a separate documentary form for television in 1963. It received a nomination for an Academy Award for Best Documentary Short, proof of the critics' and public's approval. Tensions between the East and West remained high during the mid-1960s, and *The Big Picture* played its role to record events, share them with its audience, and shape the way they interpreted them.

In each of these episodes the Berlin Wall figured as the centerpiece. It appeared in angled camera shots, both high and low, that followed the length of the barrier stretching into a distant vanishing point. It stood like a silent sentinel, brick stacked atop brick, the top crowned with thorny barbed wire. The camera offered gray-toned scenes accompanied by the sounds of heavy pounding percussion. The lens framed faces peering over sections of the wall, troubled, with eyes searching for loved ones on the opposite side. A gravelly voiced narrator read the scripted words, reminding viewers of the ideological differences between the East and West. But always, regardless of the episode, the wall figured prominently. It became the embodiment of the politics that kept the sides apart during the Cold War. It was an enduring representation for the West of the communists' denial of freedoms and liberties, and *The Big Picture* used the iconic wall to clarify the stakes of the Cold War battle.

The second major Cold War event *The Big Picture* captured was the 1962 Cuban Missile Crisis. In two separate 1963 episodes, "Pentagon Report" (TV-580) and "One Week in October (Cuban Missile Crisis)" (TV-619), the program described the events surrounding the emplacement of the Soviet nuclear-ready missiles in Cuba, the desperate diplomatic brinksmanship that followed, the blockade of the island, and the eventual removal of the weapons. Each of the episodes painted Soviet premier Nikita Khrushchev in the role of the archvillain who orchestrated the communists' plans. As the narrator in "Pentagon Report, 1963" noted, Khrushchev claimed that Soviet interventions around the world were merely to support "wars of liberation and popular revolt."[60] "We prefer to call them subversion and covert aggression" was the narrator's retort.[61] That characterization of the Soviet leader continued through the *Big Picture* episodes, whether it was describing his actions in Cuba or the controversy surrounding the Berlin Wall, which began with Khrushchev's veiled threats against Western allies' presence in that city in 1958 and culminated with the start of construction in August 1961.[62] In contrast, *The Big Picture* projected the United States in the role of champion of oppressed peoples and guardian of Western freedoms. The narration in these episodes couched the results in terms of a victory for the United States and a rebuke of communism. In both events, the Berlin Wall and the Missile Crisis, *The Big Picture* served to recount the crises to its attentive viewers, and it concluded both features with an ever-present ringing endorsement of the military: "The United States can be proud of our armed forces, alert to meet every challenge. The spirit that safeguards our country is the will to serve and the will to win of everyone in uniform."[63]

Vietnam, a Tough Sell

None of the *Big Picture* episodes seemed to carry a message that resonated in the sphere of public opinion so much as those that featured the United States' involvement in Vietnam, which was at the time considered to be an essential piece of the containment barrier. Certainly, by any count, the *Big Picture* series featured more episodes on army operations in Vietnam than any other individual subject. The APC produced forty-one between 1962 and 1971, and of those, thirty-four appeared during the last five years. By following these films during the course of the series, viewers could trace the trajectory of American military interests in that nation from an earnest commitment to stop a communist threat to presentations that seemed tragically out of sync with the political zeitgeist of the late 1960s and early 1970s. Beginning in 1962 with "Hidden War in Vietnam" (TV-562), and then "The Fight for Vietnam" (TV-574) in 1963, viewers caught the almost conspiratorial undertones of operations in the Southeast Asian jungles that targeted a danger that few Americans really appreciated. "Hidden War in Vietnam" told the story of American Special Operations Forces (SOF) soldiers, whose mission it was to train the local populace to fight and win "a dirty war, fought without uniforms on a battlefield without boundaries."[64] The episode "Fight for Vietnam" described that country's importance as "a strategic location affecting the whole of Southeast Asia," which had turned into "another battlefield of the Cold War" through the "coercive terror and false promises of Communism."[65] Examination of the narratives and intents of these *Big Picture* episodes, together with other early ones such as "U.S. Army Advisor in Vietnam" (TV-605) and "Operation Montagnard" (TV-607), makes it apparent that the CINFO produced these with the intended purpose of informing and shaping Americans' thoughts about maintaining the nation's commitment in Southeast Asia.

After the incident in the Gulf of Tonkin in 1964, the American public began to lose some of its confidence in the political and military leadership.[66] *The Big Picture* reflected this change in attitude through the production of episodes that seemed to project a harder sales pitch as a counterbalance to negative opinions regarding Amer-

Figure 3.1. Filming of an episode of *The Big Picture* in the APC studio in the presence of two South Vietnamese military technical advisors. Working closely with foreign liaisons on filming projects was another way to build strong relationships with allied nations. (Image Source: *In Focus*, August 1964)

ican involvement. "Action Vietnam" (TV-654) in December 1964, followed by "Why Vietnam?" (TV-674) and "The Unique War" (TV-680), all seem to have been produced for that purpose. Scripted to tell the story of "a dirty, many-sided, complex struggle, a twilight war, fought in shadow and stealth," they sought to describe a desperate fight by American heroes against a nefarious enemy.[67] Detailing the sacrifices and commitment of American service members, the episode "Action Vietnam" opened with footage of an army officer receiving the Medal of Honor from President Johnson for bravery on the battlefield in Vietnam. It featured a somber, staged ceremony filmed at the White House. Playing on well-worn patriotic sentiments, the *Big Picture* narrative and images continued to sell the conflict as a necessary consequence of containing the communist menace. In building a national consensus to support the war effort the producers may, however, have sacrificed reality for propaganda value. As Professor

David E. James notes in his commentary on Vietnam War documentaries, interpretive discrepancies existed between the narrative and the actual events. For example, "Why Vietnam?" takes license in discussing the sequence of historical events leading up to the war by offering a skewed view. James points out: "Blatantly misrepresenting history, [President] Johnson argued in the film that Vietnam was a defensive war."[68] Johnson's claims arrived on the heels of the manufactured Tonkin Gulf incident and are evidence of the disconnect that existed between the reality and the message in some of the *Big Picture* scripts. The audiovisual design reinforces the deception in several ways. As film scholar Claudia Springer notes, the producers of most Department of Defense compilations were confident in crafting films that communicated certain messages through the use of visual symbolism. Evidence of that practice exists in the *Big Picture* series. While the tone of the films is consistently supportive of the government's position for intervention in Vietnam, the sometimes subtle use of imagery manipulates the viewer's acceptance of that message. Springer identifies the almost Capra-like technique of using images of children to "evoke feelings of pity and outrage in the viewer."[69] This observation holds through a number of *Big Picture* episodes such as "Action Vietnam" (1965), "Why Vietnam?" (1965), and "The Unique War" (1966). Laced throughout these films are scenes of rural villages and hamlets with docile women, children, and older Vietnamese performing the tasks of daily life, innocently and simply, making them potential targets of aggression. Other scenes such as those in "Action Vietnam" stun the viewer with images of burning villages and fleeing children, with soldiers carrying dead bodies of the young and crowds fighting back flames that are consuming their livelihoods and freedoms. Background music fills the ear with the drama of the moment and feelings of frenetic panic. These films conjure an enemy that like a dark demonic shadow lurks, unseen and dangerous, haunting the lives of these "innocents" and threatening their liberties. As the narrator somberly confides, the "face and name is Communism."[70] In a well-timed symbolic gesture in "The Unique War" the camera shows a small Vietnamese boy beating a snake to death with a stick at the same moment a voice-over comments on "the threat to freedom that Communist aggression poses."[71] It was a venomous danger, threatening to poison the minds of naïve peasants. This monolithic "communism" carried "all the negative associations already embedded in the public imagination" and was central to production efforts to introduce a Manichean-like understanding of the Cold War world to viewers.[72]

Other visual connections that touch on American ideals also appear in *The Big Picture*. For example, "The Unique War" includes scenes of a cluster of Vietnamese children worshipping in a simple village church. Here, the visual and scripted narratives conflate to evoke from the American audience feelings of paternalism and anger against the godless communist interloper and to encourage the Western-style intervention of Americans come to save the day. This practice of manipulated imagery begins in episodes produced earlier in the conflict, such as "The Fight for Vietnam" (1963) and "Operation Montagnard" (1964), and it carries through to later films such as "Vietnam Village Reborn" (TV-705) (1967). Compounding these views of the villagers was the evidence of a growing divide between the Americans and the Vietnamese. As Tony Shaw notes regarding images of the war in his work *Hollywood's Cold War*, film productions that stripped villagers of any dialogue or commentary rendered them powerless. They were simply the "white man's burden," to be herded, manipulated, and tolerated as was necessary in the prosecution of the war.[73]

It is also important to note that another component of the Department of Defense films, including *The Big Picture*, was an ethnographic treatment, adopted to add texture and a veneer of sincerity to the messages. They fell, however, well short in application. In place of offering a comprehensive study of a particular people and culture, *The Big Picture* offered only clumsy, sophomoric descriptions that provided the soldier, and the viewing audience, "a special opportunity" to get to know Vietnam and its people.[74] The hope was that this type of thinly veiled ethnography could serve as a recruiting vehicle to attract the interest of service members and a catalyst to enlist a commitment from taxpayers at home. More important, as Springer notes, these films want the viewer to believe they are "receiving an intimate perspective of Vietnamese life," but they present the Vietnamese as "simple-minded, mired in tradition, and dependent on American aid."[75] These efforts to cast episodes in the light of a National Geographic cultural study fell short and instead created a dichotomy, leaving the audience to wonder about the purpose. Were the Americans there as benefactors or in a martial spirit to wage war? Even as narrators declared that "this is a war whose objective is to win the hearts and minds of the people," their voices cautioned soldiers to be wary of the enemy who often lurked among the villagers.[76] Army medics bathed children and tended to their wounds as warnings of Viet Cong guerrillas laced the narratives, while bombs poured from the underbellies of B-52s and villagers made their ambling way on bicycles. Episodes often superimposed a brutal, unconventional war over pastoral scenes of a simple people, leaving audiences to interpret the messages. This effort at an ethnographic study leaves many Vietnam-era *Big Picture* episodes coming across as awkward and contrived, cobbled together from too many competing messages. In this way, they often failed to communicate any clear meaning.

As the decade unfolded, the APC continued to produce a plethora of Vietnam-themed episodes. When protests on college campuses began to intensify in 1967, then exploded across America after the beginning of the Tet Offensive during January–February 1968, *The Big Picture* still held the line through unwavering messages of support for military involvement in that area of the globe. A favored technique employed by producers to maintain viewer interest at this time was to incorporate Hollywood stars, such as John Wayne and Bob Hope, as participants in various segments. This, however, became more difficult as the war became more unpopular. A survey of titles reveals that a majority of the episodes after 1967 were about the missions and accomplishments of specific units operating in Southeast Asia. From "Screaming Eagles in Vietnam" (TV-714) about the 101st Airmobile Division, to "The Ninth Infantry Division" (TV-746), to "The Americal Division" (TV-768) about the 23rd Infantry Division, at least fifteen episodes celebrated the patriotic achievements of the soldiers in those units, who were performing their duty as they understood it. Still, as the American public grew weary of supporting a seemingly interminable war and confidence in national leadership continued to erode, these *Big Picture* episodes appeared to be transmitting an archaic and faded message linked to a dated Cold War strategy. This contributed to some of the ire felt by members of Congress, such as J. William Fulbright, who accused the military of improperly transmitting foreign policy messages, which was beyond the scope of its responsibilities.

Eventually, as the conclusion of direct American military involvement in Vietnam drew near, together with the end of the *Big Picture* series in 1971, the APC producers crafted an episode titled "Progress to Peace" (TV-792). It was an attempt to explain the United States' exit strategy from the conflict and to bring the history of American involvement there full circle. Narrated by popular actor Raymond Burr, it explained the Vietnamization process as a natural consequence of the overall strategic scheme, wrapping it with an insouciance that obscured any admission of culpability or accountability for the final result. As Burr explained to the viewer, when the end of the 1960s arrived, "the time had come with another major change in the character of the war in Vietnam. That is, free world forces would begin to phase out of the war as the people and armed forces of South Vietnam became capable of filling the gap."[77] True or not, that was the final policy message from *The Big Picture*. Although two more episodes about the war followed, they were little more than historical summaries of unit operations in Southeast Asia.[78]

These *Big Picture* episodes, which the APC produced in a familiar, straightforward documentary format, offered a contrasting lens to a contemporary treatment of military operations in Vietnam through entertainment television. As historian Scott Laderman suggests, a strong current existed in the television industry in the 1960s that eventually carried the medium away from the war and its surrounding controversy, even as *The Big Picture* stayed the Cold War course. Early in the conflict, weekly series such as *Alcoa Premiere* (ABC, 1961–1963), and the "fictional vignettes" of the dramatic series *Navy Log* offered shows that tended toward a patriotic celebration of America's involvement in Southeast Asia, in consonance with the early *Big Picture* episodes.[79] By middecade however, fictionalized shows began to diverge and offered perspectives of American foreign policy that were both cynical and ambivalent. As Laderman notes, after the 1968 Tet Offensive, networks understood that "confronting the war's increasingly contentious politics on network television would prove difficult," and they drew back from such controversy.[80] Through the trajectory of fictionalized television's reflections of the war, *The Big Picture* remained consistent in its message for the necessity of involvement in Vietnam as a key element of America's Cold War containment strategy. This course of action eventually drew criticism from an increasing number of political elites, such as J. William Fulbright, who brought enough pressure to bear to eventually precipitate the termination of the series.

Whither Anticommunism?

Unpacking the anticommunist rhetoric integrated into the *Big Picture* narratives compels an examination of those messages to understand whether over time they changed. In reviewing the earliest episodes, produced during the desperate years of the Korean War, it is no surprise that the first narrator somberly intoned that the show was about "an army committed by you the people of the United States to stop Communist aggression wherever it may strike."[81] This hard anticommunist edge persisted through the episodes of 1950s and the early 1960s as *The Big Picture* brought audiences to the Arctic in "Operation Blue Jay" (TV-227) in 1952 and "Top of the World" (TV-543) in 1962, where the challenge was to forestall communist expansion even in the remote northern climes. That sharp focus on anticommunism, which was one of the originating goals of the show, continued as the East and West played games of Cold War brinksmanship with the construction of the Berlin Wall and the Cuban Missile Crisis. Scripted narratives consistently piqued viewers' fears of creeping communism as a singular monolithic shadowy entity that crept bogeyman-like through episodes, threatening lives, livelihoods, and liberties. Producers telegraphed those messages into the Vietnam era through the "Hidden War in Vietnam" (TV-562) in 1962, to "Vietnam Crucible" (TV-736) in 1968. There was little deviation through all these productions but for the rescripting of the show's introduction, which eliminated a description of "communist aggression" and replaced it with words that proclaimed a wider global army mission to simply protect "against aggression." It was a move away from direct provocation of a committed enemy by producers.

As domestic antiwar paroxysms increased after 1968, *The Big Picture* shifted its focus from Vietnam and anticommunist rhetoric to episodes that featured a modern army on the cutting edge of science and technology, fully engaged with local communities, the environment, and society. Although occasional episodes on Vietnam still appeared, army studios began producing titles such as "Meeting Tomorrow's Challenge" (TV-765, 1970), "A Day in America" (TV-776, 1970), "A Visit to Mars" (TV-778, 1970), and "Toward a Better Environment" (TV-808, 1971), absent any anticommunist scripting. By 1971 the geopolitical environment was changing; President Nixon was preparing to engage with the People's Republic of China and follow the path to détente with the Soviet Union. Hard words were out of place. By the time the series came to an end that year, anticommunist rhetoric had not changed—it simply disappeared.

The Big Picture was the longest-lasting informational television series of the Cold War period. Said differently: "With its breadth of distribution and length of availability, it was probably the most widely viewed series in television history."[82] Appearing weekly, in prime time and through broad syndication, it provided a window into the tense geopolitical confrontation between the East and West for millions of viewers, coming into homes and barracks, for the public and service members. It served as a useful vehicle to remind both groups of the gulf of differences between the two sides and of their responsibilities to guard against the loss of their precious freedoms. As such, it was a valuable contributor to the United States' grand strategy for containing the spread of the communist stain in the early decades of the Cold War and promoting the army's role in the effort.

4

The Big Picture through an Exceptionalist Lens

"America on the Move" (TV-549) opens with scenes of industrial machines busy at work, shiny steel wheels and lathes turning, smoke stacks belching, serious-faced men hard at their labors with heavy construction equipment sculpting the earth. Over this the narrator proclaims that after the war "there was a renewed sense of energy in the land" that lends itself to a renewed dedication.[1] His rising voice then carries viewers to scenes of the nation's capital that provide a frame for his claim: "History has selected us [America] for a decisive role in the drama which will determine whether freedom itself will endure."[2] Full of pride, the narrator confides that "a position of leadership is forced on us, for we are the strongest and most productive nation on earth," later adding, "We are less than two centuries old but no nation has ever been more strongly stirred by the knowledge of its own story."[3] It was a haughty proclamation, but it described the prevailing post-1945 mood in the United States, which spoke of a proud and exceptional people. It was a prevalent attitude that many Americans felt set us apart from the rest of the world. This chapter examines how during the first half of the Cold War *The Big Picture* provided a tool to cultivate that exceptional identity, exploiting the consensual feelings of a specialness harbored by most Americans. As the dialogue makes clear, encouraging a sense of exceptionalism was necessary to rationalize the nation's turn toward increased militarism and power projection in the postwar era. It was a key component of Cold War morale-boosting campaigns.

Exceptionalist Ideals

That exceptionalist perspective evolved from sources that are traceable to earlier times in American history. The concept of an exceptional people appeared on the shores of the New World with some of the first European arrivals. John Winthrop declared in 1630 that his new colony in Massachusetts was to be "as a Citty [sic] upon a Hill, the eies [sic] of all the people are upon [sic] us."[4] Clinging to that belief, these early Americans accepted that they were truly unique. This they evoked in their Declaration of Independence from England and their separation from the old connections with Europe. Recognizing an emerging distinctiveness by the late 1700s, essayist Hector St. John Crèvecoeur observed, "The American is a new man, who acts upon new principles; he must therefore entertain new ideas, and form new opinions."[5] Wearing that difference like a badge, by the turn of the next century Americans easily accepted the concept of a Manifest Destiny, the expression of their God-given right to multiply and expand across the blank canvas of their continent to establish a new nation. Affirmation of that exceptional identity echoed in the words of French diarist Alexis de Tocqueville, who in 1835 observed that America offered the world the best examples of equality and democracy in effect. He included in his observations that "religion is considered as a political institution which powerfully supports the maintenance of a democratic republic among Americans."[6] Thus religion found a central place in the exceptional expression, as it would in a number of *Big Picture* episodes. As the nation grew and its global role gradually changed, many Americans held fast to that idea of exceptionalism, which came to form the core of its identity. That ideal followed over the decades through victories in successive wars, which seemed to confirm Americans' belief in a unique destiny. The exceptional vision then came into sharper focus as World War II drew to a close in 1945, when America bore a triumphal banner proclaiming its resounding victory over the evils of fascism and began flexing its political and economic muscles.

As this national identity gained shape over time, it evolved into a consensus, based on an amalgam of prevailing characteristics that represented an exceptionalist ideology. Widely accepted by postwar American society, the slate of prescribed and insinuated attributes melded together the concepts of antistatism, antisocialism, anticommunism, anticolonialism, populism, and individualism, as well as educational and economic opportunity, meritocracy, and rejection of class consciousness. Blended in were other beliefs such as assigned gender roles and the centrality of the nuclear family and religion. Various conservative groups in the United States, such as the Freedoms Foundation, Christian evangelicals, a willing Eisenhower administration, and the armed forces, pressed these beliefs into service during the Cold War with the Soviet Union. Combined, they contributed to the core of an imagined identity that Washington elites expected the military and the public to accept and *The Big Picture* to communicate.

Collectively, the slate of exceptional attributes represented an ideology that resonated throughout American life, shaping its social, cultural, and political behaviors, attitudes, and self-identity during the first two postwar decades. Many of these ideas threaded through the narratives of *Big Picture* episodes such as "America on the Move" (1962). The episodes collected in this chapter portray an America working to identify who it was and to define its role in the postwar world. They address this imagined exceptional community, and as historians Benedict Anderson and Michael Kackman both note, "media of various forms are central to the constitution of a national identity."[7] Whether it is language, print media, radio, or film, each mode can serve as a vehicle to transmit the message that will collectively bind a community. It was the golden age of television, and *The Big Picture* could sell the concept of a unifying exceptional American identity through its program to members of the military and the public the better to mobilize them for the ideological struggles of the Cold War.

As the narrator in "America on the Move" suggests, this initiative carried with it a great urgency presented by "obligations of leadership which the conditions of the world have forced upon us."[8] It was a commitment that echoed the words of President John F. Kennedy's inaugural address given in January 1961 when he pledged "that we shall pay any price, bear any burden, meet any hardship, support any friend, oppose any foe, in order to assure the survival and the success of liberty."[9] The contemporary political landscape of the globe, particularly in the Third World, was changing and presenting significant challenges to the powers of the East and the West as they struggled to cope. The media had dubbed 1960 the "Year of Africa" in recognition of the seventeen nations on that continent that had thrown off colonial rule and started on the road to independence. The United States and the Soviets each rushed to provide compass points of direction. For the Americans, however, it was also a time fraught with paradox. Caught between supporting its allies, such as Britain and France, who were former colonial overlords, or committing to the spirit of freedom and liberty, the United States tended toward the latter. It was a connection that the Americans hoped to foster with the newly emergent countries, as our nation was quick to describe itself also as a "child of revolution."[10]

It was a decade of tempests, and American exceptionalism was the lighthouse in the storm to guide the United States and willing nations to the safe harbor of liberty and democracy. A litany of threats existed. The Cuban Revolution ended in 1959 with a victory for socialism, the Congo Crisis raged from 1960 to 1965, the Angolan War of Independence ran its lengthy course from 1961 to 1974, and the Dominican Civil War spent its furies in 1965. There were also missteps along the way. The April 1961 American-sponsored attempt to overthrow the Castro regime at a place called the Bay of Pigs resulted in disastrous failure for the Kennedy administration. All these followed the communist blockade of West Berlin in 1948, hostilities on the Korean peninsula from 1950 to 1953, and Soviet use of military power to subdue Hungarian revolutionaries in 1956, incidents brought to viewers' attention in the *Big Picture* episode "Army in Action—Years of Menace" (TV-645).[11] Through it all, an exceptionalist perspective could serve to bolster the national resolve when it wavered and guide the behaviors of its citizens and soldiers alike by contrasting the differences between the Soviets and the Americans. The narrative of "America on the Move" reminded viewers: "Pride of heritage, faith in freedom, are weapons of the mind and heart which have sustained and strengthened America's men at arms in troubled times before. Today, these weapons are no less valuable; indeed, they are more compellingly needed than ever in man's history."[12] Adherence to that template would steel the hearts of Americans and set the United States as the example for nations and peoples with aspirations toward freedom and a democratic way of life. It was a necessary weapon in the war against communist hegemony, and, as the narrator concluded, "as a public service, the *Big Picture* brings it to your attention today."[13]

Assessing this exceptionalist consensus as the APC scripted it into *Big Picture* episodes also reveals that it was not entirely static but did reflect change over time. Evidence of this appears in later episodes, which depict the evolution of women's roles in the military. They indicate that circumstances forced the army to accept changes in the consensual tenets of assigned gender roles. This came with an emerging fear of failure to meet recruiting goals with the advent of the all-volunteer force. That drove military elites to embrace a broader definition of women's capabilities in the hope of attracting them to satisfy shortfalls in the rank and file. In this context, *The Big Picture* not only reflected societal change but served as a vehicle to encourage change among its viewing audience.

The AFI&E Connection

During the Cold War *The Big Picture* served as a much-needed vehicle to air the messages of Americanism. As a key element in the Armed Forces Information and Education (AFI&E) Program, together with AFRS radio, information centers, command information programs, soldier newspapers, and information films, television contributed to the dissemination of messages and propaganda. As historian Thomas Palmer noted, the "Cold War shaped troop information, gave it renewed legitimacy, and provided Congressional and Executive support for indoctrination measures in the Armed Forces."[14] Conceptualized during World War I as the Morale Branch, then expanded during World War II as the Special Services Division, the idea of providing information to service members regarding the "why" of fighting and imbuing them with a sense of purpose and belief in a cause was instrumental in preparing them to fight—thus, the production of Capra's "Why We Fight" series.[15] Between the two world wars, the military information and education programs lacked rigor, sidelined by leadership who questioned their need beyond providing basic professional information to uniformed personnel. The necessity arose again during the Cold War with the Korean conflict, when elites in Washington perceived a weakening of resolve among the nation's troops, and so the army began producing films to revitalize their fighting spirit and bolster their confidence in American ideals. From this, the army produced episodes such as "Code of Conduct" and "Defense against Enemy Propaganda." So it was that *The Big Picture*, as a child of television, found its place in the arsenal of Cold War weapons.

Like each piece in the AFI&E tool kit, however, *The Big Picture* would serve a dual purpose. In one regard it was inward facing, necessary to educate and indoctrinate military members. In another, it was outward facing, producing propaganda for domestic and international audiences to provide a "Cold War education."[16] In this way, it shared contemporary news while selling American ideals. The army produced episodes such as "Challenge of Ideas" that informed and educated those in uniform as well as those watching at home or around the globe. In this context, *The Big Picture* served the information and education mission as a platform to launch propaganda that went "far beyond informing the troops."[17] As Dr. John A. Hannah, assistant secretary of defense, noted in 1953, "From the standpoint of society and the long-range welfare of the country, there is a basic obligation to inculcate the fundamental convictions of citizenship which might otherwise be lacking."[18] In short, the AFI&E program was "in the business of combatting Communism."[19]

As part of a complex communications network to transmit scripted views, production of the *Big Picture* episodes complemented ongoing propaganda initiatives by the United States Information Agency (USIA) to present everyday life in America. Through its program *Facts about the United States* it hoped to offer a perspective of "'typical citizens playing their role in daily living' to the world."[20] In parallel to this, the *Big Picture* films were able to provide a lens to observe life in the United States as well as the military and understand some of its key tenets, including presenting "America as a land of spiritual and religious vitality."[21] Most important was the hope that all these initiatives would have a positive impact on global public opinion. As Kenneth Osgood notes, if "foreigners could see ordinary Americans as individuals like themselves, working and struggling for a better life ... they would perceive the American government likewise."[22]

Exceptional Shortfalls Glossed

As important as it was to project a unified national image, the exceptionalist narrative could not mask certain cracks in the liberty bell. As historian Elaine Tyler May notes, "The real dangers to America were internal ones: racial strife, emancipated women, class conflict, and familial disruption."[23] Through the early postwar decades the shadow of Jim Crow darkened the lives of many marginalized Americans. While exceptionalist ideals trumpeted the virtues of equality, African Americans and other minority groups did not share in the benefits. Even after the May 1954 *Brown v. Board of Education* Supreme Court decision, many school systems throughout the American South remained segregated, and suburban Levittowns across the country still excluded minorities through the practice of "red-lining," placing housing loans beyond their reach. Other fractures in the exceptionalist façade revolved around the adherence to gender roles. Women were "homeward bound," trapped in exceptionalist expectations that kept them from reaching their potential outside the traditional home. In addition, society lacked tolerance toward any gender identification or sexual orientation outside of those that the exceptionalist ideal recognized as normative. As May notes, anticommunists turning "their wrath on homosexuals" and "gay baiting" was not an uncommon practice.[24] The exceptionalists drew a "direct connection between communism and sexual depravity," as they saw it.[25] The consensus dictated that deviation from the prescribed norm threatened the family by opening the door for infiltration through blackmail and manipulation. The exceptionalist model did not account for this list of inconsistencies.

Despite these real life tempests, *The Big Picture* continued to pass the message of American exceptionalism, cleanly glossing over any democratic shortcomings by not addressing them in its episodes. For example, the APC produced no shows that specifically addressed race or diversity, and only eight that focused on women's contributions during an eighteen-year span.[26] Instead, the APC continued to craft narratives for the series that would demonstrate the exceptionalist ideals and through them shape and inform the thinking of service members and the American public. This was important to solidify an exceptional core that was consistent with domestic politics and to prepare the messages for delivery to occupied and Third World nations. This was consistent with policy programs such as *Militant Liberty* (discussed later in this chapter). The series presented its messages in key narrative frames that addressed foundational ideals, demonstrated exceptional lifestyles, spoke of the centrality of religion, and provided exceptional historical references from America's past.

Foundational Ideals

Serving as a primer to remind and educate the American public and service members of its exceptionalist character, the *Big Picture* episode "Preamble to Peace" (TV-373) was one of the first to focus on the nation's founding principles. Produced in 1957, following a time of heightened tensions stirred by the dark energies of the McCarthy communist witch hunts, it made clear its purpose when it gently chided, "We sometimes lose sight of some of the basic facts about the origins and structure of our government."[27] Reviewing the Preamble of the US Constitution, the episode reminded the audience of the benefits of life in a democratic society and the need to preserve those liberties. It also trumpeted the army as one of the important guardians of those sacred privileges. Worth noting is that among the targets of McCarthy's anticommunist purge directed against the army at the time were several employees at the US Army Signal Corps laboratories at Fort Monmouth, New Jersey, former home of the APC, as well as information officers at I&E and the AFRS. Labeled security risks, they fought for years to expunge the stain from their records.[28] The timing of the release of this episode suggests that the APC crafted it to deflect criticism of the army and as a reaction to the corrupted extremes of patriotism.

Expanding more widely on the concept of selling tenets of Americanism was the 1961 episode "Challenge of Ideas" (TV-512). Noted for its sharp castigation of communist philosophies, it continued the momentum set by earlier episodes and served as a tour de force of American exceptionalism through its employment of a phalanx of popular guest narrators. Once again, it drew clear lines, West against East, an exceptional America as a light against the shadows of darkness. No less a contributor was the episode, "Our Heritage" (TV-684), produced several years later, in 1966. It also revisited the nation's founding principles by guiding viewers through an examination of the Declaration of Independence and providing a narrative that appeared scripted to educate and stir patriotic sentiments. The host of the show was Dr. Frank C. Baxter, a well-known professor from UCLA and television personality of the day. He lectured viewers about the reasons for the American Revolution and how the ideas of liberty found their way into the wording of "our crown jewel," the Declaration.[29] In his presentation he reminded the audience that "out of our heritage has come human liberty, democracy, and the birth of a great nation."[30] The film featured patriotic segments of marching bands and children reciting the Pledge of Allegiance. It appeared on television at a time the United States stood on the cusp of deeper involvement in Southeast Asia. The timing of this episode, like the others, suggests that they appeared at moments when the American leadership may have perceived a softening in the public's resolve to support long-term strategic policies. In that regard, *The Big Picture* offered a tonic to revitalize Americans' commitment to the national policies by refreshing their understanding of underlying ideologies. No less a document than the Declaration of Independence served as an embodiment of those sacred principles and so was central to an episode such as "Our Heritage" that peddled the exceptionalist ideals.

Main Street, USA

Aside from tutorials on the fundamentals of Americanism, episodes demonstrating an exceptional lifestyle were also available among the pages of the *Big Picture* catalog. The APC producers of the series seemed to understand that an effective way to engage their viewers was by walking them down the streets of America, following in the paths of citizens just like them, people to whom they could relate. One example from 1956 appeared in "Pictorial Report No. 26" (TV-353). Although the episode was a compilation of contemporary news reports from around the army, one item of note was a story of how a small southern town was exercising its patriotic duty. It focused on Galax, Virginia, and described how residents there were working through the local chamber of commerce to form a US Army Reserve unit to celebrate the town's centennial. The ranks filled rapidly with "American men proud to answer their country's call."[31] As the narrator described, it was a "warm-hearted story of a people determined to keep American democracy safe. For they know that freedom is everybody's business."[32] The episode concluded with a patriotic celebration, complete with a parade down Main Street featuring marching bands, floats, and the newly uniformed Army Reserve unit. Understanding the public relations value of the situation, the CINFO invited the assistant secretary of defense to a special ceremony for the presentation of a DOD Reserve Unit Award to the town's chamber of commerce. The CINFO also noted that the episode promoted an exceptional but positive story that "will serve as an example to other communities who have potential personnel for similar Reserve units."[33]

"Ottumwa, U.S.A." (TV-387), produced in 1957, offered a similar patriotic perspective. The narrator introduced the episode with a gentle admonition noting that in contrast to their communist counterparts, "we as a free people, who believe in the true form of liberty, have many times been incoherent and lack the verbal ability to explain or defend completely what liberty is."[34] The remedy was to take the viewer on another tour of a true American community whose members personified that understanding, as a means of demonstrating the living application of those ideals. APC producers chose Ottumwa, Iowa, nestled in the American heartland, because it was there "we have found a living example of everything we call our American way of life."[35] Placing great importance on the production of this episode, the APC employed two of its best writers at the time, Reginald Wells and Harry Middleton, to construct the story. Wells was at one time a filmmaker for the *March of Time* series of newsreels, and later was a founding editor of *Sports Illustrated* magazine. Middleton was a noted journalist who later served as a speechwriter for President Johnson from 1967 to 1969. Their script followed the activities of an army recruiter as he interacted with citizens of the town during the course of his day. It was a clever device used by the writers to weave together the actions of individual townsfolk as they exercised their liberties, at home, work, play, and worship, and their responsibilities to defend those freedoms by enlisting. The last action was further illuminated by the comment that the "biggest responsibility young men face is military duty."[36] By itself, that observance served as an important pitch for increasing enlistments, especially at a time when army manpower levels were approaching a critical post–Korean War low.

The CINFO observed the completion of the Ottumwa production in a letter to the manager of that town's chamber of commerce. He revealed in the message that Ottumwa was to receive a special certificate signed by the secretary of the army recognizing their behavior as "an outstanding example of good military-civilian relations."[37] The plan included a presentation of the award at the world premiere of the episode, which the army planned to take place in the town. Aside from assorted dignitaries, the army band and chorus would be in attendance at the ceremony to contribute to the atmosphere. To organizers it appeared to be a successful blending that celebrated both *The Big Picture* and American exceptionalist ideals. In addition, the film might be useful in combatting any lingering resistance from towns not inclined to welcome new military installations. Still, "Ottumwa, USA" would be a peg on which America could hang its exceptionalist cap.

It may be no small coincidence that the producers of the sitcom *M*A*S*H*, which aired on the CBS television network from 1972 to 1983, chose Ottumwa as the hometown of one its central characters, Corporal "Radar" O'Reilly. Writers of the show presented the series as an irreverent critique of the Vietnam-era US military and scripted barbs of exceptionalist values. Radar, a down-to-earth farm boy from Iowa, was often the target of fast-talking doctors who mocked his simplistic belief in those prescribed American values. Although *The Big Picture* had disappeared from American television screens by 1971, for more than a decade afterward *M*A*S*H* served as the antithesis for its exceptionalist message, and Ottumwa as the convenient lightning rod for its carping bolts. This was not unlike the shadow that *The Phil Silvers Show* cast over earlier episodes of *The Big Picture*. Although its comedic repertoire focused more on military life, like *M*A*S*H* it also served to challenge exceptionalist messages through its irreverence and mockery.

Similar to "Ottumwa, USA," the APC expounded the civil-military connection through episodes of *The Big Picture* that also featured the Boy Scouts, an organization often closely associated with traditional American ideals. The story "U.S. Army and the Boy Scouts" (TV-520) addressed the Scouts' long relationship with the army. Scouting was, the narrator explained, "One of the few institutions to balance the rather softening effect of our modern way of life," which might cause American youth to stray from a full appreciation of prescribed American values.[38] The narrator acknowledged that the Scouting program was sponsored by "schools, business clubs, churches and the like," all those important American institutions closely associated with American traditions and ideals. He also added that from the founding of the Boy Scouts, "the United States Army has been one of its chief supporters."[39] The script assured the audience that Scouting would "help our sons, cousins, and younger brothers develop the initiative, the resourcefulness, the character, the quick-thinking and the leadership they really need."[40] The episode underscored that comment when it concluded with a summary by the narrator, John Daly, who revealed that five of seven current astronauts were Scouts. For good measure he noted that President John F. Kennedy had been a member of Troop 2, Bronxville, New York.[41]

The civil-military connection was growing stronger in the 1950s, particularly with the coming of war on the Korean peninsula. As historian Bruce Cumings suggests, it was that conflict and "not World War II that occasioned the enormous military base structure and the domestic military-industrial complex to service it."[42] By 1952 "the aircraft industry was booming again," and "defense and aerospace accounted directly or indirectly for 55 percent of employment in the country."[43] Employment was on the rise and the economy was robust. The overseas base structure was growing, so that in the ten years between 1950 and 1960 the number of military service members deployed overseas nearly doubled from just over 300,000 to 600,000.[44] This was an entirely new reality for the United States, and most Americans who had never been comfortable with the idea of a large standing military were skeptical. It did not help to allay their fears either when President Eisenhower voiced his concerns in his final news conference, remarking that the armament industry was so pervasive that it carried an "almost insidious penetration of our minds."[45] He went on to comment that it left most Americans thinking that "the only thing the country does is produce weapons and missiles."[46] Hollywood contributed its own perspective of these emerging fears with films such as *Rally Round the Flag* (1955), which offered a comedic look at Americans struggling with the fears of an emerging national militarism. In this atmosphere of concern, an organization such as the Boy Scouts provided a convenient bridge between the military and the public. The military had a long-standing association with the Scouts, and that relationship held potential for allaying fears of expanding militarism. *The Big Picture* provided a useful vehicle through its many films featuring a kind and nurturing military working closely with the youths in episodes such as "The U.S. Army and the Boy Scouts." It suggests that the producers scripted these programs to depict bonds of patriotism and trust to deflect any concerns among viewers regarding perceptions of emerging militarism and to win over an anxious public, although documentary evidence was not found to show that the OCINFO had this in mind as a purpose.

Many of the *Big Picture* episodes throughout the series also celebrated the concept of a traditional American home, which was particularly central to the exceptional consensus. As historian Elaine Tyler May notes, "home" offered a refuge in the uncertain times of the early Cold War. As such, it "prompted Americans to create a family-centered culture" that would provide security.[47] This was a security that was akin to diplomat George Kennan's containment strategy, which in the early Cold War period described America's geopolitical initiatives to curtail the spread of communism and to protect the exceptional American way of life. This, the United States accomplished through special military alliances, such as NATO and SEATO, and the forward stationing of military forces in Europe and Asia. All this the APC featured in a series of *Big Picture* episodes.[48] For Elaine Tyler May, the home became a microcosm of the Cold War global struggle with the creation of boundaries to protect the American family from "the hazards of the age."[49] These hazards included, among a number of things, the dangers of nuclear war, deviation from traditional gender roles, and any perceived moral weakness or degeneracy, "which allegedly led to communism."[50] It was that home, the "locale of the good life, the evidence of democratic abundance," that was an icon of a superior West and the primary bulwark against threats to the exceptionalist consensus. *Big Picture* writers often worked to weave this conception of "home" into their episodes. Images frequently appeared showing parents in a tight-knit family unit living within the constructs of expected gender roles, consistent with the nation's exceptionalist beliefs. Episodes such as "Ottumwa, USA," "Pictorial Report No. 26," and "The Soldier's Christmas" (TV-745) all bore witness to this concept by showing mothers and fathers welcoming soldiers home for the holidays, serving family meals, guiding children through important decisions, and following the routines expected of their roles. The key overall was to ensure an understanding of the American way of life and to allow the average viewer to associate with their fellow Americans on the screen, and thus make a meaningful connection with their own lives within the "imagined" exceptional community. Subsequent *Big Picture* episodes, such as "The American Way of Life" (TV-476) and "A Day in America" (TV-776), followed similar story lines, all scripted to meet the audience on a personal level, reinforce consensual familial ideals, and remind Americans "why we fight."

In God We Trust

Believing that religion held a central place in the life of America, President Truman called for the creation of the President's Committee on Religion and Welfare in the Armed Forces in October 1947. Its mission was to encourage a wholesome lifestyle for uniformed personnel through participation in religious and recreational activities with local communities.[51] Following that thread, the secretary of defense organized the Armed Forces Chaplains Board later in 1949 with the purpose to advise the nation's military leadership on matters of faith and to develop "uniform religious policies."[52] Many members of the American clergy sought to cultivate a wider understanding that religious belief was an essential underpinning of the foundational American values and to ensure its inculcation to the armed forces' set of values. Following this, the army began including a program of mandatory religious instruction, which received the title "Character Guidance." New recruits attended a series of lectures led by chaplains, while other soldiers received the training on an annual basis. It centered on the "belief that people were moral beings whose sense of right and wrong stemmed from religion."[53]

Picking up on that energy, the *Big Picture* producers focused on the particular tenet of religion to emphasize the exceptional American way of life. Separated out for special focus, the APC created at least six unique episodes that featured the ways in which this characteristic appeared woven into the fabric of the American identity, including its place among army values. The first films on the subject, "The Army Chaplains" (TV-190) in 1952 and "Christmas in Korea" (TV-244), appeared when America and the West were locked in a sharp ideological battle with the communist East during the early Cold War years of the Korean conflict. As was noted then, the freedom of worship enjoyed by the democratic nations and the atheism of the communists was among the significant differences between the two sides. To help distinguish that divide, President Eisenhower introduced the phrase "In God We Trust" as the national motto in 1956.[54] The distinction was also fostered through the belief that America "was to be more than the policeman of the globe—it was the new savior of the world by Divine appointment."[55] These episodes served to remind service members of the strong spiritual connection that reached as far back in American history as the Revolutionary War. For example, a favorite stained glass window found in many military chapels of the period featured the image of George Washington kneeling in prayer at Valley Forge.

"Religious Emphasis Day in Philadelphia" (TV-407), which aired in 1958, spoke of a unique event organized in that city when 6,000 military members were invited to worship and participate in specially scheduled activities with the citizens. Introducing the episode was the comment that "religion has always been a vitally important part of life for men in our armed forces. . . . The American serviceman and woman have long been encouraged to express their faith according to their beliefs."[56] Although this episode touted the link between religion and the exceptional consensus, it unfortunately fell short of wider inclusiveness when the narrator commented that service members of "all faiths," Catholic, Protestant, and Jewish, would be present to worship. There was no mention of other religions or spiritual groups on the margins of society.

These types of *Big Picture* episodes aired in parallel with Hollywood's production run of "biblical sagas" such as *The Robe* in 1953, *The Ten Commandments* in 1956, and *Ben-Hur* in 1959. Although they ran as competition with television, it is evident that the subject matter of the films meshed well with programming on the small screen as both were appropriate for the time and added greater ammunition to the propaganda war against "Godless communism."[57] Other offerings on television included Catholic bishop Fulton J. Sheen's inspirational weekly, *Life Is Worth Living*. Conservative Christians considered him a significant contributor to understanding and appreciating the American way of life. Known for his anticommunist and antisocialist rhetoric, Sheen won awards from the conservative faith-based Freedoms Foundation and an Emmy for Outstanding Television Personality in 1952.[58] Sheen's program was among those contemporary shows that espoused "the strategic position religion assumed in the Cold War era."[59]

Within the armed forces' Chaplain Corps, a budding evangelical movement had arisen during the mid-1950s, driven by the anticommunist zeitgeist and supported in large part by President Eisenhower and his administration. At the time, it encouraged an American civil-military religious connection, thus opening the door for the inclusion of evangelical Christianity into service-directed character education.[60] As such, it was also not uncommon for exceptional themes to find their way into the homilies of military chaplains or to find resonance in productions such as *The Big Picture*. Seen by the president as another piece in the bulwark against the spread of communist dogma, the civil-religious connection resonated outside the chapel and into military life through other means of communication. It appeared in articles in all editions of the *Stars and Stripes* newspaper and in a plethora of regularly scheduled television shows available to military audiences through the AFN radio and television networks. *The Big Picture* helped illuminate this connection through episodes such as "The Chaplain and the Commander" (TV-532, 1961) that spoke of the close working relationship between chaplains and the military chain of command. It noted that legacy by claiming that "since Lexington and Concord clergy men in uniform have served American troops in peace and war, from Bunker Hill to the Brandenburg Gate," a reference to the divided city of Berlin.[61] Other connections appeared in "The Army Chaplain—Yesterday and Today" (TV-538, 1961), and "The Bridge" (TV-737, 1968). Each episode addressed the role of the chaplaincy both in the history of the military and in performance of contemporary duties to service personnel. Continuing through the 1960s, the influence of the evangelical right had insinuated itself into the lives of military members from the pulpit, in training, and through print media, radio, and television, with its message of anti-communism and American exceptionalism. As historian Lori Bogle notes, "The postwar military establishment engaged in religiously oriented indoctrination during Troop Information and Education (TI&E) programs in its continuing efforts to fulfill its constitutional and 'God-given' duty to provide for the common defense."[62]

As cameras focused on scenes of Independence Hall, the pealing of church bells and the sweeping intonations of choral strains invited viewers into the episode "Religious Emphasis Day in Philadelphia." Even without the prompting of a script the connection was clear: spirituality and exceptionalism existed together in the foundation of American ideals. Liturgical musical scores floated in the backgrounds. Scenes captured civilians and military personnel of various faiths sitting together worshipping as the camera played over their faces, etched with solemnity and an understanding that faith and freedom were inseparable. Regardless of the setting of the place of worship—in a chapel, in a jungle, on the hood of a jeep—the camera framed the scenes in an almost Rockwell-like canvas that gripped the viewer and sought to create a bond of warm familiarity and understanding. This the producers achieved by bathing the scenes in bright natural light whenever possible. These productions loosed the full weight of the APC's aesthetic craft to carry the exceptional message that the "belief and trust in God forms the basis for true national security."[63]

During the time of these productions, John C. Broger was serving as director for the AFI&E.[64] He brought with him the experience gained serving as a postwar founder of the Far East Broadcasting Company (FEBC), a Christian ministry broadcasting primarily in Asia. In 1954, Adm. Arthur W. Radford, then serving as chairman of the Joint Chiefs of Staff, had invited Broger to act as a consultant and create an ideological framework for the military along conservative Christian lines. The result was a program titled *Militant Liberty: A Program of Assessment and Evaluation of Freedom.*[65] It published a comprehensive booklet that the military leadership intended to serve as guide to assist the armed forces in understanding the ideals of the American way of life and to assist in the transmission of those ideals abroad, to foreign audiences to motivate them to "be more militant in their belief of liberty."[66] Thus, military elites were actively inviting Christian evangelicals into the information and education process to shape and inform the thinking of service members.

Militant Liberty differed from other informational programs, particularly those initiatives of the USIA, which it directed toward Third World nations. As historian Kenneth Osgood notes, the difference resided in the methodology. USIA programs worked toward "sharpening perceptions and attitudes" toward America and its ideals, while *Militant Liberty* worked to inspire action.[67] In the context of each approach, vehicles such as the *Big Picture* transmitted messages to shape perceptions and inspire action through episodes such as "Soldier in Panama" (TV-283) and "You in Japan" (TV-354) during the 1950s, and later "U.S. Army in the Andes" (TV-686) in 1963. As the narrator for "You in Japan" noted, that nation was "rededicated to democratic pursuits, and realigned in friendship with the West" through positive actions taken by the US military that included inculcation of American values and ideology.[68] This was necessary to deflect periodic eruptions of communist anti-American agitation. As eager as the military elites were to follow the guidelines of *Militant Liberty*, it eventually fell victim to budgetary constraints and interdepartmental bickering as the State Department saw the program as too resource-intense and aggressive.

A more direct influence on exceptionalist idealism came from a consortium of conservatives and evangelicals. The conservative Christian-based Freedoms Foundation was one of several organizations courted by President Eisenhower in the early 1950s to develop, define, and promulgate American ideals to the military and a wider public audience. Established in 1949, the Freedoms Foundation sought to reestablish the nation's Christian heritage and believed, as the president did, that the country was battling the Soviet East for the minds of men. This came at a time of widespread conservative anticommunist backlash in the United States that included the heavy-handed tactics of Senator Joseph McCarthy (R-WI), who in 1950 claimed, "Today we are engaged in a final, all-out battle between communistic atheism and Christianity."[69]

The Freedoms Foundation incorporated its ideas into an "American Credo," which included many of the tenets of Americanism and a specific link to the centrality of religion that maintained an abiding belief in a Christian God.[70] The Freedom Foundation was among the first conservative groups to begin working closely with Broger's AFI&E and the Armed Forces Radio and Television Service (AFRTS).[71] Its agenda was to disseminate anticommunist and conservative political and economic views to service members as well as the American public. Captivated by this initiative, especially the spiritual aspect, Eisenhower consistently lent his support while still in uniform, then afterward as president of Columbia University, and later when he assumed the presidency of the United States. Many of the Freedoms Foundation's ideas resonated in Eisenhower's presidential directives and foreign policy strategies for prosecuting psychological warfare in the struggle for the minds of mankind. The Freedom Foundation, funded by conservative groups, was active in transmitting its exceptional message of the centrality of spirituality for five decades.[72] Its charter included joining with the armed forces to develop a set of national core values that would inspire an ideological and spiritual reawakening in America.[73] This civil-military link suggests that military elites had little difficulty using *The Big Picture* as a vehicle to transmit those conservative Christian exceptionalist messages through its religious-themed narratives.

Those episodes that focused on the tenets of religion aired at a time that the United States was cultivating a special connection with those nations it was developing as part of its containment strategy. For example, narration in these *Big Picture* films addressed spiritual worship as a common cultural ground between the Americans and Germans, noting that in the early postwar years, "the spiritual fabric of Germany also needed a rebuilding."[74] This was a time to build one of many important cultural and social bridges with a nation that formed a critical section of the Cold War containment barrier of communism. The United States was eager to exploit it. The visual evidence, presented in the episode "People to People" (TV-430), was black-and-white footage showing military units rebuilding churches and using cranes to lift recast bells up to newly raised steeples. It also appeared in regularly scheduled joint worship services, announced in the European editions of the *Stars and Stripes,* which brought together American military personnel and their families with their German neighbors in a comfortably bound community of faith. Peering into the camera during the episode the "USAREUR Story (Part II)" (TV-542), the commander, Gen. Bruce C. Clarke, emphasized the importance of religion by noting that "it too is a vital part of our lives. We like to feel we are a religious army. USAREUR has constructed 253 chapels throughout Europe for its troops. Protestant, Catholic, and Jewish services are conducted regularly."[75]

The Big Picture captured all of this, and through these episodes it reinforced the centrality of religious worship in American life. That theme continued through the course of the series, as the show's producers never strayed far from the traditional set of exceptional tenets during the late 1960s, even during the period of the countercultural upheaval. Episodes such as "Of Soldiers and Altars" (TV-690), which aired in 1966, reflected this continuing theme. Scripted to describe the "extensive religious activities and facilities provided by [the] US Army Chaplaincy in CONUS and overseas for members the army and their dependents" the film's narrator emphasized "the Founding Fathers' dependency on a divine creator" and the "deep undergirding spiritual values upon which our nation is based."[76] Maintaining that perspective, the narrative described the exceptional "protection of divine providence" that had graced America's past as well as the "deep religious principles" that will guide its future endeavors.[77] The APCs switched to the use of 16 mm color format for this film, thereby infusing life and energy into the production. Stained glass windows in chapel scenes seemed to come to life, and the diversity of congregations became more obvious. Notable in the episode also were several scenes composed of young people, civilians and soldiers alike, discussing and condemning the tendency of others of the same age who too quickly followed popular trends and abandoned a faith-based lifestyle. In this way, the episode used the benefits of camera, sound, and settings to bring home the importance of faith to the exceptionalist consensus.

Continuing to emphasize the centrality of religion as late as 1968, the *Big Picture* series aired shows such as "The Soldier's Christmas" (TV-745), which focused on the celebration of that holiday around the globe with visits to various military posts and field locations, including those in Vietnam. It featured footage of soldiers receiving packages from home, exchanging small gifts, decorating Christmas trees, and arriving home to the welcoming arms of loved ones. The blend of background seasonal chorals and music provided by the army chorus and band, together with emotionally charged colored footage, emphasized the importance of the holiday for service members and their families. The episode again underscored the understanding that religious worship was a uniquely exceptional characteristic of the uniformed services and worked to apply a human face to the army, which was under increasing scrutiny by the media, politicians, and much of the public for its presence in Southeast Asia. Unfortunately, the *Big Picture* catalog was again found wanting for its lack of some depth. Other than the Christian celebration of Christmas, also found in "Christmas in Korea" (TV-244), no other religious holiday drew consideration, and unfortunately this was a lost opportunity to expand and welcome greater religious inclusiveness and perhaps also cultivate greater public support.

The Past Is Prologue

Similar to those with a spiritual theme, historical episodes also played a role in transmitting the exceptional message to *Big Picture* audiences. Unpacking that collection makes it is possible to group those that the APC produced with a historical narrative into two categories: informational and exceptional. The former provided straightforward information regarding specific army units, individuals, or events in American military history (a discussion of this is in the next chapter), while the latter offered an exceptional perspective wrapped in a motivational historical narrative. It is the second group that this study addresses here, for its contribution in communicating the message of an exceptional consensus.

Among the first of the motivational episodes produced by the APC was "Soldiers' Heritage" (TV-412), which aired in 1958 during the same troubling period of McCarthyite witch hunts directed at the army. Its production suggests it followed the same line as other *Big Picture* episodes that the APC crafted to deflect threats of communist corruption of American ideology. "Soldiers' Heritage" provided a short, but triumphal, history of the army's role in the nation's wars that writers laced with exceptional and patriotic expressions. It began with a salute to the individual soldier, offering a "tribute that reaches back across the developing story of the nation itself" to the army, "which has fought to preserve the nation's integrity and indeed its very life."[78] Woven into this script were exceptional references to America's "recognition of its Manifest Destiny to be strong enough to support freedom beyond its own shores" and rhetoric that asked, "What are the beliefs for which men will fight? They range from faith in a nation which strives under God to achieve its destiny" to "a capacity for honor."[79] Producers and military elites considered these to be God-sanctioned actions that encouraged popular support of national interests at home and abroad. These productions aired as the United States was beginning to dedicate increasing amounts of its national treasure toward its involvement in Southeast Asia. Those episodes such as "Hidden War in Vietnam" (TV-562, 1962) and "The Fight for Vietnam" (TV-574, 1963) served as platforms for that exceptionalist message justifying our obligation to insert ourselves whenever, and wherever, we perceived a threat to our ideology. Cut from the same cloth were two other episodes, "American Soldier" (TV-627, 1964) and another version of "The Soldier's Heritage" (TV-754, 1969), which told comparable stories about America's obligation of leadership. So similar were the scripts and the footage of all three that it was apparent that APC producers pulled the material from their archives, dusted it off, and repackaged it for a subsequent presentation. These last two episodes echoed the same sentiments as the first, regarding the American soldier's role as guardian of sacred liberties, and repeated many of the same words and phrases. In that regard, a visit to the Tomb of the Unknowns in Washington, DC, was a common point of introduction for all three films.[80] Similarly, *Big Picture* producers used that memorial in the closing sequence of all three versions of the episode "Prelude to Taps," which aired in 1962, 1967, and 1971 (TV-533, 597, and 788). The differences between all the productions were little more than aesthetic, changing from black-and-white to color film as technology changed, featuring new narrators as the years passed, and restaging old scenes with new actors. This lent it a feel of immutability, a ritual that producers repeated periodically to renew faith in the core exceptionalist values that were not changing.

Still, a consideration of the changing zeitgeist between the mid-1950s and the late 1960s might recommend an examination of the reason the message in the trio of episodes remained unchanged. In the first film, "American Soldier," the message was a reaction to perceived threats from enemies both foreign and domestic, the communists and the McCarthyites, who on one hand were plotting to undermine the democratic system and on the other to villainize the army. In the last two, the same message served as an important foil to deflect criticisms of the military and to bolster the traditional exceptional consensus at a time it was fracturing under internal societal pressures from the counterculture movement. In this context, APC producers may have seen little need to alter scripts if the same message found utility in both circumstances. However, a deeper analysis also offers a suggestion that the transmission of a too-consistent message over time revealed a fatal flaw. The inability or unwillingness of APC producers to alter the exceptional message within the later episodes, and to adopt a new approach that recognized the changing times, may have eventually rendered *The Big Picture* irrelevant. By 1969, when the series fell under attack in Congress for budget excesses and perceptions that it was attempting to influence foreign policy, it may have already been doomed. A *Stars and Stripes* article noted its demise in July 1971 with the comments that it had fallen victim to "changing times and changing tastes," and the army needed "time to come up with something that, it feels, is more relevant to the problems of the service today."[81]

A survey of the remaining *Big Picture* episodes reveals additional historically exceptional episodes that were intended as motivational films but that in part also drew criticism. Among these were "The Common Defense" (TV-433), and "To Keep and Bear Arms" (TV-557). As the first title might suggest, the episode, which aired in 1958, referenced that particular phrase in the US Constitution, using it to form a link between the intent of the original framers and the responsibilities of the army, together with the navy and the air force, in the past and present. It enthusiastically endorsed the military's efforts to defend and preserve the nation's exceptional founding principles, and again it trumpeted America's obligation: "We can never afford to drop our guard so long as the threat of aggression continues to exist."[82]

The second episode, "To Keep and Bear Arms," which aired in 1963, referenced the Bill of Rights of the Constitution and the right of the American people to keep and bear arms. Through a series of historical reenactments, it told a story of the musket and rifle in close association with the militia and the army during the nation's development. It reminded viewers that "the rifle is part of our history" and described weapon ownership as a fundamental right and responsibility.[83] However, more than being a simple historical review, as were the earlier episodes, it also served as a platform for the National Rifle Association (NRA). Embedded within the footage of the show was a shorter public relations film about that organization. It spoke of its establishment and the NRA's enduring relationship with the army, particularly with regard to joint training and competitions that it sponsored. The narrator underscored that link by commenting, "Since the NRA aids the national defense the army has always extended its fullest cooperation."[84] The shorter film addressed its support of the Civilian Marksmanship Program (CMP) in league with the military, and its purpose to "prepare America's youth" by training them with weapons.[85] The scripted narrative not only provided a historical background but also encouraged viewers, military and civilian alike, to become involved in gaining and maintaining marksmanship skills. This appeared in the 1968 *Congressional Record* and was part of the organization's "special public service publicity campaign."[86] With that information becoming a matter of public record, the *Big Picture* series found itself drawn to the center of criticism from progressive leaders in Congress, who considered this as evidence of an external organization bearing too much influence on the military and using it as a platform to further its own needs. This became particularly evident in this episode through footage from the NRA that advocated the blocking of proposed legislation that endorsed stricter gun-control laws. It was accompanied by a charge that "fresh attempts are made each year to introduce undesirable firearms legislation," describing how that would inhibit, among other things, the lawful recreational use of personal weapons.[87] It also drew a parallel between outlawing firearms and outlawing automobiles, noting that each depended on the responsible use of the owner, not the object. The timing of this episode also contributed to making it controversial. Just a few short years after it aired, the nation suffered the assassination of two popular and influential figures in 1968: the Reverend Martin Luther King Jr. and Senator Robert Kennedy. By its association with the rifle advocacy group the army fell under scrutiny, and the *Big Picture* episode, which featured the NRA, also fell out of step with the popular political mood of the country. Historical or not, through episodes such as "To Keep and Bear Arms" some political leaders, such as Thomas J. Dodd (D-CT) and Mike Mansfield (D-MT), perceived the series as selling an exceptional message that was no longer necessary or appropriate, and they introduced legislation to control gun ownership, which passed in 1968.[88]

As World War II came to a close, Americans felt a surge of triumphalism that blossomed into an exceptional vision of their nation. It was an attitude that included a collection of tenets that were unique to the United States, and set it apart from the rest of the world. Working to transmit that consensus, the government employed a variety of print and visual media. Among the vehicles used was the *Big Picture* series. During the first decades of the Cold War, it served as a vehicle to remind members of the armed forces, and the American public, of those exceptional qualities by informing and encouraging an understanding of the nation's foundational ideals. By the late 1960s, however, as the mood of the nation changed, the exceptionalist consensus fell under scrutiny as being inappropriate and out of touch with prevailing cultural attitudes. Regardless of changes in the cultural atmosphere, the *Big Picture* producers continued to script episodes that sold images of an exceptional American way of life. In the long run, the show's producers risked the loss of some of its audience, and *The Big Picture* in due course became considered by some viewers to be irrelevant and eventually was discontinued.

5

A Big Picture of the Army Way of Life

It was with a measure of pride that Col. William Quinn introduced a discussion about the history of the US Army's First Infantry Division, titled "The Big Red One" (TV-210), in 1952. It was one episode he had developed in a short series named the *Blue Badge* that APC producers incorporated into a series of the earliest *Big Picture* episodes (TV-210 through TV-222). But "The Big Red One" was not only the first in Quinn's series, it was also the first film dedicated to a historical study for the *Big Picture* catalog. Following it in quick succession were several other studies of military units. These introduced a large number of historical films that the APC produced for informational purposes. Beginning with the historical informational films, this chapter examines those *Big Picture* episodes that the Astoria studios created to inform and educate service members, their families, and the public about the army way of life, the third subject category of this study.

History of the Army

A quick survey of the *Big Picture* catalog reveals that at least eighty-six episodes were devoted to historical subjects. At approximately

10.4 percent of the total number produced by the APC, "historical" is the largest subcategory within the series. This is unsurprising considering that APC's archive was a treasure trove of video footage collected by Army Signal Corps cameramen over the years. As such, it provided the American audience with the greatest video exposure to their army. For the *Big Picture* producers it offered repeated opportunities to display past achievements, highlight moments of triumph, and demonstrate how the writers wove the army's glories into the tapestry of the national story. It provided points of connection with veterans who still remembered recent past conflicts, and it piqued the curiosity of viewers interested in military history. John Labella recalls:

> When I was young I was fascinated with the history that was presented on *The Big Picture*, especially the military history. In fact, that program as well as the *West Point Story*, also a series of that period, got me thinking about going to West Point. As I got older and still watched the program, I was more interested in the shows focusing on the battles in World War Two.[1]

Within the sequence of production, the great majority of these episodes aired prior to 1966 and the United States' deeper involvement in Southeast Asia. Of these, most featured the American experience in World War II, focusing on battles and theaters of operation. Titles about operations included "D-Day Convoy to Normandy" (TV-213), "U.S. Sixth Corps" (TV-219), and "Invasion of Southern France" (TV-220). Episodes about specific battles included "Battle of Salerno" (TV-406), "Battle of the Bulge" (TV-413), and the critically acclaimed "Battle of San Pietro" (TV-431). Several years afterward, 1964–1965, the APC produced an epic twelve-episode history series under the collective title "Army in Action" (TV-634 through TV-643, TV-645, and TV-646), which guided viewers from the buildup for World War I to the final victory in World War II. It addressed all major actions and areas of the globe that the army operated in during that period of time. The series echoed the form of earlier compilation documentaries, utilizing reels of combat footage backed by dramatic musical scores, guided by serious narration. On the whole, it was the most concerted effort by APC producers to package and present an informational minidocumentary program through *The Big Picture*.

By comparison, *Big Picture* films about specific army wartime operations in the Pacific Theater did not appear until the late 1950s, after the show had already aired a large number of those stories concerning European operations. This may have been a conscious decision made by the governing board of the APC in considering a public television schedule already saturated with Pacific Theater offerings: *Crusade in the Pacific* (1951–1952), *Victory at Sea* (1952–1953), and *Navy Log* (1955–1958). The reason may also have been that the army acted as the chief branch among the services that fought in Europe, and it served only a secondary role behind the navy and marines in the Pacific. In that regard, emphasizing action from the European theater would tell a better story to viewers. Nevertheless, the few tales from the Pacific included "Battle of Manila" (TV-417) and "Pay Off in the Pacific" (Part One) and (Part Two) (TV-480 and TV-481). Taken together, these episodes about the European and Pacific Theaters of war were principally informational and adhered closely to scripts that presented historical facts and overviews alone. They minimized the use of motivational and exceptionalist rhetoric, except for what a viewer might extract as a matter of patriotic pride in the army's successes.

Historic episodes that focused on senior military leaders were also plentiful. Again, the majority emerged from World War II. The first two were "The General Bradley Story" (TV-398) and "The General Marshall Story" (TV-408). Close on their heels were episodes on Generals MacArthur, Eisenhower, Hap Arnold, and George Patton, and Admiral Nimitz. This collection appeared onscreen between 1958 and 1959. Each was a well-scripted biography that shared personal information and celebrated the officer's wartime accomplishments. Some, such as "The General MacArthur Story" (TV-416) made a public appearance amid great fanfare. The Sperry Rand Corporation arranged a special showing for political elites in Washington, DC, that included the US Army Band and Chorus and an invitation to the secretary of the army.[2] Timing was important too, especially to have the widest impact with the television audience. The army aired the episode during the week leading up to the December 7th anniversary of the attack on Pearl Harbor. One of the new vice presidents of the corporation,

Figure 5.1. A production still from the filming of the episode "Hall of Heroes" (TV-803). The kneeling soldier was an actor hired for the part, and the three standing behind him in uniform were actually lieutenants assigned to the APC. Casts often included a mixture of military and civilian personnel. (Image Source: Army Pictorial Center)

Lt. Gen. (Ret.) Leslie R. Groves, provided a ringing endorsement of the film: "It is one of the best things I have seen from the standpoint of increasing the public's respect for the competency of the Army. I think also that it will be quite beneficial to West Point."[3] Still, as much attention as the army's special premiere generated for *The Big Picture*, one important viewer refused to watch the show about MacArthur— President Dwight Eisenhower, who had a strained relationship with his former colleague. Instead, he requested a substitute from the army. In its place, the APC forwarded a copy of "The General Marshall Story" to the White House.[4] In the case of another episode in development, "The Eisenhower Story" (TV-435), the president declared his desire to exercise a prerogative to vet the film prior to its release. Subsequently, it was on 21 May 1959 that the CINFO reported, with some measure of relief, Ike's approval to the army chief of staff.[5]

A following series of episodes regarding most of the same collection of leaders appeared as restructured presentations during the 1963 season. Popular contemporary television and movie stars such as Raymond Massey, Ronald Reagan, and Walter Matthau introduced each of these. It was Matthau who in turn reminded viewers that "a nation's greatness depends on the quality of the leaders it produces in times of crisis. We Americans have been very fortunate in this respect."[6] Although script writers laced the episodes with statements such as this, which plucked at patriotic chords, the films were good opportunities for sharing of historical information about the army's leadership with audiences and for certain actors to appear in a popular television setting.

Another possibility for the development of a plethora of historical films, with the emphasis on World War II, was the profile of the members of Congress. Approximately 50 percent of representatives and senators in the bicameral body were veterans in the Seventy-Ninth through the Eighty-First Congresses (1945–1950). That number increased to 60 percent during the Eighty-Second through the Eighty-Sixth Congresses (1951–1960), and continued an upward trend to 70 percent by 1970.[7] Collectively, a majority of these individuals saw service between 1941 and 1945. An argument exists that the large postwar percentage of veterans in the legislature figured into the initial calculus of determining the number of historical titles to produce. Although it is difficult to establish a direct correlation, or intent, it would make sense that these types of episodes would appeal to veterans as a group, and could foster a sentimental link between the army and profiled members of Congress. Such a link might be beneficial to the army during budget negotiations or discussions of manpower cuts.

Other historic episodes that appear in the *Big Picture* catalog focused on special topics. These included titles such as the three-part "The History of Aviation" (TV-502 through TV-504) and the two-part "Beyond the Call" (TV-575 and TV-576), which provided an overview of acts of valor throughout American military history and the soldiers who received the Medal of Honor for their bravery. A special episode on the "D-Day Anniversary" (TV-762) appeared in 1969 to mark the landing of Allied forces on the beaches of Normandy twenty-five years earlier. This presented a moment for the army to celebrate past victories at a time the public was heavily criticizing the military for its involvement in Vietnam. The timing of its release suggests that it might have offered a brief respite from those attacks and served to deflect some small amount of that criticism by reviving faded memories of the army's past golden moments. Still, evidence that the APC was feeling any pressure from the OCINFO to construct a bulwark through these *Big Picture* productions is not present among archived documents.

The similarities shared by all of these historical episodes are that they opened a window into a particular aspect of military life, satisfied viewer expectations regarding historical narratives and wartime footage, and did it all in a safe space. Historical videos may have drawn criticism for their aesthetics, but seldom did they draw criticism for being too political in content. The information they provided was a matter of record, with the past little influenced by the political present. This suggests that the viewing audience had less reason to reject *Big Picture* informational films about historical topics for any reason other than lack of interest in the subject material. There was, however, an occasional element of criticism generated internally. In one instance, this arose from the five-member *Big Picture* board that reviewed ongoing projects. When considering the 1959–1960 season, Col. John Weaver, troop information chief and board chair, voiced his concern that previous episodes had too often leaned heavily on past accomplishments. He suggested instead, that with the approaching season "what we want to do in the future is to show today's Army—to change that image from old-fashioned, slow, cumbersome . . . to one of a modern essential, quality and vital force that merits the support of John Q. Public."[8] This seemed especially important at a time the army was struggling to declare its relevancy to Congress. The conclusion of the board was to cancel proposed biographies on Generals Joseph Lawton Collins and Courtney H. Hodges, together with an episode on the WACs and another on Hawaii, then the newest state. They considered the WAC story too sterile and the two biographies uninteresting. The episode on Hawaii did not fit into the overall strategy of projecting the image of a modernizing army, although a year earlier, in 1958, *The Big Picture* did air "Alaska—The Outpost

State" (TV-422).[9] In the short term, historical episodes such as those mentioned did not air, and those that emphasized the army's techno-logical prowess did. However, as a survey of the *Big Picture* catalog re-veals, historical episodes began a comeback between 1962 and 1965, offering the largest number of subcategory titles until those on the Vietnam conflict appeared.

Informing and Educating

Another important category of films for soldiers and their families addressed the wide variety of informational, instructional, and edu-cational opportunities available to them in the army. These offered a view into information outlets as well as schools and technical train-ing. The first such episode produced by the APC was "The Citizen Soldier" (TV-184), which highlighted informational and educational opportunities for the soldiers both on and off duty. As the narrator noted, "It is possible for a soldier to leave the army today far better educated and informed than when he came in."[10] Complementing this film was "Information and Education Overseas (Part I), Depen-dent Schools (Part II)" (TV-198). Produced in 1952, it also focused on the two parts of the army's Troop Information and Education (TI&E) program. The first of these was the free dissemination of information about ongoing current events around the globe through command briefings and presentations. It addressed the unrestrained freedom of information enjoyed by service members through the Armed Forces Radio and Television (AFRTS) networks and the *Stars and Stripes* newspapers, which were both key pieces of this effort. The narrator introduced the episode by asking, "How can we make it possible for the soldiers we send overseas to have a part of America with them?"[11] The answer he offered was "Surely a vital part of living in this country is the chance to read and hear about the issues confronting us."[12] To provide a link to this understanding, the APC produced *Big Picture* episodes on AFN, "The Story of American Forces Network" (TV-583), and the popular newspaper, "The Story of *Stars and Stripes*" (TV-482) in 1960. Later, "All the Word to All the Troops" (TV-810) in 1971 com-bined both to show that the American armed forces were "the best informed group of military personnel in the world."[13] In this regard, one can again consider historian Benedict Anderson's ideas regarding the concept of an identifiable community, formed through cultural artifacts such as print, audio, and visual media. These existed in military communities at home and abroad in the forms of AFN, the *Stars and Stripes*, and television series such as *The Big Picture*. They served as a unique common forum to shape and bind the military community through common knowledge and an informed consciousness. In this, *The Big Picture* arguably played an important role as a medium that was accessible to military members, acting in the role of a common, familiar forum.

The second important part of TI&E was an overview of the types of classes offered to members of the military and the unique school system for dependent school-age children that the armed forces had established for families stationed overseas. The army considered this essential for soldiers because, as the narrator noted, "a lot of guys wouldn't get an education at all if it weren't for the army education program."[14] It was considered essential for their children because as the narrator, Carl Zimmermann, confidently concluded, "There is something solidly American here in this school system that embraces the whole world."[15] The episode served as an advertisement to encourage soldiers to continue their education, explained the system that could assist them, and provided the American public a brief look into the lives of the military families living overseas. This became increasingly important as American military communities overseas began to rapidly multiply in number, and swell in size, after the army welcomed the first families to West Germany in April 1946.

The army continued to sell its information and education programs through *The Big Picture* for the two decades it aired. Among the titles the APC produced between 1954 and 1963, were "Education in the Army" (TV-279), "Army Technical Schools in Europe" (TV-282), "Opportunity to Learn" (TV-540), and "Tools for Learning" (TV-571). Even as late as 1970, with the episode "The Largest School House in the World" (TV-785) the army was using educational opportunities as enticement for recruiting, particularly among those who were searching for employment. Each of these films described an aspect of the army's effort to prepare its soldiers for their participation in a modernizing military. The first, "Education in the Army," shed light on the sobering statistic that the military classified one out of every three new recruits as "Mental Group 4," with a dangerously low cognitive ability, "so low as to handicap their performance as soldiers."[16] As the film explained, that condition was unacceptable if they were to keep pace with the "demanding technical jobs necessary to keep a complex modern army operating."[17] The other episodes provided insight into other schools for general education, from grammar school level to college, and those for technical skills.[18] "The Largest School House in the World" also addressed the army's transitional program for instruction in a variety of skills that could carry over into the civilian world. This collection of films stated the need for continuing to educate the American soldier and discussed opportunities that were available to them. Similar to other APC releases, these *Big Picture* episodes appeared at a time when the army was struggling to meet its postwar recruiting and retention goals. They offered enticements for recruits wanting to serve in the military as well as those soldiers eager to bolster their educations or attain some technical skill. In that regard, the narrator's casual comments that the cost to each individual was free except for some ancillary costs, such as books, greatly added to the inducement. As a recruiting and retention tool, the opportunity to advance individual education was very appealing and reflected the exceptionalist tenet of upward mobility through education.

The army also emphasized other unique educational opportunities. Among these were language training. The *Big Picture* episode "Army Language School" (TV-200) was another early effort by the army to inform its ranks, and the public, about training they might not know existed and to generate interest for participation. The focus in this film was on the armed forces' school at the Presidio at Monterey, California. There, soldiers trained on the "weapons of words," the languages and customs of the nations to which they would eventually be assigned.[19] This, the narrator explained, was essential to helping them become better ambassadors for the United States. Although the weaponization of language as a Cold War strategy may have appeared awkward, the army saw this as essential, considering the growing demands of "America's world responsibilities" in countries linked to the common defense of the West.[20] The APC revisited the subject of language study again in 1959 with "U.S. Army Language School"

(TV-492) and in 1970 with the presentation of "Language Power for Peace" (TV-779). In the latter, they addressed the Defense Language Institute (DLI) in Monterey, emphasizing the expansion of the facilities that would eventually include up to fifty different language study programs. Just as the earlier episode had done, these last two served as much as an internal sales pitch as a public relations vehicle.

The spectrum of training opportunities in the army was broad, and the service used *The Big Picture* as a primary vehicle to showcase the variety. Seeded throughout the catalog were episodes that addressed specialized training alongside basic education. Examples include episodes about legal training, "Soldiers at Law" (TV-739); the warrant officer training program, "Call Me Mister" (TV-759); and training for musicians, "The Army's Music Men" (TV-811). It also featured occasional training films that benefited military members, their families, and civilian employees alike, such as the episode "Mouth-to-Mouth Resuscitation" (TV-495). Nearly two dozen separate *Big Picture* films emphasized training in the army, serving as inducements for recruitment and retention, as well as providing a window into the army way of life.

Army Leadership

Leadership development is important to the military, and *The Big Picture* served as a platform to provide an understanding of this key aspect of the service, because more than in almost any other profession, a defined rank structure is necessary for command, control, and discipline. The APC produced approximately a dozen episodes that outlined the path to the officer ranks for enlisted soldiers and interested civilians. These included discussions of the Reserve Officer Training Corps (ROTC), the US Military Academy at West Point, and the Officer Candidate School (OCS) system. Among the first episodes to follow this theme were "ROTC Summer Training" (TV-323) and "Graduate: Reserve Officers' Training Corps" (TV-391), which aired in 1955 and 1957 respectively. These provided insight into the program for college students by emphasizing the contributions individuals could make—"ROTC offers opportunities for men with leadership abilities to become officers"—and the help they could receive "for whatever future they plan."[21] The ROTC program was also the largest source of officers for the military, and *The Big Picture* offered the public a view into the process of procuring new leaders by answering the question posed early in the films by the narrator: "How does the nation find its officers?"[22] A follow-on episode, "R.O.T.C.—A Pattern for Progress" (TV-609), was described as an "unusual chronicle" that spoke about the benefits of remaining in the service for officers, and like many other *Big Picture* productions it incorporated several of the same scenes as the earlier episode. It also reiterated that to the ROTC graduates, "our nation owes no small part of its security in a troubled time," recognizing the long history of contributions made by them since the program's inception during World War I.[23]

Of the three sources of leaders that *The Big Picture* addressed, at least nine related episodes featured West Point. In these films, the series stressed the competitive nature of the entrance requirements to the academy and gave comprehensive overviews of the life of a cadet through to receiving a commission as an active duty army officer. West Point was introduced to viewers in "Duty, Honor, Country" (TV-186) as "a name that's synonymous with your country's history" and as "an institution dedicated to the defense of freedom."[24] Aired during the ongoing Korean War conflict, in 1952, the episode was scripted by APC producers to resonate in the patriotic timbre of viewers' hearts with the pounding percussion of martial music, footage of sweeping vistas of the campus, statues, and parades, and a peek into the activities of a cadet's daily life. The *Big Picture* was able to capitalize on the skills of the APC cameramen to introduce a lively overview of the academy that explained its connection with American history and its central place in the development of military leaders. Other episodes such as "The Making of a West Pointer" (TV-321) in 1955 and "West Point—Education for Leadership" (TV-515), which aired in 1961, followed suit. They appeared during the army's period of effort to prove to Congress and the public its relevancy in the defense of the Cold War West. It offered an inspirational reminder of contributions made by past graduates and of the school's "roots in the very heart of America."[25] West Point continued to remain a favored subject of the APC producers, which was evident in subsequent episodes about the school and the large number of video biographies of general officers who once stood among its ranks, leaders such as Eisenhower, Bradley, MacArthur, and Patton. Still, West Point was only the second of a trio of sources for leaders of the early Cold War army. The last was the OCS system.

The Big Picture series introduced OCS to service members and the public through two episodes, "OCS Fort Sill" (TV-521), and "The OCS Story" (TV-715). The armed forces considered it to be the most important pathway for members of the enlisted ranks to advance to commissioning as an officer. As such, OCS was also consistent with the exceptionalist tenet of upward mobility for service members. Similar to the ROTC and West Point episodes, these aired during periods when the army was dealing with manpower issues: the first in 1962, as recruiting and retention were suffering, and the second in 1967, when many young men were actively avoiding military service during the Vietnam conflict. The films served as recruiting tools to encourage interest among eligible members of the public as well as enlisted soldiers already serving in the army. As the narrator explained to the viewing audience, OCS was "one of the prime sources of the junior officers" who were providing America with the leadership it required as the nation's "global military commitments" continued to grow.[26]

Besides appealing to patriotic ardor, the appearance of six additional West Point episodes between 1955 and 1964 suggests another purpose for their production—recruitment. During this time the army was suffering depressed manpower levels. A survey of the numbers reveals that enlisted personnel levels for the army had fallen from 1.6 million in 1952 to 756,932 by 1961.[27] That drawdown, mandated by the Truman administration, was a cause of worry for military elites. In parallel, the number of active duty army officers had dropped from a post-1945 high of 148,000 in 1952 to approximately 99,000 in 1961.[28] In addition, the US Military Academy had seen the corps of cadets shrink in size from 1,726 in 1952 to a low of 1,701 in 1958, then rise slowly to 1,854 in 1964.[29] By comparison, the rolls of the United States Naval Academy reflected numbers that were more than double for each of those respective years: 3,576, 3,483, and 3,980.[30] The army needed to attract qualified candidates for the academy, to satisfy its need for more active duty officers. This became necessary as the nation found itself engaged in dangerous games of brinksmanship with the Soviets during the Bay of Pigs invasion of April 1961, the Berlin Wall crisis of August 1961, and the Cuban Missile Crisis of October 1962.

The last opportunity *The Big Picture* had to effect an understanding of leadership development in the army was the 1971 episode "Young American Leaders" (TV-804). It was a cumulative work that gave yet another overview of the leadership programs available through OCS, ROTC, and West Point. Unlike previous episodes, however, APC writers had purposely scripted this one. It contained contrasting comments throughout the film from young men that reflected the existing societal divide. There were remarks made by individuals opposing military service: "training soldiers in college is contributing to the mess the world is already in" and "it's like losing years of your life."[31] Opposing these were contrary views from West Point and ROTC cadets, who opined that leadership was rewarding, as was serving the nation. Still, as even-handed as this script might initially appear, it became readily apparent that its purpose was to deflect negative criticisms directed at the military. Noting that all young Americans shared "a restless search for meaning" in their lives, the narrator narrowly observed, "A very vocal minority pursue their search by disruption and often violence."[32] The closing scenes provided a coda with the statement "Never have so many young Americans had greater opportunities to move forward toward leadership in the service of their country."[33] In this context, *The Big Picture* had again declared itself a vehicle to sell the army's leadership programs, inform the public, and shape Americans' thoughts about the contemporary military.

Toward a Diverse Army

A regular viewer of *The Big Picture* series might have noticed a growing change in the demographics of the army over time. Early episodes incorporated footage from the Korean conflict that on occasion coincidentally flashed images of racially integrated army units in combat, training, or other activities. But the topic of integration was never the specific subject of any one *Big Picture* episode. Although President Truman had provided the mandate for the armed forces to take the necessary steps, through Executive Order 9981 on 26 July 1948, reality did not keep pace with the expectation. Still, over the two-decade span of its existence, The Big Picture was on hand to capture the important, yet gradual, trajectory of change as well as shortcomings, and to provide a record. Big Picture episodes served as embodiment of the political messaging that pressed for greater inclusion and diversity in the military, a movement that was slowly gaining momentum in society.

By 1949, African Americans serving in the army accounted for 12.4 percent of the enlisted ranks.[34] This was slightly higher than their proportion of the total American population, which at the time was approximately 10 percent. That same year, however, African Americans accounted for less than 2 percent of the officer corps.[35] By 1954, the same year that the Supreme Court decision in Brown v. Board of Education dismantled the apparatus of inequality in the schoolhouse and public accommodations, the proportion of African American enlisted personnel had risen to 13.7 percent.[36] That year they also accounted for 3 percent of the officer ranks.[37] In parallel, as those service members entered the military, so did their families. As the number of white dependents increased in the United States and at overseas stations, the number of Black dependents did also. Although many Americans still lagged behind in accepting a more diverse society, the army continued to work toward the necessary adjustments, albeit there were still many challenges along the way. In reflecting these changes, The Big Picture had mixed success.

Until 1962, Black soldiers rarely appeared in episodes. Stories such as "The History of Cavalry" (TV-382) and "A Pictorial History of the U.S. Cavalry" (TV-647) showed Black soldiers only in background footage, conducting menial tasks, such as stable hands caring for horses. There was never any mention of the often-decorated 10th Cavalry Regiment, the "Buffalo Soldiers," a segregated unit formed after the American Civil War that was most famous for its participation in the history of the American West and the Spanish American War. Similarly, the episodes "Army Transportation Corps" (TV-204) from 1952 and "An Army Moves" (TV-610) from 1964, which both addressed the history of that branch, neglected to address the contributions made by Black soldiers. Neither mentioned the Black teamsters who regularly drove wagon trains of supplies westward across the American landscape or the famous Red Ball Express that whisked much needed supplies to American forces fighting in Europe during World War II.[38] Although several other films made by the Army Pictorial Service for the War Department prior to 1951 lauded their accomplishments, the *Big Picture* series missed these opportunities to broadcast the history of the two famous units. That was also the case with the famous 442nd Infantry Regiment, which saw extensive combat during World War II. Composed almost entirely of Nisei, second-generation Japanese Americans, it was the most decorated army unit during the war.[39] There is brief notice in the episode "U.S. Sixth Corps" (TV-219) of the 100th Infantry Battalion, also composed of Nisei, during the Italian campaign from Naples to Cassino, but the *Big Picture* catalog carries no episode recognizing these units' achievements.[40] As a result, it also missed another chance to celebrate past moments of diversity in the army. This was true with marginalized groups such as Asians, Hispanics, and Native Americans throughout the film series. The first two rarely appeared in any episode unless it was coincidental. The last appeared merely as bit players in the history of the American West, or as an obstacle to progress. Episodes such as "The History of Cavalry" described "hostile Indians who made war on the pioneers carrying civilization to the Buffalo lands," together with an attitude that always projected them as "the enemy in the West."[41] Casting a slightly different light, the episode "OCS Fort Sill" included a segment of a visit to the post museum. There, the narrator seems to boast that the guide, PFC Benjamin Clark, was the great-grandson of the Comanche chief Quanah Parker. Displays of Native American artifacts appear in the film, together with the modest comment that they are "memories of the American Indian who played a critical role in the destinies of the army cavalrymen."[42] Those words however, lacked any amplification, although the narrator added as an aside that "Indians of other tribes are also employed on post."[43] These trite depictions of marginalized Americans were unfortunate, reflected poorly on the military's efforts, and tarnished the image it wanted to project. This was true throughout the 1950s. With the start of the next decade, however, the *Big Picture* series did record some change.

As mentioned, beginning in the early 1960s the APC produced

Big Picture episodes on the US Military Academy, the ROTC program, and OCS. These programs served as founts of leadership for the army, and stories about them also offered a special view into the greater dynamic of integration of the military. The episode "OCS Fort Sill," filmed in 1961, showed Black enlisted soldiers among the ranks of OCS candidates, as well as Black soldiers filling leadership positions as sergeants and officers. The same was true of "The OCS Story" (TV-715), which also showed Black soldiers participating in a military that appeared to function more fully as an integrated force. "R.O.T.C.—A Pattern for Progress" (TV-609), which aired in 1964, offered segments in which Black missile crewmen raced to accomplish their assigned tasks alongside their white colleagues. The episode "Science Moves the Army" (TV-668), produced in 1966, included footage of integrated technicians and scientists. Focusing on the activities of the Army Tank Automotive Center, it included a lengthy scene showing two Black microbiologists working in a laboratory to find a solution to a problem. They were also shown attending meetings and lectures. These images supported the army's purpose of selling its diversity even in terms of its civilian employees. They came at time when the service most needed them, with enlistments flagging and domestic racial tensions increasing. Those images not only served as a visual record to depict change over time, but in themselves communicated a revision of ideals that expanded definitions of inclusion and diversity to match the need for change in American society and to serve a functional need in the military. More than making a progressive statement, they seemed to be a response to existing racial tensions outside the military and a means to maintain unity and discipline within its ranks.

Those *Big Picture* episodes aired against a contrasting backdrop of racially tense flashpoints that were exploding across the United States between the late 1950s and the mid-1960s. In September 1957, President Eisenhower ordered troops from the army's 101st Airborne Division to Little Rock, Arkansas, as a protective escort for Black students attempting to attend the high school there. In 1962, there was racial tension as James Meredith attempted to enroll in the University of Mississippi, and in 1963 television news cameras exposed national audiences to the brutal police employment of dogs and water cannons against Black protestors in Birmingham, Alabama. These tragedies, however, foreshadowed a positive impulse that witnessed the March on Washington for Jobs and Freedom in August 1963 and passage of both the 1964 Civil Rights Act and the 1965 Voting Rights Act. Enacted to resolve the desperate situation in the nation, these actions also ameliorated the negative impression of America that the media was broadcasting globally. This provided fodder for the United States Information Agency (USIA) and encouraged the release of films from Hollywood that portrayed American society dealing with the difficult issues at home.[44] Similar to the big screen, television followed suit, developing shows that began to engage with racial challenges.[45]

The efforts of the army and the APC to produce *Big Picture* episodes that depicted the military as more racially diverse suggest that it was inspired by those energies that were driving both conflict and change in America. The military had much to gain, and nothing to lose, by embracing a new reality that would continue to be reflected in subsequent productions. Policies facilitating integration of the military encouraged recruitment, enhanced unit discipline and cohesion, and improved race relations. In that context, it is also possible to consider that the Department of the Army, through the CINFO, took calculated steps to use *The Big Picture* as a mechanism to shape and inform thinking about integration of the military. This, however, remains conjecture since documentary evidence is lacking that such a use of the series was a matter of discussion at APC production board meetings or in directed guidance received from the OCINFO. Still, it is possible to make the argument that those episodes that featured Black people in leadership positions, for example, did more than reflect ongoing change. They instead precipitated that change by demonstrating possibilities and successes. Airing these episodes through the AFRTS offered a wider circulation, particularly among forward-deployed units. Those episodes could not have come soon enough, as the military also found itself embroiled in instances of racial conflict at home and abroad. Among the most noted were a riot between African American and white soldiers on New Year's Eve 1955 at the Baumholder training area in West Germany and a race riot at McNair Barracks in Berlin in September 1970.[46] Although the military authorities worked to quash any media release of the former, the latter received wide press coverage when another armed military unit arrived on the scene to restore the peace.

By the time the APC was investing its resources in creating a series of *Big Picture* episodes about the Vietnam War in the early 1960s, Black service members began appearing regularly on film. No longer relegated to menial tasks or appearing as vague figures moving in the background of footage that celebrated the accomplishments of a white military, they emerged to shoulder responsibilities and assume leadership roles in America's modern army. They also faced common dangers with fellow soldiers in Vietnam. Among the several episodes that depicted this was "The Ninth Infantry Division" (TV-746), which aired in 1968. Episodes showed Black soldiers sharing the burdens and responsibilities, and sometimes paying the ultimate price of military service with increasing frequency. This was the aspect of integration that the *Big Picture* series presented to members of the military, their families, and the public. It was an army that was working to embrace integration as a way of life.

Over the years the *Big Picture* series continued to offer a visual record of demographic change for the army, and in some regards it may have facilitated greater inclusion. In this context it also traced the gradual acceptance of women into the ranks, using its cameras to capture their presence and contributions. From the official beginning of the Women's Army Corps in July 1943, the military purposely suppressed the number of females in uniform. For example, military regulations intentionally kept their percentage low by dictating that the numbers of female officers, warrant officers, and enlisted personnel in the army could not exceed 2 percent of men's strength in each category.[47] Still, the army struggled to meet those limited goals. By 1960 there were only 5,034 women in the armed forces stationed overseas, representing 0.008 percent of the end strength total.[48] Although that percentage grew slightly with increased military operations beginning with the Korean War, it remained relatively low until the Department of Defense disbanded the WACs in 1978 and fully integrated women into the armed forces. At that time, the number of women in uniform began to increase noticeably, from 2 percent of the total army force to 10 percent.[49] These numbers differed significantly from those of women who served as nurses in the US Army and Navy Nurse Corps, which formed during World War II. Those percentages were always greater, and the military continued to recognize their presence.[50] In this regard, the *Big Picture* catalog featured a number of titles that recognized and addressed the accomplishments of women in uniform.

Altogether, eight separate episodes released by the APC through *The Big Picture* between 1952 and 1970 specifically addressed the female demographic. The first two, "Women in the Army" (TV-191) and "The WAC Is a Soldier, Too" (TV-277), aired in 1952 and 1954 respectively, close on the heels of fighting in Korea. The APC scheduled the second to air on Christmas Day 1954 with the hope of possibly garnering a large television audience. Both episodes highlighted the contributions of women, and as army chief Gen. Matthew Ridgway commented at the opening ceremonies for the new WAC Training Center in September 1954, "The privilege of serving the United States in uniform is no longer limited to men."[51] *The Big Picture* captured these proclamations as the dictates of a postwar manpower shortage echoed on film with Ridgway's additional comment that "the task of keeping our nation strong and free, requires the efforts and talents of all our citizens, men and women alike."[52] Footage from the episode reflected those words as the army worked to embrace inclusion. Racially integrated platoons of women marching, drilling, sitting in classes together, and standing alongside one another in formations pronounced this as the new army way of life, an example to follow, even as the nation as a whole was still struggling to accept the integration of its own schoolhouses full of children.

By 1970, the APC had produced a more comprehensive look at the WACs. In an episode titled "The Feminine Touch" (TV-780), *The Big Picture* focused on the continued integration of women into the military. Although they were not fully absorbed into the regular army, the duties and responsibilities of the women in uniform had increased significantly from the early 1950s. The female narrator emphasized that the military no longer relegated women solely to clerical duties and that more than one hundred occupational specialties were available.[53] Concurrent film footage showed images of women working as computer programmers, warehouse specialists, and instructors. The episode featured WACs in a variety of leadership roles as officers and noncommissioned officers, managing, instructing, and leading other women. Racial integration appeared frequently as well, in groups of women marching, training, and sharing off-duty time. One of the most interesting aspects of this *Big Picture* episode, however, was the time it spent describing the WAC's involvement in training women of other nations. The script discussed how the army had stationed American WAC advisors in South Vietnam to train the women of that nation to serve in many of the same roles. These included clerical duties, computer programming and security positions at military airfields. American WACs were also assisting in the organization of an OCS for female recruits in South Vietnam. The film noted that the United States was concurrently conducting a similar assistance program in South Korea for women in that nation. This particular *Big Picture* episode offered viewers a comprehensive review of the contemporary Women's Army Corps, complete with recruiting enticements such as unique job positions, opportunities for leadership, and travel to exotic lands. It also touched patriotic sentiments by offering a chance of "belonging to something with roots that reach deep."[54]

Consequently, one of the most important aspect of these episodes was their utility as a recruiting tool to fill the ranks of the military. In June 1968 the army published the *Army 75 Personnel Concept Study*.[55] One of the key assumptions of the study was the continuation of the draft into the 1970s. As historian Beth Bailey notes, understanding the public's "mounting anger over the draft," the army leadership considered how they might "reduce the number of unwilling soldiers in its ranks."[56] The reality they came to was that "the future of the Army . . . might very well depend on women" to fill the rolls.[57] By 1971, expressing concerns that the soon to be all-volunteer force (AVF) might suffer shortfalls in its manning goals, the secretary of the army, Robert F. Froehlke, supported a plan to "double the size of the Women's Army Corps to 23,800 enlisted women by June 30, 1978."[58] The army then raised that goal to 50,400 by the end of 1979.[59] As the *Big Picture* episodes had noted, it was the changing nature of warfare during the Cold War that increased the availability of new occupational specialties for men and women both. In that regard, a need to fill the ranks appeared by the 1950s, and the sales pitch through all available means, including *The Big Picture*, intensified. As Beth Bailey observes, in some regard, "the move to an all-volunteer force jumpstarted a gender revolution in the military."[60]

Although it is interesting to note that a visual record of women in uniform does exist in the *Big Picture* episodes, continuing to unpack this production initiative introduces some other considerations. For example, it is evident that the army was reacting to a manpower shortfall and that women offered a largely untapped resource. So the APC crafted several *Big Picture* episodes to draw their attention to possible enlistment. However, there is no evidence that the APC planning board specifically set a goal to further the women's rights movement or set that as a framework for development of future story lines. While that visual imprint of inclusion is laudable, assessing this series of films as anything other than a reflection of institutional or societal changes is difficult. The scripted narration in a number of the episodes is in terms that are less than affirming of fuller gender inclusion and equality. For example, the narrator for "The WAC Is a Soldier, Too" (TV-277) condescendingly refers to female enlistees as "every girl" and notes that the WACs place great value on "meticulous grooming and feminine grace" while in uniform.[61] The accompanying film footage for this episode shows new enlistees giggling as they try on gloves and hats, which the narrator notes were styled for them by a well-known designer. This was certainly not a concern for male enlistees. The music that follows the video footage is lighthearted and dances along like a Disney feature full of woodwinds, flutes, and strings, absent the martial brass-and-bugle fare of other *Big Picture* productions. By 1970, little had changed in the treatment of women in uniform with the production of "The Feminine Touch" (TV-780), which still featured a patronizing narration and appeared to treat women as little more than augmentees to men in uniform.

The Big Picture followed its focus on the WAC by airing a different perspective of women in the service through episodes about the Nurse Corps. This alternate tack was more respectful and considered the longer history of the nurses' association with the military through numerous wars. In 1954, the APC aired "Nurses in the Army" (TV-290), the first of several films to explore the responsibilities and duties of women in that key role. It also carried a celebratory tone from the beginning, honoring the "great and heroic achievements of our army nurses," who braved "the same dangers endured by the troops which she accompanied into combat."[62] Similar to the WAC episodes, it too included video footage of mixed-race groups of nurses living and working together, in a manner that was much more purposeful and intended than in the *Big Picture* films featuring male service members. These were candid shots, not structured scenes, and they transmitted a message of accepted racial inclusion and diversity. But in contrast to the WAC episodes, those that featured the army nurses were more somber and spoke of their significant contributions made during World War II and the Korean conflict.

Subsequent episodes about army nurses sent other important signals. The *Big Picture* film "The Army Nurse Story" (TV-516), which aired in 1961, presented several nascent concepts of women's rights. In this half-hour docudrama, nurses and actresses shared the story of some nurses' decisions to join and remain in the service. Each nurse appeared on screen as a commissioned officer, in ranks varying from lieutenant to colonel, in a position of responsibility. The episodes portrayed higher-ranking nurses in positions of independent decision-making. The producers also wove into the background story line the concept of a single-parent family headed by a strong woman. Most interesting was the presentation of a scene in which a nurse considers rejecting a marriage proposal to remain in the corps, which she confessed was a personally fulfilling career decision. This script presented some groundbreaking ideas that contradicted the contemporary expectation of assigned gender roles. These portrayals ran counter to the exceptionalist consensus that framed traditional ideas that endorsed prescribed behaviors. In this context, and at least in this one instance, *The Big Picture* had adopted a very progressive position.[63] The episodes "The Army Nurse: Soldier of Mercy" (TV-667) followed in 1965, and "The Army Nurse" (TV-783) in 1970. Each reiterated the key points about the history of the Nursing Corps and exhibited the same displays of inclusion and integration as earlier films. Although they did back away from the edgy social commentary that was found in "The Army Nurse," they did both include scenes with groups of racially integrated nurses, white, Black, and Asian, performing duties in the service of sick and injured soldiers. Just as

Figure 5.2. The episode "The Army Nurse" (TV-516), which aired in 1961, featured women serving in leadership positions and making choices that placed career above traditional roles. In this scene a nurse refuses a proposal of marriage that could jeopardize her career progression. The producers of the *Big Picture* series embraced gender inclusion more quickly than racial integration.

important, they showed images of female officers in positions of leadership and women braving the dangers of field service in Vietnam. The last episode expanded the concept of inclusion by addressing the "common bond men and women" share in the nursing profession, as it showed both male and female nurses engaged in duties together.[64]

The Big Picture provided a window into the emergence of increased diversity and inclusiveness in the army, and in this regard it also served as a model of democratic behavior in terms of public relations. Although the APC produced no single episode to address these challenges directly, it is apparent through study of the films that the military was moving in the proper direction to amend this deep fault. In this context, *The Big Picture* revealed the successes, as well as the continuing shortfalls, but it did also offer the example of a system that in one way was a step ahead of the rest of American society. This provided an important, and encouraging, view of army life.

Dispelling Morale Problems

The one nonprofit organization that is most readily identifiable for its relationship with the armed forces is the United Service Organizations Inc. (USO). Popular images abound in print and visual media of entertainers traveling to wartime locations to practice their talents for the amusement of American service members, sponsored by the USO. Created in 1941, at the direction of President Franklin Roosevelt, to provide for the morale and recreation services of uniformed personnel and their families, the USO first saw service during World War II. As historian Sam Lebovic notes, during that war "Americans were quick to interpret the shows as evidence of the uniquely democratic, free, and liberal nature of the U.S. war effort."[65] One contemporary entertainer observed that "under the stress of war, entertainment is more and more being thought of as a part of our way of life."[66] Between 1941 and 1948 the USO camp shows entertained more that 212 million soldiers, in forty-two countries, more than 428,000 times.[67] The relationship between the military and the USO was well established. After 1950, the USO found life again in supporting troops involved in the Korean conflict, then Vietnam. Many well-known contemporary entertainers joined the organization's entourages during these years as Hollywood rushed to prove its patriotism during those trying times. Along with collaboration in the film studios, this formed yet another tight connection between Hollywood and the military. Most important, the USO's presence on the battlefield maintained a morale-boosting connection to home for service members who stood in harm's way or at isolated locations. The *Big Picture* series captured the essence of the USO through a collection of several episodes that proffered a salute to its contribution to the military way of life. This was as critical during times of conflict as it was during the times of tenuous peace during the Cold War. As Lt. Gen. William E. Hall of the Continental Air Command observed, "Today's servicemen do not have the satisfaction of occasional action of some kind, which in itself frequently dispels morale problems."[68] Instead, he noted, they bore the strain of simply being "vigilant watch dogs of our security."[69] The need for boosting morale was just as critical, as General Hall added: "My feeling is that the USO's mission is quite as urgent under the 'cold war' conditions in which we live today."[70] For those service members, the USO was a necessary palliative to feelings of boredom and disconnectedness from home.

The first *Big Picture* episode that focused on the entertainment organization was "United Service Organization (USO): Wherever They Go" (TV-467), which aired in 1959. Relying on footage captured by army cameramen during World War II and Korea, it offered a general background on the origins of the USO and its mission. Opening the episode was film of Bob Hope, whose name became synonymous with the organization, conducting one of his iconic comedic monologues before a crowd of amused servicemen in Alaska. The important message communicated throughout the show was that the USO was possible only through the generous support of the public, as the narrator noted: "The story of your own efforts" made the organization a success.[71] A follow-on episode, with a similar title (TV-697), aired in 1967 and reiterated many of the same highlights about the USO's past. A 1971 episode, "USO—30 Years of Service" (TV-817), carried the same message and the same uplifting scenes of entertainment and support to service members, both on and off stage. All three episodes opened with introductory routines by Bob Hope, but none recycled older footage, instead incorporating new scenes and new videos from entertainers in Korea, then Vietnam. It carried the same familiar reminders, directed toward the public, that "today the USO is on active duty with our troops all over the world."[72] In addition, the *Big Picture* script also informed viewers that during the previous three decades the USO had entertained "more than twenty million Americans of all services."[73] This established a nostalgic link with many veterans watching at home who shared warm memories of the many al fresco overseas performances. At the conclusion of the second episode the chairman of the board of the USO, Harvey Firestone Jr., provided an acknowledgment of gratitude with his comment: "We are most grateful to the army for this truly 'big picture' of the worldwide activities of the USO and their effect on morale and military performance."[74]

The Big Picture served to tell an important story about army life, and it continued to elicit public backing for the USO's untiring efforts. Much of the cinematography told the story. Cameras framed the appreciative stares of service members gazing up at entertainers

Figure 5.3. Bob Hope entertaining the troops in Vietnam in 1968 as part of a USO tour. By the late 1960s, Hope's name had become synonymous with the organization. The *Big Picture* catalog listed at least five separate episodes featuring the USO. Hope headlined each of them. Altogether, he appeared in seven episodes, more than any other entertainer. (Image Source: US Army)

on stage, or captured them crowding around a celebrity to grip their hand. Films recorded scenes of effusive performers giving their all for the troops, with the video record of *The Big Picture* telling the story to the public and potential donors. Clips of comic routines or songs provided the soundtracks, as did the cheering throngs of troops. These high-energy audiovisual productions from the APC sold the USO while making connections with veterans and the folks back at home.

The women that the USO brought to the various theaters of military operations came out of patriotic duty and with the hope of bringing a touch of home to millions of service members. But the presence of these female dancers, actors, musicians, and singers also served as a contrast to those other women serving there in uniform or as nurses. The USO, and the military, expected the costumed women to perform a gender-specific behavior on stage. It was a representation of prevailing notions of sentimental sexuality that was a norm of traditional behavior, and *The Big Picture* accommodated it. Just as the show offered a view into advancements made by women toward greater inclusion and increased equality in the military through episodes about the WACs and nurses, it also provided contrasting snapshots of women still bound by the expectations of traditional gender roles during the first half of the Cold War. In these moments, through episodes about the USO, *The Big Picture* unintentionally provided visual evidence of the contradictions existing in the military, as well as in society.

A special episode honoring all entertainers who traveled overseas to combat areas during World War II aired in 1964. As actress Celeste Holm, the narrator, noted, it was "a documentary thank you note" to the performers from the army.[75] They were in her words "soldiers in greasepaint," which was also the title of the film.[76] It featured many popular performers of the time, including comedians Bob Hope, Jack Benny, and Joe E. Brown, whose son died while in the service early in the war. Many of these performers appeared in other episodes as well, but the army produced this special edition to offer thanks to them all. The episode also included footage of Hollywood stars working to sell war bonds from coast to coast on the home front. Like other films from the *Big Picture* catalog, the APC released this production to underscore the close relationship between American entertainers and the military, promote their patriotic efforts, and ensure their continued support in the future. As the narrator reminded viewers, "the Cold War can be just as hard to fight as any kind."[77]

Bob Hope's association with the USO entertaining troops is noteworthy because of his dedication but also because of his undaunted exceptionalist patriotism. His support of the military, and by association the nation's foreign policies, gained recognition through close personal relationships with several presidents, including Eisenhower, Nixon, Kennedy, and Johnson. The last two leaders bestowed on the entertainer the Congressional Gold Medal in 1962 and the Presidential Medal of Freedom in 1969. But it was Hope's "hawkish determination to support the troops no matter the righteousness of the cause" that eventually drew criticism, especially during the Vietnam conflict, when the public began seeing his brand of patriotism as mawkish and over the top.[78] Still, his work with the USO and his love of country "became an ingrained part of his brand and a symbol for the larger imbrication of the American war machine, capitalism, and the entertainment industry."[79] The military needed him to sell their way of life and American ideals, and as *The Big Picture* revealed, Hope delivered.

The 1968 episode "To Serve a Soldier" (TV-744) offered another perspective of entertainment and recreation for soldiers in their off duty time. It focused on the Army Special Services and the facilities, service clubs, and rest and recreation activities they provided. As the film emphasized, the Special Services were there to support the army both in the States and overseas. In particular, the episode included many minutes of footage addressing the recreation services available in Vietnam. Scenes of smiling soldiers playing sports, enjoying showers, watching movies, dancing, or swimming at the Vung Tau beachside resort provided the public a view of the army caring for its own. But, in a way, these same scenes might also suggest a dissonant understanding of the war in Vietnam when compared with the raw colored combat footage of other *Big Picture* episodes such as "Screaming Eagles in Vietnam" (TV-714). In that context, the APC released "To Serve a Soldier" in the midst of eight episodes that year that featured army units engaged in various missions in that country. For this reason, it had the potential to offer the public a bifurcated view of soldiers at war and at recreation that may have appeared disconnected and difficult to resolve. It offered a contrast between the brutality of combat and "suffocating luxury" just miles apart.[80] Nevertheless, this episode hewed closely to a theme of rest, relaxation, and care. In that fashion, it also included footage of the USO visiting the country with its key emissary Bob Hope once again in the lead of a troop of popular contemporary performers.[81]

Not all of the army's talent came from the professional guild. As *The Big Picture* showed, much of it came from within, by the soldiers themselves. Two particular episodes, "Army Talent Show" (TV-315) from 1955 and "The Song of the Soldier" (TV-725) from 1968, offered a view into this unique aspect of army life. They described a historical perspective of soldiers performing for themselves over the course of years. But they also introduced the public to the way that "professional talent finds its way into uniform" in the contemporary army, not as actors in APC productions, but rather on the stage before live audiences of the public and peers.[82] A case in point from the first episode was the popular contemporary comedic actor Ken Berry, who got his start performing in uniform before his peers.[83] "Song of the Soldier" was unique because it featured the US Army Chorus and Band in a well-orchestrated and performed production in Washington, DC, that won an Emmy award in 1968. If these types of episodes didn't attract interest for their entertainment value, they did offer a way in which *The Big Picture* was able to put a human face on the individual in uniform, show another dimension of life in the ranks, and show that the military cared about the service members. However, as much as morale and welfare were a means to ensure that soldiers were fit to fight, so was physical readiness.

Fitness for America

Both President Dwight D. Eisenhower and his successor, President John F. Kennedy, appreciated the attribute of physical fitness. Each had experiences with that dimension of military training from their service during World War II, and each understood that a fit nation and a fit military were requirements driven by the exigencies of the new postwar world. In 1956, Eisenhower issued Executive Order 10673 that launched the President's Council on Youth Fitness to revamp, create, and oversee a new series of fitness initiatives.[84] Kennedy followed with his own project to improve the fitness of America's young people with the White House Committee on Health and Fitness. During the 1961–1962 school year it published a booklet, *U.S. Physical Fitness Program*, that outlined a fitness test to challenge students at all grade levels.[85] These two sets of presidential initiatives came at a time when Cold War tensions between the East and West were at a peak, and the government brought all national resources and goals to focus on besting the competition. *The Big Picture* reflected this dynamic and the army's efforts to prove that it was up to the physical standard of the demanding times.

An episode titled "Sports for All" (TV-248), about army intramural sports, was the first mention of physical fitness by *The Big Picture*. Cameras captured soldiers at training, "harder than most athletes," and learning to "play as a team so they will fight as a team."[86] The Olympic Games was another arena where *The Big Picture* featured the American military's physical prowess, in the episode "Helsinki Olympics" (TV-250). At Helsinki, Finland, in the summer of 1952, Signal Corps cameramen captured the competition, focusing on the various events in which the army and other services participated. Nearly every sport had military team members, but the episode followed those events where service members excelled. This included crew, pentathlon, track and field, and boxing. By the end of the film, the narrator proudly proclaimed that the military had totaled over thirty medals, with the army alone capturing nine.[87] The timing of the episode, near the end of the Korean conflict, provided appropriate ammunition for the ongoing propaganda war between the East and West, and it showcased the level of fitness that the president expected of all the American armed forces.

Subsequent episodes, such as "Shape of the Nation" (TV-582), "The Army's All-Americans" (TV-568), and "Operation Scoreboard" (TV-656), celebrated the fitness of the armed forces and used their physical proficiency as an example for the rest of the nation. "Shape of the Nation," which aired in 1963, answered President Kennedy's call for the country to invest in its own health with his concern that "we were getting to be a nation of spectators," who were grown too dependent on labor-saving conveniences of contemporary life.[88] This *Big Picture* episode, starring repeat narrator comedian Bob Hope, served as the president's clarion call for all citizens to "join in a great national effort to build a strong and better America."[89] To shake viewers into awareness, the script touted the superior physical fitness of Eastern Bloc nations and included footage of their successes over the West in a number of sporting and athletic competitions. Also sobering were the statistics that of civilian men called up for service during the 1961 Berlin Wall emergency, the military rejected three out of five for physical reasons.[90] "The Army's All-Americans" also from 1963, celebrated those American athletes who set an example by donning a uniform during World War II and the Korean War. During various on-screen interviews they underscored the need for physical fitness and encouraged the building of a "nation-wide team of All-Americans."[91] In a similar manner, "Operation Scoreboard," which appeared a year later, was a salute to the military's efforts to maintain the fitness of its fighting forces as a "regular and necessary part" of its daily life.[92] The episode included interviews with several well-known contemporary sports figures, announcers, and coaches who praised the army for sponsoring athletic programs for its soldiers, and it celebrated athletes who over the years had served in the military during times of national mobilization. The *Big Picture* show was more than a simple salute to the military, however; it was a public service announcement in support of President Lyndon Johnson's mandate on physical fitness and sports that followed a line similar to that of his predecessors.[93] Each leader had witnessed a softening of Americans living in a post-1945 culture of leisure, and each used the military lifestyle of physical readiness as an example for the nation to follow. For this, *The Big Picture* served as a convenient, available platform.

Civilian Partners Support the Troops

Although it was not until 1968 that the APC had dedicated a specific episode to the army's civilian partners, they had been supporting the United States' military since the earliest days with George Washington, filling roles such as teamsters, gunsmiths, guides, and scouts. "The Army's Civilians" (TV-726) was an attempt to share the scope of that partnership and "the many ways in which they contribute to our nation's security."[94] At the time of the airing of this episode, in June 1968, the army was employing 416,280 civilians globally, in a variety of service and support roles, including those deployed in support of the armed forces in Vietnam.[95] This included 20,000 positions converted from military to civilian in that country.[96] In this regard, the army was employing more civilian employees than any other government agency except the US Post Office, "to perform essential but non-combat tasks."[97] The spectrum of jobs at home and abroad, for men and women, included maintenance and lab technicians, computer technicians, clerks, medical professionals, and schoolteachers for the worldwide Department of Defense Schools System. The contributions of the civilian partners working alongside the uniformed members were intrinsic to the success of the army's global military mission by introducing skill sets and experience that military members did not possess. They also provided stability through contracts that often required them to remain onsite for up to five years, when normal military rotations were annual.[98] *The Big Picture* provided a lens into this unique and seldom understood union that bound the military more closely to the American government employees.

From early in the series, during the period of the conflict in Korea, *The Big Picture* had featured footage of army civilians using their skills to support the military. The first episode to discuss the essential roles they performed was "Tools for a Modern Army" (TV-208), which aired in 1952. In this film, which focused on evolving machines and weapons systems, it was clear that the army's success in the fields of science and technology depended on a capable corps of civilian technicians. As the narrator somberly noted, by the end of World War II, "scientists and engineers became as important as the military commander."[99] The episode depicted the work done by civilians as the key to modernization in an increasingly dangerous world, as they strove to provide "better tools for a modern army."[100] This was at a time the army was beginning to grapple with the other services for diminishing resources and to ensure its relevancy during the Cold War. Subsequent episodes continued to make the public and service members aware of the close working union between civilians and the military.

"Science Moves the Army" (TV-668) and "Pioneering for Tomorrow" (TV-815), aired in 1966 and 1971 respectively, emphasized the way that the efforts of civilian scientists, engineers, and technicians continued to be central to the army's modernizing efforts. Comments such as "military and civilian personnel are facing space age problems" and "tomorrow's battle may well be decided by students in college today" served as evidence of that solidarity of effort, as well as a recruitment pitch to entice the next generation of American scholars to become involved in the adventure of the future, through the US Army.[101] "Pioneering for Tomorrow" focused on the network of army laboratories and research facilities spread across the nation, and it included footage of activities at the Natick Laboratory near Boston and the Harry Diamond Laboratories outside Washington, DC. In this film, *The Big Picture* showcased the research and development efforts of the US Army Materiel Command (AMC) and its essential core of professional civilians, disclosing that they were at the time involved in over 500 ongoing projects.[102] This series of episodes was important for making viewers aware of the ways in which the work of the civilian scientists, engineers, and technicians complemented the life of the contemporary military. That was a cause to celebrate, however, as it also suggested that the army was welcoming an even closer collaboration between the military and civilian industry, as elements such as the AMC were operating on the margin between the two. This ran contrary to outgoing President Eisenhower's fears expressed in January of 1961 when he warned of the possibility of "an incestuous relation between the military, Congress, and industry."[103] In that regard, *The Big Picture* provided a testimony to the former, while acting as an inadvertent witness to the latter.

Another view of civilian interaction with the military that *The Big Picture* provided was the use of foreign nationals at military facilities overseas. As with many of their civilian counterparts in the United States, the military employed foreign nationals in a variety of support services and technical roles, as managers and skilled workers. As the episode "Foreign Nationals" (TV-314) explained, the use of this source of civilian manpower at overseas facilities in the early postwar years freed American soldiers for training and missions. Focusing on the occupation army in Korea, Japan, and West Germany, the film qualified the use of foreign nationals as a money-saving strategy for the United States, which paid host-nation workers at the lower local wage rates rather than at salaries comparable to those of Americans. As the narrator also explained, this bolstered the recovery of those occupied nations, thus forestalling the intervention of communism, which often worked to exploit nations with struggling economies. At the time of its airing in 1955, the episode noted that the US Army was employing approximately 100,000 Japanese, "thousands" of Korean citizens, and more than 130,000 nationals in Western Europe.[104] The narrator also expressed the hope that this additional interaction between the Americans and the local populace would continue to foster stronger relations among the nations and friendship between individuals. Eventually, foreign nationals began filling other positions, such as security guards monitoring access points to American military facilities and workers in post exchanges, movie theaters, and other recreational facilities. Employment of local nationals (LN) also suggests that linking their livelihoods with the United States military would encourage their support of an American presence in their country. Codification of that commitment to employ certain numbers of non-American citizens in specially designated jobs began in the 1950s and is still part of the specially negotiated status of forces agreements (SOFA) between the United States and those nations hosting the US military, such as South Korea, Germany, and Japan.[105]

Although the episode "Foreign Nationals" did feature the close working relationship between LNs and Americans, it did not cast a light on the occasional moments of tension that arose. These usually occurred during periods of increased unemployment in the host nation, when American civilians and military dependents were competing with the local populace to fill any available slots in American military facilities. This sometimes resulted in the renegotiation of employment contracts between host communities and local American military commanders who retained the hiring authority. The absence of any mention of labor disputes between LN employees and their American managers suggests that the series producers felt their appearance in *Big Picture* films could tarnish the image of bonhomie they were working to project between the military and civilian workers and between the United States and its allies.

The Big Picture revealed the emphasis the government placed on the tight relationship between the army and its civilian employees around the world. It served to celebrate their contributions, attract their participation, and inform the public of this unique association. Footage captured President Johnson as he described the civil servants in laudatory terms: "men and women of broad vision with new answers and good ideas," who were "building sound and satisfying personal careers making their own positive contributions to the country's strength and security."[106] At a time when the military was drawing heavy criticism for its involvement in the Vietnam conflict, episodes such as "The Army's Civilians" went a long way to cementing the bonds between the civilian community and the army.

The Military as a Good Neighbor

Throughout the *Big Picture* catalog there were episodes that addressed the interaction of army units with surrounding communities both as partners and as a resource in times of need. The military was always proud of its participation in this type of relationship and used it as a valuable public relations tool to exhibit the ways soldiers did "work with, and for, local populations."[107] The episode "Operation Noah" (TV-318) recounted the catastrophic floods that swept through the northeastern United States in the wake of a series of hurricanes in 1955. Noteworthy was the assistance that the army, through its Corps of Engineers, provided to help communities recover, including providing food and shelter for those who suffered losses.

Another film, crafted specifically to tell the story of civil-military cooperation was "Alexandria: City of Understanding" (TV-375), produced in 1957. Inspired by the Alexandria Chamber of Commerce, it told the story of that city's close historical relationship with the military. It also celebrated the military's place in the modern life of the community. The narrator claimed that the average citizen of Alexandria "finds daily contributions made by the military to his community life. In turn, he has been welcoming the military man to a fuller participation in his own activities."[108] Scenes showed military facilities that employed numerous Alexandrians, as well as service personnel attending religious services and participating in other group activities. It was the citizen who "has come to recognize the military as a cross-section of his own

American neighbors," a comfortable position for the army.[109] Following that theme, "Your Military Neighbor" (TV-675), produced in 1966, listed the ways that the soldier was present in the ongoing lives of many other communities. It contained images of servicemen participating in disaster relief efforts, organizing Armed Forces Day parades and activities, working with local youth in sports or Scouting programs, providing medical assistance when needed, attending religious worship together, and "raising his family in the best American tradition."[110] That theme of soldiers serving as "double-duty Americans" was particularly evident in certain episodes about army reserve units and was central to selling the army as a reliable neighbor.[111]

Several *Big Picture* episodes—"Alaskan Earthquake" (TV-670) from 1964 and "The Army's Other Role" (TV-812) and "Citizen Soldier—Community Leader" (TV-816), which both aired in 1971—were also attempts by the army to continue to market itself and its reservists as good partners and neighbors and to exhibit the close link between units and the local communities. The first two films addressed the army's wider participation in disaster relief and assistance operations, identifying military units as perfect for the job with their personnel, equipment, and training. The second episode provided an admirable history of the army's response to various catastrophes, beginning with the 1871 Chicago Fire and following through a litany of floods, hurricanes, tornadoes, and blizzards. The narrator applauded the army for "extending its helping hand to people everywhere in their hour of need."[112] This episode also emphasized the close cooperative relationship that the army and the American Red Cross shared in supporting disaster relief efforts. As an acknowledgement, retired army general Alfred M. Gruenther, who was then serving as the president of the aid agency, commented that "time after time I have seen the army respond promptly and effectively in disasters," and "as president of the Red Cross I want to thank the army for this magnificent service."[113] The third film in the series focused on the army's participation in community service, featuring soldiers from reserve units constructing Little League baseball fields, working with Boys and Girls Clubs, serving as leaders for Boy Scout troops, building parks, roads, and schools, and cleaning up rivers. It was emphasized that reservists "live, work, and train in communities throughout the United

States" and were excellent neighbors.[114] The army drew much-needed praise from all these episodes.

The APC producers introduced the disaster relief films with dramatic music and scenes of rushing tsunamis, collapsing buildings, floods, and raging fires. Scripted narration describing the suffering and anguish of civilian communities accompanied footage of desperate attempts at rescue by individuals and local authorities. But as viewers would expect, the army soon appeared on location with the same timing of the cavalry come to the rescue in a Western film. Stark videos showing the army participating in search and rescue operations, providing shelter and food, transporting supplies, and clearing roads on heavy equipment–filled television screens. Images flashed by of dirty-faced, blanketed children receiving care from uniformed personnel. *The Big Picture* was on the job capturing the actions of the contemporary army as it worked shoulder to shoulder with civilian partners to save lives and salvage the day. As a public relations vehicle, episodes such as these were well worth the cost of their production.

This collection of APC efforts was important to the army as it was beginning to lick its public relations wounds from the tarnished image it suffered during the height of the Vietnam conflict. Although it was clear in the films that reserve units did occasionally deploy to Vietnam, usually in support roles, the overall focus of the soldiers' responsibilities in these episodes was on national and community service, not combat. In this context, Army Reserve units offered a possible alternative for young men seeking to avoid the draft and active-duty service that might place them in harm's way in the waning days of the war. That understanding fed the waiting lists for acceptance into Army Reserve units that grew longer as the war dragged on. In parallel, the episodes that focused on community service also gained importance as the army began to look toward its future and cast about for ways to continue to fill its ranks as the projected end of the draft loomed in June 1971. In February 1971, however, President Nixon and the Department of Defense petitioned Congress to extend conscription. Although it was a politically contentious issue, the request passed in Congress, and the draft continued for two more years. December 1972 saw the end of an active ground combat role for the United States in Vietnam, and the last conscripts reported for duty in June 1973.[115]

Unfortunately, the impact of these films on the army's recruiting and retention efforts could not be fully realized when the military turned to an all-volunteer force because the APC terminated the *Big Picture* series in late 1971. However, as some of the last episodes produced, these provided the viewing audience with positive parting images of the soldier as a reliable community partner and neighbor, bringing "concrete evidence of his friendship wherever he serves."[116]

A unique connection the army had established during the postwar decades was with young men. One of the earliest was the military's long-standing association with the Boy Scouts, especially the army's invitation for Scouts to share in the adventure at Camp Century in the northern reaches of the globe in the "U.S. Army and the Boy Scouts" (TV-520). But the connection with young Americans was more extensive. One example was with a special community depicted in the episode "Boys Town, U.S.A." (TV-346). After explaining the purpose of the home and organization, the film focused on the army's 353rd Military Police Company, a US Army Reserve unit. Recent graduates of the Boys Town School filled most of its ranks. Created purposefully by the army, in conjunction with the faculty and clergy, the unit afforded an opportunity for the members of the student body who had recently turned eighteen years of age to participate in the military as reservists. It was one of many options offered to the young men who might have been lacking clear future goals and was another way the army was supporting a local community by producing "young citizens of whom the nation may be proud."[117] Although public reaction was generally positive, some criticisms were directed at the program. An example was a reproach the dean-registrar of Freed-Hardeman College, Tennessee, a private Christian school, fired at the APC. He charged that the film's producers had intentionally scripted the episode on Boys Town to "publicize the Roman Catholic Church."[118] A letter from the acting chief of the R-T Branch of the APC sought to deflect the dart by emphasizing that "the Army is non-sectarian."[119] This assurance seemed to mollify the dean's concerns.

A second association between the army and young men appeared in the 1959 episode "Army Digest No. 3" (TV-479). It described a long-standing relationship between the Second Squadron, 102nd Armored Cavalry Regiment, of the New Jersey Army National Guard and a group of teens between the ages of fifteen and seventeen. Attracting these youth from the local West Orange, New Jersey, area, the unit formed the Junior Essex Troop. Aside from its ascribed purpose to "keep alive a tradition and a way of life" through training its young cadets in horsemanship skills, it also trained them in the basic military craft.[120] This additional skill set included drill and ceremonies, marksmanship, discipline, and leadership. All of this was to prepare them for their role "as citizens, both military and civilian, of tomorrow."[121] Although the episode made no mention about the number of these young cadets who eventually pursued a military career, it was evident that the army was investing a significant amount of time and resources in shaping their thoughts about a future career in uniform. As these *Big Picture* episodes suggest, the army's efforts through its Boys Town initiative and the Junior Essex Troop were about not only cultivating community relations, but also developing a recruitment pool at a time that enlistments and retention among the ranks were sagging in the late 1950s.

The *Big Picture* series dedicated a significant portion of its catalog to episodes that informed and educated service members, their families, and the public about the army way of life. It provided windows for viewers into how the army was educated and led, how it was trained and entertained, and who filled its ranks. Just as important, *The Big Picture* showed how the army was dealing with contemporary issues such as integration and diversity, and its successes and shortcomings as it faced each challenge. It also created a narrative that projected the army as a service of the people and for the people through episodes that featured soldiers extending a helping hand when needed and being good neighbors. This third subject category of the film series stands separate from the other two in that it was less about selling an ideological message or describing a strategic vision in a Cold War geopolitical sense. It was, instead, more about telling the story of who the individuals in the army were, what their way of life was, and how they worked to improve community relations and public opinion about the military. By doing so, it placed a human face on the person in uniform, with the purpose of making their presence more acceptable in communities throughout the nation and in locations around the globe.

Conclusion

On March 19, 1960, the Pacific Edition of the *Stars and Stripes* proudly noted that

> unlike "Crusade in Europe" or "Victory at Sea," "The Big Picture" covers today's newsworthy activities of the army at home and overseas with occasional flashbacks to World War II and Korea. Although the "Big Picture" has held a rather coveted position in the television medium, the army has tried to maintain high standards in production. This February marked the third straight year the series has won an award from the Freedoms Foundation at Valley Forge, Pa.[1]

Just over decade later, with a hint of resignation, the *Stars and Stripes* announced the termination of the series: "The Army's award-winning 'Big Picture,' probably the oldest television production on the air, is finally coming to an end, the victim of changing times and changing tastes. . . . There are several reasons for cancelling the half-hour show. One is the fact that the army wanted for some time to come up with something that, it feels, is more relevant to the problems of the service today."[2] The other reasons noted for termination included mounting production costs and a shrinking audience, although at the end, the series was carried by "426 commercial, educational and cable television stations," and 51 stations on the AFRTS overseas network.[3] This was a larger total than at any other time in the show's two-decade history, but in the end that knowledge did not stay the hand of the decision-makers in the Pentagon. Still, in the window of time from earliest episodes in 1951 to the last in 1971, the APC successfully produced 823 *Big Picture* episodes, beginning with miles of recovered black-and-white combat footage and finishing with sophisticated state-of-the art television technology. Through it all, APC production teams crafted stories that defended the service, described its role in the Cold War, emphasized the ideals of an exceptional America, and shared a window into the army way of life. By unpacking this extensive collection of films, investigating scripts, and reviewing available videos, this study reveals the mix of complicated agendas, narratives, and energies that frame the simple intentions of the producers. These episodes generally elevated the service and celebrated its achievements by sharing newsworthy activities.

As the first tense decade of the Cold War unfolded, *The Big Picture* highlighted the army's capabilities and its future potential, and through that established its continuing relevancy. The APC produced episodes that featured the army trumpeting its embrace of technological advances as well as its ability to operate in extreme climes. A litany of films spilled out of the APC studios in the early to mid-1950s that featured an army determined to gain distance over competing military branches in the Capitol Hill budget battles by riding the contrails of Nike guided missiles. The producers launched episodes featuring those missiles in rapid succession: "Guided Missiles" in 1953, "Army Ballistic Missile Agency" in 1956, "Missile Man" in 1957, and "Missile on Target" in 1958. Following those up was the film "Army Satellites," which aired in 1958 when the army breached the thermosphere with its Explorer I satellite program. In parallel, the army was also exploring new regions on Earth as it went about conquering the hostile landscape of the Arctic Circle. The *Big Picture* episodes "Operation Blue Jay," "Exercise Arctic Night," "Operation Lead Dog," and others were offerings to both Congress and a wider viewing audience about the army's ability to operate where the other services were less able to venture. To ensure a solid connection with the American public, the APC producers even brought along the Boy Scouts to share in the adventure.[4] In these episodes the army made its pitch for relevancy, and dollars, in the emerging Cold War strategic scheme. It was a matter of survival, and *The Big Picture* offered a convenient means to allow the army to step through the small screen into American living rooms and appeal directly to the public with video evidence. Although the army eventually lost authority over the nation's missile program to the air force, it was nevertheless able to demonstrate its ongoing relevance in the age of the atom and the missile.

As an examination of the episodes has revealed, the Cold War cast a long shadow across the *Big Picture* catalog. The scripts of many APC episodes dealt with the East-West tensions and celebrated the army's mission, and in that, they served as another advertisement for its relevancy. That is evident in more than half the *Big Picture* episodes, and it was the key to informing service members and the public about the army's contributions. A cascade of titles that focused on the individual in uniform— "Soldier in Berlin," "Soldier in Europe," "Soldier in Panama," "Soldier in France"—combined with others such as "United State Army Europe" and "The Border Watchers" to describe the army's responsibility to enforce the nation's strategic containment strategy to keep the communists at bay. This Cold War collection also told of key alliances with partners in "Decade of NATO," "Southeast Asia Treaty Organization (SEATO) Nations," and other "Partners in Freedom." In parallel, *The Big Picture* also provided video footage of American service members extending the hand of friendship and engaging with local nationals through "German Youth Activities," "Operation Friendly Hand," and "People to People," winning hearts and minds in the contest with the East. *The Big Picture* both educated Americans and hawked the army's important position manning the ramparts of freedom during the Cold War. In this, it was a success.

Another public relations victory for the army appeared in its role in disaster relief and its partnership with the American Red Cross. A number of episodes lauded the service's commitment to response with rapid, comprehensive aid whenever catastrophe struck. *Big Picture* episodes such as "Operation Noah" spoke of flood relief, and "The Army's Other Role" addressed the army's participation in a litany of relief operations that spanned several decades. Just as impressive was the army's work to position itself as a good neighbor through Army Reserve units that helped with local community projects and participated in youth programs such as Scouting and team sports. The visual evidence provided in the episodes "Your Military Neighbor" and "Citizen Soldier—Community Leader" included soldiers building a Little League baseball field and joining in Boy Scout events. Again, this exposure through the television series contributed to the service's credibility as a reliable community partner. In these films *The Big Picture* again served as a positive image maker for the army.

During its production years the APC developed a large number of *Big Picture* episodes to tell the story of the army way of life in a simplistic, informational format. Shows about military history, which included biographies, spoke of heritage and legacy. The public generally accepted these for their educational, yet sometimes banal, content. Also present in this group were those episodes that shed light on educational and leadership programs, entertainment, and physical fitness and training, as well as the military's civilian component. The significance of these video records of military life appeared not in the scripted content alone, but also in the realization of change that was taking place in the contemporary army. These reflected American society at its best, and occasionally at its most disappointing. Episodes such as "The OCS Story" and "West Point—Education for Leadership" provided insights into those programs but over time began to include footage of racially mixed classes of soldiers and leaders. This reflected changes not only within the military but also within the fabric of society. By the time the series began airing episodes on Vietnam, video footage showed a well-integrated army performing its mission and conducting combat operations. The same was true for "Nurses in the Army" and "An Army Moves," which provided information about programs involving women, but also addressed the growth of inclusion as the contributions, and sacrifices, made by women were increasingly recognized. This also included their greater participation in the leadership structure of the army, which the video record offered in such episodes as "The Feminine Touch," which aired in 1970—although its title was a bit denigrating in suggesting a difference in gendered influence in the military. Overall, however, *The Big Picture* did shed a positive light on the service's efforts to keep pace with societal change. Still, consideration of those same episodes also reveals unfortunate shortcomings.

Just as inclusion and diversity increased in the army to reflect greater democratization of the military, it was still incomplete, and *The Big Picture* recorded the shortfall. For example, episodes such as "The History of the Cavalry" discussed Native Americans narrowly, only in terms of being "the enemy in the West." Any positive references were absent from the catalog of films.[5] Just as obvious were shallow references to other marginalized groups. Hispanics and Asians rarely appeared in footage unless it was coincidental. A glaring absence among the *Big Picture* episodes was any reference to the most decorated army unit in the history of American warfare, the 442nd Infantry Regiment. Perhaps the fact that Nisei, second-generation Japanese Americans, composed more than 90 percent of its ranks was a consideration. Although Hollywood did produce a feature-length film on the unit's World War II exploits, it did not exist among *Big Picture* episodes. As far as the army had come, this registered as a shortcoming. As disappointing as these gaps were, they did not resonate with the same negative energy as the controversies that emerged to grip the television series.

The Big Picture found itself twice entangled in controversy during its two-decade existence. The first reflected the army's close association with the NRA. The episode "To Keep and Bear Arms" was an exceptionalist celebration of Americans' rights under the Second Amendment of the Bill of Rights to possess firearms. The film's script saluted that individual liberty as intrinsic to the American way of life, long connected to the existence of the United States through its historical past. But embedded in the episode was a promotional clip from the NRA that touted a link between gun ownership and personal rights. As part of that narrative, the NRA sponsors encouraged viewers to pressure their congressional representatives to act against any legislation that might, in any way, limit the exercise of that right. However, with the shooting deaths of the Reverend Martin Luther King Jr. and Senator Robert Kennedy in 1968, the question of gun control emerged as an active issue on Capitol Hill. As a result, "To Keep and Bear Arms" was a casualty of the heavy fire the NRA began receiving from many progressive legislators. By association,

The Big Picture found itself under scrutiny, this time for its support of a nonprofit but politicized organization. In this the series was caught in a controversy that worked to undermine its credibility, as it was perceived as failing to grasp the new American cultural and social zeitgeist, resulting from its myopic adherence to selling a dated exceptionalist consensus.

The storm clouds of controversy gathered a second time for *The Big Picture* from the airing of an extensive series of episodes on Vietnam. As early as 1962, with the airing of the first episode, "Hidden War in Vietnam," the tone was set. The entire production—title, script, video scenes, and action sequences—told the viewer that this was going to be a special war, different from previous conflicts in World War II or Korea. From the opening scene, with Gen. Paul D. Harkins leaning in toward the camera to confide that this was "a war which is hidden and stealthy as it is relentless and exhausting," to its final frames, the script spoke of a shadowy conflict.[6] The early Vietnam *Big Picture* episodes invited the viewer in as a confidante in this new military venture. By way of shaping public opinion and cultivating support for a military presence in that region of the globe, they revealed the "U.S. Army Advisor in Vietnam" in 1962, strove to answer the question "Why Vietnam?" in 1965, and described it as "The Unique War" in 1966. Episodes that followed until 1971, the final year of the series, continued to sell the war even as public and political support collapsed. The slavish devotion to the cause, as evidenced by the catalog of seventeen Vietnam-related titles generated between 1968 and 1971, ultimately undermined the credibility of the television series. *The Big Picture* eventually fell out of step with public thinking and societal acceptance as it continued to peddle the war and a long-jaded exceptionalist ideology. In that context, as military and conservative elites continued to use the series as a platform for affecting national policy decision-making, it soon became a lightning rod that drew bolts of criticism from Capitol Hill lawmakers. Progressives such as Senator J. William Fulbright saw this as evidence that the army was stepping beyond its prescribed responsibilities and duties, and as the *Congressional Record* noted, *The Big Picture* was culpable. As this study revealed earlier, this led to censure and contributed to the demise of the series.

Certain other observations emerged from this study of *The Big Picture* and its catalog of films. The first is the close association the APC and the army shared with Hollywood. It was a symbiotic relationship that began in the decades before World War II, endured through those turbulent years, and continued into the age of television. The military benefited from the positive public exposure on the big screen, and Hollywood studios from the availability of military equipment and facilities for film production. The studios were also able to prove their patriotism and dedication to national defense. None of this changed with the advent of the Cold War. Unpacking that relationship during this study revealed a great reliance by the APC on the talents and skill set of actors and stagehands who contributed to the production of the *Big Picture* series. Some actors and directors got their start in the army's Astoria studios, others enhanced their careers, but in the end it was the television show that benefited from the infusion of professionalism and star power.

Another observation that emerged from the study of *Big Picture* episodes is the manner in which Christian evangelism informed and shaped military thinking. Episodes with titles such as "The Army Chaplains," "Religious Emphasis Day in Philadelphia," "The Chaplain and the Commander," "The Army Chaplain—Yesterday and Today," and "Of Soldiers and Altars" emphasized the centrality of Christianity and religion in the formation of the tenets of Americanism within the army. *The Big Picture* captured this, and in this collection of episodes, together with others such as "Challenge of Ideas," stressed their importance as an inherent strength, and necessary condition, of the American way of life.

One lingering question about the *Big Picture* series concerns its too sudden termination. Although evidence indicates that the army was bowing to external pressures from groups such as Senator Fulbright's congressional coterie, why the APC ultimately ended the show is unclear. It was an award-winning production, it continued to attract a wide viewing audience, and it was still able to communicate a variety of messages through the medium of television. Studios were still in place, as were teams of writers, directors, and cameramen. Costs had mounted, and budget constraints had an impact on production, but limiting the number of episodes and their extravagance might have been an easy solution.[7] In the end, the army shows that followed never carried the same impact nor possessed the same longevity. The American public, and historical memory, have long forgotten most of these. With the disappearance of *The Big Picture* the army surrendered a key piece of media terrain that might have served it well into the future as it continued to defend its relevancy and maintain its connectivity with the American public.

During its two-decade run, *The Big Picture* established itself as a window into the life of the army, selling the service and an exceptional American way of life, telling stories of its history and accomplishments, and adding a human face to those who stood in the rank and file. It never escaped criticism, but served as a useful, enduring public relations tool. As Kenneth D. Alford recalls fondly, he did watch *The Big Picture* at least twice a week growing up. It provided him with a sense of the military, and he enjoyed the history and patriotic tone of the episodes. By itself the show never inspired him to join the army, but he later enlisted for several years during the height of the Cold War.[8] Although an official count is impossible to estimate, one source postulates that millions of Americans watched the show at some time during its production run.[9] Still, in the end, the screen faded to black on the final episode, absent any invitation to "be with us again next week."[10] All that was said about the facility that once produced the longest lasting television series was that "it's closed now and empty of people. . . . Its complex of buildings that house motion picture sound stages: film, tape, and sound equipment—dead storage and entertainment history—are enclosed by wire and guarded by military policemen."[11] This was almost a too quiet a fade to black for a series born in the flash and bang of war.

The Big Picture Catalog

The term "Not Used in *Big Picture* Series" indicates the APC chose not to produce or air the episode; the term "Not Available" indicates that the episode does not appear in any reference or archive.

TV 169	The First Forty Days in Korea
TV 170	The Turning of the Tide
TV 171	The United Nations Offensive
TV 172	Chinese Reds Enter the War
TV 173	United Nations Forces Escape the Chinese Trap
TV 174	United Nations Consolidate below the 38th Parallel
TV 175	United Nations Forces Push the Chinese Back
TV 176	The United Nations Offensive Continues
TV 177	The UN Forces Cross the 38th Parallel
TV 178	The Reds Launch Their Expected Spring Offensive
TV 179	United Nations Forces Counterattack
TV 180	The Korean Cease-Fire Talks Begin
TV 181	The UN Line Is Stabilized While Truce Talks Continue
TV 182	The Mission of the Army
TV 183	The Army Combat Team
TV 184	The Citizen Soldier
TV 185	The Combat Soldier
TV 186	Duty, Honor, Country
TV 187	The Army Reserve Team
TV 188	Army Aviation (Withdrawn from the series)
TV 189	The Army Medical Corps
TV 190	The Army Chaplains
TV 191	Women in the Army
TV 192	The Eyes and Ears of the Army

TV 193	Enough and On Time
TV 194	Citizen, Soldier and Taxpayer, Too
TV 195	(Not Used in Big Picture Series)
TV 196	A Day in Korea
TV 198	Information and Education Overseas (Part I), Dependent Schools (Part II)
TV 199	We Never Stop
TV 200	Army Language School
TV 201	Civil Assistance, Korea
TV 202	Pictorial Report No. 1
TV 203	Follow Me
TV 204	Army Transportation Corps
TV 205	All American
TV 206	Truth Is Our Defense
TV 207	Pictorial Report No. 2
TV 208	Tools for a Modern Army
TV 209	The Great Gun (Not Used in *Big Picture* Series)
TV 210	The Big Red One
TV 211	The Work Horse of the Western Front
TV 212	The 1st Cavalry Division and the 41st Infantry Division
TV 213	D-Day Convoy to Normandy
TV 214	The 6th Infantry Division
TV 215	The Red Bull Attacks
TV 216	All-American
TV 217	The Famous Third Army
TV 218	Blood and Bullets
TV 219	U.S. Sixth Corps
TV 220	Invasion of Southern France
TV 221	The 7th Infantry Division
TV 222	29th Infantry Division
TV 223	Third Korean Winter
TV 224	Seventh Army
TV 225	Fire Power Artillery
TV 226	Special Services
TV 227	Operation Blue Jay
TV 228	Ranger Ready
TV 229	Double Duty American—Reserves

TV 230	Alaska
TV 231	Report from the Provost Marshal General
TV 232	Soldier in Berlin
TV 233	Armored Force
TV 234	Army Aviation
TV 235	Korean Wind-Up
TV 236	Pictorial Report No. 3
TV 237	Hawaiian Defense
TV 238	Soldier in Europe
TV 239	The Soldier Patient
TV 240	Pictorial Report No. 4
TV 241	The Republic of Korea (ROK) Soldier
TV 242	Atrocities in Korea
TV 243	German Youth Activities
TV 244	Christmas in Korea (Withdrawn from the series)
TV 245	Guided Missiles
TV 246	A Second Life
TV 247	The Quartermaster in Europe
TV 248	Sports for All
TV 249	This Is Aberdeen
TV 250	Helsinki Olympics
TV 251	Pictorial Report No. 5
TV 252	Alaskan Scout and Alaskan Command
TV 253	Pictorial Report No. 6
TV 254	Japan-Our Far East Partner
TV 255	Rebirth of Seoul
TV 256	The Steel Ring
TV 257	Engineer Mission
TV 258	This Is First Army
TV 259	This Is Second Army
TV 260	This Is Third Army
TV 261	This Is Fourth Army
TV 262	This Is Fifth Army
TV 263	This Is Sixth Army
TV 264	Pictorial Report No. 7
TV 265	TV in the Army
TV 266	Exercise Flash Burn

TV 267	NATO: Partners in Peace
TV 268	Okinawa: Keystone of the Pacific
TV 269	Soldier in Austria
TV 270	Battlefields of Yesterday
TV 271	Armed Forces Assistance to Korea
TV 272	Pictorial Report No. 8
TV 273	Ice Cap
TV 274	Fifteen Forty-Five Hours
TV 275	Military District of Washington
TV 276	John Garand: M-1 Rifle
TV 277	The WAC Is a Soldier, Too
TV 278	Pictorial Report No. 9
TV 279	Education in the Army
TV 280	Airborne to Battle
TV 281	Soldier in Britain
TV 282	Army Technical Schools in Europe
TV 283	Soldier in Panama
TV 284	The Lodge Act Soldier
TV 285	Defense of Japan
TV 286	Pictorial Report No. 10
TV 287	Nerves of the Army
TV 288	Time to Go
TV 289	24th Infantry Division in Korea
TV 290	Nurses in the Army
TV 291	NATO Maneuvers
TV 292	M48 Patton Tank: "Birth of a Tank"
TV 293	Aid to Nationalist China
TV 294	25th Infantry Division in Korea
TV 295	Ordinance in Europe
TV 296	First Cavalry Division in Korea
TV 297	Second Infantry Division in Korea
TV 298	Airborne Medic
TV 299	Pictorial Report No. 11
TV 300	Role of the Army
TV 301	The 7th Infantry Division in Korea
TV 302	Third Division in Korea
TV 303	Civilian Soldiers

TV 304   Pictorial Report No. 12

TV 305   Pan American Games

TV 306   This Is Fort Belvoir

TV 307   Pictorial Report No. 13

TV 308   The Atom Soldier

TV 309   Army Postal Service

TV 310   The Medical Service Corps

TV 311   Pictorial Report No. 14

TV 312   Army Information School

TV 313   Pictorial Report No. 15

TV 314   Foreign Nationals

TV 315   Army Talent Show

TV 316   Operation Gyroscope

TV 317   Pictorial Report No. 16

TV 318   Operation Noah

TV 319   Japanese Self-Defense Forces

TV 320   Escape from a Prisoner of War Camp

TV 321   The Making of a West Pointer

TV 322   Pictorial Report No. 17

TV 323   ROTC Summer Training

TV 324   Pictorial Report No. 18

TV 325   Military Police Town Patrol

TV 326   Division in Europe

TV 327   War Games: "Operation Sage Brush"

TV 328   Soldier in France

TV 329   Pictorial Report No. 19

TV 330   Pictorial Report No. 20

TV 331   Military Justice

TV 332   Army Reserve History: "The Whites of Their Eyes"

TV 333   Pictorial Report No. 21

TV 334   Arctic Gear: "Exercise Moose Horn"

TV 335   (Not Available)

TV 336   Operation Friendly Hand

TV 337   "Exercise Arctic Night"

TV 338   The Guns Are Silent

TV 339   Mountaineers in Khaki: Mountaineer and Cold Weather School

TV 340   The New German Army
TV 341   Pictorial Report No. 22
TV 342   Pictorial report No. 23
TV 343   Army Flight Training: "Above the Best"
TV 344   Army in Review
TV 345   Focus on the Middle East
TV 346   Boys Town, U.S.A.
TV 347   Pictorial Report No. 24
TV 348   Historic Fort Monroe
TV 349   Letter from the Mojave
TV 350   Pictorial Report No. 25
TV 351   Pentomic 101st
TV 352   Soldier in Hawaii
TV 353   Pictorial Report No. 26
TV 354   You in Japan
TV 355   The Big Picture Salutes the Red Cross
TV 356   Artillery: "King of Battle"
TV 357   Army Ballistic Missile Agency
TV 358   Pictorial Report No. 27
TV 359   DEW Line: Distant Early Warning System
TV 360   Defense against Enemy Propaganda
TV 361   Traditions and Achievements in the Army
TV 362   War Games: "The Aggressor"
TV 363   Weather: Friend or Foe
TV 364   Operation Mercy
TV 365   Army Diver's School
TV 366   Research and Development in the Arctic
TV 367   Pictorial Report No. 28
TV 368   Inland Waterways
TV 369   Warfare Tech: "Progress"
TV 370   Fifty Years of Aviation
TV 371   Mister Army
TV 372   Pictorial Report No. 29
TV 373   Preamble to Peace
TV 374   Provide for the Common Defense (JOCO)
TV 375   Alexandria: City of Understanding
TV 376   Pictorial Report No. 30

TV 377   Brush Fire—Korea

TV 378   Southern European Task Force (SETAF)

TV 379   Pictorial Report No. 31

TV 380   42nd Rainbow Division

TV 381   What Makes a General

TV 382   The History of Cavalry

TV 383   Engineer Supply Mission

TV 384   Missile Man

TV 385   Our Sons

TV 386   Many Roads to Glory

TV 387   Ottumwa, U.S.A.

TV 388   42nd Field Artillery Group

TV 389   Armored Combat Power

TV 390   Army Newsreel No. 1

TV 391   Graduate : Reserve Officers' Training Corps

TV 392   Pictorial Report No. 32

TV 393   Individual Protection against Atomic Attack

TV 394   Pentomic Army

TV 395   Special Services (USAREUR)

TV 396   Atomic Battlefield

TV 397   Army Satellites

TV 398   The General Bradley Story

TV 399   Your Defense

TV 400   Far East MAAGS

TV 401   Fire Brigade

TV 402   Why NATO?

TV 403   Southeast Asia Treaty Organization (SEATO) Nations

TV 404   Missile on Target

TV 405   (Not Used in Big Picture Series)

TV 406   Battle of Salerno

TV 407   Religious Emphasis Day in Philadelphia

TV 408   The General Marshall Story

TV 409   Army Newsreel No. 2

TV 410   First Sergeant

TV 411   Aerial Mobility

TV 412   Soldiers' Heritage

TV 413   Battle of the Bulge

TV 414	Salute to the Canadian Army
TV 415	Story of a Squad
TV 416	The General MacArthur Story
TV 417	Battle of Manila
TV 418	Seven-Year-End Report
TV 419	Pictorial Report No. 33
TV 420	A Debt Is Honored
TV 421	Pentomic Seventh Army
TV 422	Alaska—The Outpost State
TV 423	Okinawa—Bastion of the Pacific
TV 424	USMAAG Germany
TV 425	The Stilwell Story
TV 426	Flying Soldiers
TV 427	The Patrol
TV 428	Code of the Fighting Man
TV 429	Character Guidance
TV 430	People to People
TV 431	Battle of San Pietro
TV 432	Thayer of West Point
TV 433	The Common Defense
TV 434	Canine College
TV 435	The Eisenhower Story
TV 436	The Admiral Nimitz Story
TV 437	The General Hap Arnold Story
TV 438	The Unseen Weapon (CBR)
TV 439	Nike-Hercules—A Reality
TV 440	The Quartermaster Story
TV 441	Battle for New Guinea
TV 442	The Fort Monmouth Story
TV 443	West Point Summer Cadet Training
TV 444	The General Pershing Story
TV 445	Summer Storm
TV 446	Winter War
TV 447	War's End
TV 448	Phantom Fighters (10th Special Forces)
TV 449	A Sharper Sword and Stronger Shield
TV 450	Airborne Soldier

TV 451	Korea Today
TV 452	Look toward Tomorrow
TV 453	History of the Signal Corps
TV 454	Washington Soldier
TV 455	Germany Today
TV 456	Operation Discovery
TV 457	Army Medicine
TV 458	History of Firepower
TV 459	The Joe Mann Story
TV 460	Signal Soldiers
TV 461	Operation Danville
TV 462	The Army—A Deterrent to Aggression
TV 463	Army Digest No. 1
TV 464	One Army
TV 465	The Army's "First"
TV 466	Army Digest No. 2
TV 467	United Service Organization (USO): Wherever They Go
TV 468	The General Patton Story
TV 469	Ranger—Mark of a Man
TV 470	Tularosa Frontier
TV 471	Top Soldier
TV 472	The Seventh Army Story
TV 473	Project Man
TV 474	I Am the Guard
TV 475	Arms for Tomorrow
TV 476	The American Way of Life
TV 477	Operation Cartwheel
TV 478	Old Glory
TV 479	Army Digest No. 3
TV 480	Payoff in the Pacific (Part One)
TV 481	Payoff in the Pacific (Part Two)
TV 482	The Story of *Stars and Stripes*
TV 483	Army Digest No. 4
TV 484	Battle of North Africa (Part One)
TV 485	Battle of North Africa (Part Two)
TV 486	They Were There
TV 487	Army Digest No. 5

TV 488	Big Picture Highlights
TV 489	Eighth Army Shield of the Free World
TV 490	Army Digest No. 6
TV 491	Decade of NATO
TV 492	U.S. Army Language School
TV 493	Dateline: West Berlin
TV 494	Operation Lead Dog
TV 495	Mouth-to-Mouth Resuscitation
TV 496	History of Maneuvers
TV 497	(Not Used in *Big Picture* Series)
TV 498	(Not Used in *Big Picture* Series)
TV 499	(Not Used in *Big Picture* Series)
TV 500	(Not Used in *Big Picture* Series)
TV 501	(Not Used in *Big Picture* Series)
TV 502	History of Aviation (Part One)
TV 503	History of Aviation (Part Two)
TV 504	History of Aviation (Part Three)
TV 505	Partners in Progress
TV 506	Breakout and Pursuit Story of "Operation Cobra" (B&W—1961)
TV 507	STRAC Fourth
TV 508	Broken Bridge
TV 509	Role of Armor
TV 510	Special Digest
TV 511	Army Digest No. 8
TV 512	Challenge of Ideas
TV 513	Infantry Operations
TV 514	City under the Ice
TV 515	West Point—Education for Leadership (B&W—1961)
TV 516	The Army Nurse Story
TV 517	The Military Police Story (B&W—1961)
TV 518	Silent Warriors
TV 519	Korea and You
TV 520	U. S. Army and the Boy Scouts
TV 521	OCS Fort Sill
TV 522	Global Frontiers
TV 523	The Army's Music Men (B&W—1961)

TV 524	CDEC
TV 525	U.S. Army Cold Weather and Mountain School
TV 526	Army Digest No. 9
TV 527	Patrolling
TV 528	Caribbean Command
TV 529	Military Assistance Program (Part One)
TV 530	U.S. Army in Berlin: Timetable for Crisis (Part One) (B&W—1962)
TV 531	Exercise Swift Strike
TV 532	The Chaplain and the Commander
TV 533	Prelude to Taps
TV 534	The Eagle's Talon
TV 535	Military Assistance Advisory Group: Iran
TV 536	U.S. Army in Berlin: Checkpoint Charlie (Part Two) (B&W—1962)
TV 537	Operation Readiness
TV 538	The Army Chaplain—Yesterday and Today
TV 539	This Is the Infantry
TV 540	Opportunity to Learn
TV 541	The USAREUR Story (Part I)
TV 542	The USAREUR Story (Part II)
TV 543	Top of the World
TV 544	Solid Punch
TV 545	This Is Our Strength
TV 546	The Famous Forth
TV 547	Special Forces
TV 548	Military Assistance Program (Part Two)
TV 549	America on the Move
TV 550	Patterns of History
TV 551	Strike Command
TV 552	Soldier Statesman
TV 553	This Is How It Is
TV 554	Sky Divers
TV 555	The Aggressor (See also TV 362)
TV 556	Mobility
TV 557	To Keep and Bear Arms
TV 558	Take Command

(Catalog lists two titles as TV 559)

TV 559	United States Army Pacific (USARPAC)
TV 559	Climb to Glory (Part One) (B&W—1963) Story of the 10th Mountain Division
TV 560	Road to the Wall
TV 561	Guerrilla, U.S.A.
TV 562	Hidden War in Vietnam
TV 563	Testing for Tomorrow
TV 564	Alert CONARC (Part One)
TV 565	Men in Training—CONARC (Part Two)
TV 566	Dragon's Teeth (B&W—1963)
TV 567	The Soldier Is Tops (B&W—1963)
TV 568	The Army's All-Americans
TV 569	Salute to the Navy
TV 570	COMZ
TV 571	Tools for Learning
TV 572	Command Decision: The Invasion of Southern France (B&W—1963)
TV 573	Firepower, Mobility, Communications: "Modernization"
TV 574	The Fight for Vietnam
TV 575	Beyond the Call—Part I (The Medal of Honor) (B&W—1963)
TV 576	Beyond the Call—Part II (The Medal of Honor) (B&W—1963)
TV 577	Recall
TV 578	The Third Challenge: Unconventional Warfare
TV 579	Beachhead: Anzio (B&W—1963)
TV 580	Pentagon Report
TV 581	Salute to MATS
TV 582	Shape of the Nation
TV 583	The Story of American Forces Network
TV 584	Alaskan Scout (B&W—1963)
TV 585	Special Forces Advisor
TV 586A	At a Moment's Notice
TV 586B	Salute to the Air Force
TV 587	Fortress in the Sea (B&W—1963)
TV-588	Famous Generals—Pershing (B&W—1963)

TV 589	Famous Generals—MacArthur (B&W—1963)
TV 590	The Big Picture—Famous Generals—Eisenhower (B&W—28 min—1963)
TV 591	Famous Generals—Bradley (B&W—28 min—1963)
TV 592	Famous Generals—Marshall (B&W—28 min—1963)
TV 593	A Nation Sings (B&W—1963)
TV 594	Famous Generals—Patton (B&W—1963)
TV 595	Famous Generals—Arnold (B&W—1963)
TV 596	Famous Generals—Stilwell (B&W—1963)
TV 597	Prelude to Taps (Color—1964)
TV 598	Operation Amigo
TV 599	Climb to Glory (Part One)
TV 600	Climb to Glory (Part Two) (B&W—1963)
TV 601	Paris 44 (B&W—1964)
TV 602	The Measure of Our Defense
TV 603	I Am a Soldier
TV 604	Mapping Adventure
TV 605	U.S. Army Advisor in Vietnam
TV 606	Seventh Army Checkmate to Aggression
TV 607	Operation Montagnard
TV 608	Point of the Spear
TV 609	R.O.T.C.—A Pattern for Progress
TV 610	An Army Moves (B&W—1964)
TV 611	Soldiers in Greasepaint (B&W—1964)
TV 612	AEF in Siberia (B&W—1964)
TV 613	Pershing Joins the Ranks
TV 614	Battalion Commander
TV 615	D-Day
TV 616	Thailand
TV 617	Partners in Freedom
TV 618	Third Army
TV 619	One Week in October (Cuban Missile Crisis)
TV 620	Traditions and Achievements (B&W—1964)
TV 621	Salute to the U.S. Coast Guard
TV 622	Medal of Honor
TV 623	How Sleep the Brave (Color—1965)
TV 624	Thayer of West Point (B&W—1964)

TV 625	Old Glory (B&W—1964)
TV 627	American Soldier
TV 628	The West Berlin Struggle
TV 629	Wings at the Tree Tops (US Armed Helicopters)
TV 630	Infantry School: "Wherever Brave Men Fight"
TV 631	Iran
TV 632	NATO: The Changed Face of Europe
TV 633	American on the Move
TV 634	Army in Action—The Winds of Change (B&W—1964)
TV 635	Army in Action—The Three Faces of Evil (B&W—1964)
TV 636	Army in Action—Flames on the Horizon (B&W—1964)
TV 637	Army in Action—The Spreading Holocaust (B&W—1965)
TV 638	Army in Action—The Slumbering Giant Awakes (B&W—1965)
TV 639	Army in Action—Global War (B&W—1965)
TV 640	Army in Action—The Tide Turns (B&W—1965)
TV 641	Army in Action—The Victory (B&W—1965)
TV 642	Army in Action—The Years Between (B&W—1965)
TV 643	Army in Action—The Cobra Strikes (B&W—1965)
TV 644	World Trouble Spots (B&W—1965)
TV 645	Army in Action—Years of Menace (B&W—1965)
TV 646	Army in Action—The Finest Tradition (B&W—1965)
TV 647	A Pictorial History of the U.S. Cavalry (B&W—1965)
TV 648	Battle of St. Vith—Part I (B&W—1965)
TV 649	Battle of St. Vith—Part II (B&W—1965)
TV 650	Tried by Fire—Part I (B&W—1965)
TV 651	Tried by Fire—Part II (B&W—1965)
TV 652	Prologue to Leadership
TV 653	A Soldier's Warranty
TV 654	Action Vietnam
TV 655	Assignment Iran
TV 656	Operation Scoreboard
TV 657	Exercise Desert Strike
TV 657	Bridge at Remagen—Part I (B&W—1965)
TV 658	Bridge at Remagen—Part II (B&W—1965)
TV 659	Tigers on the Loose—Part I (B&W—1965)

TV 660	Tigers on the Loose—Part II (B&W—1965)
TV 661	Exercise Desert Strike
TV 662	Drill Sergeant
TV 663	Berlin Duty
TV 664	Icecap (B&W—1965)
TV 665	Assignment Taiwan
TV 666	EOD (Explosive Ordinance Disposal)
TV 667	The Army Nurse: Soldier of Mercy
TV 668	Science Moves the Army
TV 669	United States Strike Command
TV 670	Alaskan Earthquake (B&W—1966)
TV 671	Army Medical Research
TV 672	Your Army Reports: Number 1
TV 673	M-60: King of Armor
TV 674	Why Vietnam?
TV 675	Your Military Neighbor (B&W—1966)
TV 676	Operation Roll-Up
TV 677	Your Army Reports: Number 2
TV 678	Your Army Reports: Number 3
TV 679	Army Missions Unlimited
TV 680	The Unique War
TV 681	The Army in Taiwan
TV 682	Not for Conquest
TV 683	Lifeline of Logistics
TV 684	Our Heritage (B&W—1966)
TV 685	Your Army Reports: Number 4
TV 686	U. S. Army in the Andes
TV 687	Firepower for Freedom (Color—1966)
TV 688	Something to Build On
TV 689	Your Army Reports: Number 5
TV 690	Of Soldiers and Altars (Color—1966)
TV 691	Chopper Pilot (Claws for the Eagle) (Color—1967)
TV 692	Your Army Reports: Number 6
TV 693	The Red Diamond (Color—1967)
TV 694	(Not Available)
TV 695	A Nation Builds under Fire
TV 696	Your Army Reports: Number 7

TV 697   USO Wherever They Go (Color—1967)
TV 698   Alaskan Centennial (Color—1967)
TV 699   The Army's Floating Workshop
TV 700   Your Army Reports: Number 8
TV 701   US Army Combat Development Command
TV 702   To Answer the Call (Color—1967)
TV 703   Probe and Pursue
TV 704   The Army and Vietnam
TV 705   Vietnam Village Reborn (Color—1967)
TV 706   The Inner Ring
TV 707   Your Army Reports: Number 9
TV 708   Stay Alert, Stay Alive
TV 709   It's Up to You Basic Combat Training (Color—1967)
TV 710   Shotgun Rider
TV 711   The I in Infantry—The Individual (Color—1967)
TV 712   The Pershing
TV 713   Your Army Reports: Number 10
TV 714   Screaming Eagles in Vietnam (Color—1967)
TV 715   The OCS Story (Color—1967)
TV 716   The Big Red One in Vietnam
TV 717   Ready around the World (Color—1968)
TV 718   Your Army Reports: Number 11
TV 719   Army Transportation   Key to Mobility (Color—1968)
TV 720   The Sky Soldiers (Color—1968)
TV 721   Physical Fitness (Color—1968)
TV 722   Your Army Reports: Number 12
TV 723   When the Chips Are Down (Color—1968)
TV 724   Ready to Strike (Color—28 min—1968)
TV 725   The Song of the Soldier (Color—28 min—1968)
TV 726   The Army's Civilians (Color—28 min—1968)
TV 727   CONARC Headquarters of the US Soldier
TV 728   The Army Triangle (Color—1968)
TV 729   Your Army Reports: Number 13
TV 730   (Not Available)
TV 731   The Senior Soldier
TV 732   The Role of U.S. Combat Engineers in Vietnam
          (Color—1968)

TV 733   Platoon Leader (Color—1968)
TV 734   Your Army Reports: Number 14
TV 735   Fight for Life (Color—1968)
TV 736   Vietnam Crucible
TV 737   The Bridge (Color—1968)
TV 738   USARPAC (Color—1968)
TV 739   SoldiersatLaw (Color—1968)
TV 740   (Not Available)
TV 741   Men with a Mission (Color—1968)
TV 742   Meeting the Need (Color—1968)
TV 743   Your Army Reports: Number 15
TV 744   To Serve a Soldier (Color—1968)
TV 745   The Soldier's Christmas (Color—1968)
TV 746   The Ninth Infantry Division (Color—1968)
TV 747   The Big Green Lab (Color—1969)
TV 748   The First Air Cavalry Division (Color—1969)
TV 749   Logistics in Vietnam (Color—28 min—1969)
TV 750   West Point—The Army Challenge (Color—1969)
TV 751   Equal to the Environment (Color—1969)
TV 752   The Army Air Mobility Team (Color—1969)
TY 753   Seek and Strike (Color—1969)
TV 754   The Soldier's Heritage (Color—1969)
TV 755   The Voice of Command (Color—1969)
TV 756   The Silver Rifles (Color—1969)
TV 757   Korea Revisited (Color—1969)
TV 758   Ranger (Color—1969)
TV 759   Call Me Mister (Warrant Officer) (Color—1969)
TV 760   Your Army Reports: Number 16
TV 761   United States Army Europe (Color—1969)
TV 762   D-Day Anniversary (B&W—1969)
TV 763   NATO—The Changed Face of Europe (Color—1969)
TV 764   The Fourth Infantry Division (Color—1969)
TV 765   Meeting Tomorrow's Challenge (Color—1970)
TV 766   The Golden Knights—The Army Parachute Team
         (Color—1969)
TV 767   The Men from the Boys (Color—1969)
TV 768   The Americal Division (Color—1969)

TV 769   Your Army Reports: Number 18 (Color—1969)
TV 770   The 11th Armored Cavalry Regiment (Color—1969)
TV 771   Scout Dogs (Color—1969)
TV 772   82nd Airborne Division (Color—1970)
TV 773   Testing at Aberdeen (Color—1969)
TV 774   The Combat Infantry Soldier
TV 775   What Makes a Modern Army? (Color—1970)
TV 776   A Day in America (Color—1969)
TV 777   What Price Confidence (Color—28 min—1970)
TV 778   A Visit to Mars (Color—1970)
TV 779   Language Power for Peace (Color—1970)
TV 780   The Feminine Touch (Color—1970)
TV 781   Engineering for Tomorrow (Color—1970)
TV 782   The Spirit of Fort Benning (Color—1970)
TV 783   The Army Nurse (Color—1970)
TV 784   Fort Sill—The Field Artillery Center (Color—1970)
TV 785   The Largest School House in the World (Color—1970)
TV 786   The General Bradley Story (Color—1970)
TV 787   8th Infantry Division (Color—1970)
TV 788   Prelude to Taps (Color—1971)
TV 789   The Border Watchers (Color—1970)
TV 790   The Army's Helping Hand (Color—1970)
TV 791   Fort Bliss—Heart of Army Air Defense (Color—1970)
TV 792   Progress to Peace (Color—1971)
TV 793   Recondo (Color—28 min—1970)
TV 794   US Army Alaska (Color—1972)
TV 795   The Third Armored Division—Spearhead (Color—28 min—1970)
TV 796   The Guns at Springfield (Color—1971)
TV 797   (Not Available)
TV 798   The Might of the Pen (Color—1971)
TV 799   The Fourth Armored Division (Color—1971)
TV 800   Mapping a Better Tomorrow (Color—1971)
TV 801   The Third Infantry Division (Color—1971)
TV 802   The Twenty-Fourth Infantry Division (Color—1971)
TV 803   Hall of Heroes (Color—1971)
TV 804   Young American Leaders (Color—1971)

TV 805	Vision to Victory (Color—1971)
TV 806	There Is a Way (Color—1971)
TV 807	The 1st Infantry Division in Vietnam (1965–1970) (Color—1971)
TV 808	Toward a Better Environment (Color—1971)
TV 809	Mission in Action (Color—1971)
TV 810	AII the Word to All the Troops (Color—28 min—1971)
TV 811	The Army's Music Men (Color—1971)
TV 812	The Army's Other Role (Color—1971)
TV 813	(Not Available)
TV 814	The Making of the Soldier-Policeman (Color—1971)
TV 815	Pioneering for Tomorrow (Color—1971)
TV 816	Citizen Soldier – Community Leader (Color—29 min—1971)
TV 817	USO 30 Years of Service (Color—1971)
TV 818	(Not Available)
TV 819	The U.S. Army in Space and under the Sea (Color—1971)
TV 820	(Not Available)
TV 821	(Not Available)
TV 822	Materiel Readiness (Color—1971)
TV 823	Drill Sergeant (Color—1971)

Notes

Introduction

1. Ernie Pyle, *Here Is Your War: The Story of GI Joe* (New York: World Publishing, 1945), 304. In 1943, Pyle was covering the war front in Northern Africa.

2. "Army to Issue Video Series of Combat Pix," *Billboard*, 15 December 1951, 5.

3. "Army to Issue Video Series of Combat Pix," 5.

4. J. William Fulbright, *The Pentagon Propaganda Machine* (New York: Liveright, 1970), 70. The recognition of the importance of the series as an informational platform for the army served as a magnet to draw much of the criticism that this study addresses.

5. See RG 111, motion pictures 111-LC-30189 through 111-30197, National Archives at College Park, Maryland.

6. See *Big Picture* film "Why NATO?," ARC Identifier 2569670/Local ID 111-TV-402.

7. John A. Hannah, "Doctrine for Information and Education," *Army Information Digest* 8, no. 7 (July 1953): 4.

8. See *Big Picture* film "America on the Move," ARC Identifier 2569784 /Local ID 111-TV-549. This episode appeared close to the time of the Cuban Missile Crisis.

9. See *Big Picture* film "The Feminine Touch," Local ID 111-TV-780, accessed 14 August 2018, https://www.youtube.com/watch?v=th43sM7P2Fc.

10. See *Big Picture* film "Your Military Neighbor," Local ID 111-TV-675, accessed 18 August 2018, https://www.youtube.com/watch?reload=9&v=M loNbS1kjtw.

11. See Anna Froula and Stacy Takacs, eds., *American Militarism on the Small Screen* (New York: Routledge, 2016), 2.

Chapter 1. "Welcome to *The Big Picture*"

1. Jan Uebelherr, "Carl Zimmermann, 96, Was Silver-Haired Dean of Milwaukee Broadcast News," *Journal-Sentinel*, 11 April 2014, http://archive .jsonline.com/news/obituaries/carl-zimmermann-96-was-silver-haired -dean-of-milwaukee-broadcast-news-b99241298z1-254968761.html/. During the war, NBC's *Army Hour* regularly broadcast Zimmermann's reports. He received the Bronze Star medal for frontline reporting.

2. Carl Flint would serve as the chief, Services Films Office, of the Production Division, for the Army Pictorial Center, 1954–1963. William Brown would also work for the APC in the Production Division.

3. Kirby had previously served as the chief of Radio Branch, Bureau of Public Relations, in the War Department during World War II. See George Raynor Thompson, Dixie R. Harris, Pauline M. Oakes, and Dulany Terrett, *The Signal Corps: The Test, December 1941–July 1943* (Washington, DC: Center of Military History, 2003), 194–195.

4. See *Big Picture* film "The First Forty Days in Korea," ARC Identifier 2569439/Local ID III-TV-169. To underscore his credibility, Zimmerman wore his military uniform complete with four left-sleeve hash marks, each reflecting six months of experience in a combat zone.

5. See *Big Picture* films "The First Forty Days in Korea," ARC Identifier 2569439/Local ID III-TV-169, through "The UN Line Is Stabilized While Truce Talks Continue," ARC Identifier 2569451/Local ID III-TV-181.

6. See *Big Picture* film "The First Forty Days in Korea," ARC Identifier 2569439/Local ID III-TV-169.

7. See "The First Forty Days in Korea."

8. See *Big Picture* films "The United Nations Offensive," ARC Identifier 2569441/Local ID III-TV-171 and "The UN Forces Cross the 38th Parallel," ARC Identifier 2569447/Local ID III-TV-177.

9. Paul M. Edwards, *To Acknowledge a War: The Korean War in American Memory* (Westport, CT: Greenwood Press, 2000), 16.

10. For a comprehensive explanation of the American exceptionalist model see Seymour M. Lipset, *American Exceptionalism: A Double-Edged Sword* (New York: Norton, 1996).

11. Historian Christian Appy explains this as a dimension of 1950s culture: fighting to protect loved ones at home, with the military serving as a "military melting pot of democratic values." See Lisa M. Mundey, *American Militarism and Anti-Militarism in Popular Media, 1945–1970* (Jefferson, NC: McFarland, 2012), 6.

12. For examples see *Big Picture* episodes, "The Citizen Soldier" (TV-184), "NATO Maneuvers" (TV-291), "Southeast Asia Treaty Organization" (TV-403), and "Alaskan Earthquake" (TV-670).

13. For examples see *Big Picture* episodes "Citizen, Soldier, and Taxpayer Too" (TV-194), "The Soldier Patient" (TV-293), "People to People" (TV-430), and "Your Military Neighbor" (TV-675).

14. Mundey, *American Militarism*, 28.

15. Nicholas Worontsoff Jr. (retired, Spring, TX), correspondence with the author, 9 September 2018. The referenced episode was "The Fort Monmouth Story" (TV-442).

16. D. J. Kinney, "Selling Greenland: The Big Picture Television Series and the Army's Bid for Relevance during the Early Cold War," *Centaurus* 55 (2013): 346.

17. Letter from MG H. P. Storke, CINFO, to MG L. L. "Chubby" Doan, Chief Armor Section, US Continental Army, 24 January 1958. The letter acknowledged receipt of the recommendation by the OCINFO. RG 319.4.1-a1, National Archives and Records Administration, College Park, MD (hereafter NARA).

18. Memo from COL W. L. Weaver Chief, TID, to COL W. L. Slisher, Chief Information Section, Fifth US Army, 21 September 1959. RG 319.4.1-A1 47–20–311.25, General Correspondence, 1959, NARA.

19. Memo from Weaver to Slisher.

20. Lawrence H. Suid, *Guts and Glory: The Making of the American Military Image in Film* (Lexington: University Press of Kentucky, 2002), 62. Here Suid is describing the production of military-related films by the navy in particular, but all services in general, and their agendas of garnering support.

21. Kinney, "Selling Greenland," 348. See also Andrew Bacevich, *The Pentomic Era: The U.S. Army between Korea and Vietnam* (Washington, DC: National Defense University Press, 1986), and Brian McAllister Linn's *Elvis's Army: Cold War GIs and the Atomic Battlefield* (Cambridge, MA: Harvard University Press, 2016).

22. Kinney, "Selling Greenland," 348.

23. See *Big Picture* films "Salute to the Navy" (TV-569, 1962), "Salute to the Air Force" (TV-586B, 1963), and "Salute to the U.S. Coast Guard" (TV-621, 1964). The episode celebrating the navy aired close on the heels of the Cuban Missile Crisis and included footage of nuclear-ready missiles on parade in Red Square.

24. See US Congress, House, *Subscription Television: Hearings before the Committee on Interstate and Foreign Commerce*, 85th Cong., 2d sess., 1958,

490–492. AMVETS is the American Veterans service organization that advocates for its members. Founded in 1944 by veterans, it has a congressional charter.

25. US Congress, House, *Subscription Television*.

26. Charles O. Porter (OR). "The Pledge of Allegiance to the Flag," 103 Cong. Rec. A4173 (1957).

27. "Report of the National Rifle Association," 114 Cong. Rec. 16506–16507 (1968).

28. J. William Fulbright (D-AR). "Introduction of a Bill Requiring the Secretary of Defense to Submit Regular Reports with Respect to the Kinds and Amounts of Information Released for Distribution to the Public by the Department of Defense," 115 Cong. Rec. 37249–37250 (1969).

29. Christopher H. Sterling and John M. Kittross, *Stay Tuned: A History of American Broadcasting* (Mahwah, NJ: Lawrence Erlbaum, 2002), 279.

30. They were NBC, CBS, ABC, DuMont, and their affiliates.

31. David Halberstam, *The Fifties*, reprint (New York: Ballantine Books, 1994), 184.

32. Gary R. Edgerton, *The Columbia History of American Television* (New York: Columbia University Press, 2007), 103.

33. Halberstam, *The Fifties*, 186.

34. Frieda Barkin Hennock, President Truman's FCC commissioner, and first female to fill that position, was responsible for the task of sorting things out.

35. William Boddy, *Fifties Television: The Industry and Its Critics* (Urbana: University of Illinois Press, 1990), 49.

36. Boddy, *Fifties Television*, 50.

37. NBC was established in 1926, CBS in 1927, ABC in 1943, and DuMont in 1946.

38. Edgerton, *Columbia History of American Television*, 103.

39. Edgerton, 103.

40. "Television Facts and Statistics," Television History—The First 75 Years: 1950–1959, accessed 17 April 2018, http://www.tvhistory.tv/facts-stats.htm.

41. Thomas Doherty, *Cold War, Cool Medium: Television, McCarthyism, and American Culture*, rev. ed. (New York: Columbia University Press, 2005), 4.

42. Doherty, *Cold War*, 5.

43. Jonathan Kahana, *Intelligence Work: The Politics of American Documentary* (New York: Columbia University Press, 2008), 273.

44. Doherty, *Cold War*, 2.

45. Although the HUAC hearing followed on the heels of Senator Estes Kefauver's televised investigation into organized crime in America, it was the anticommunist forum that generated more Cold War angst among Americans. See Doherty, *Cold War.*

46. Alan Nadel, "Cold War Television and the Technology of Brainwashing," in *American Cold War Culture,* ed. Douglas Field (Edinburgh: Edinburgh University Press, 2005), 152. The sobriquet "Tail Gunner Joe" is in reference to Senator Joseph McCarthy's World War II service in the US Army Air Corps.

47. Alex McNeil, *Total Television,* rev. ed. (New York: Penguin Books, 1996), 141.

48. See Thomas Doherty, *Projections of War: Hollywood, American Culture, and World War II,* rev. ed. (New York: Columbia University Press, 1993).

49. Nancy Bernhard, *U.S. Television News and Cold War Propaganda, 1947–1960* (Cambridge: Cambridge University Press, 2003), 135.

50. Bernhard, *U.S. Television News,* 133.

51. Bernhard, 135.

52. That would have been equivalent to eighty-five shows of thirty minutes each during that year for the DOD. See *Encyclopedia.com,* s.v. "Hollywood and Television in the 1950s: The Roots of Diversification," accessed 21 April 2018, https://www.encyclopedia.com/arts/culture-magazines/hollywood-and-television-1950s-roots-diversification.

53. Bernhard, *U.S. Television News,* 135. As a snapshot, the US Census Bureau records the total population of the United States as 151.3 million in 1950.

54. The *March of Time* series consisted of short documentary-style films on contemporary subjects created for theater viewing. It ran from February 1935 until August 1951. Their length varied between two and twenty minutes.

55. Established in 1940, the award named after philanthropist and businessman George Peabody honors excellence in radio and television in seven categories: news, children's programming, entertainment, documentaries, education, interactive programming, and public service. It is the oldest electronic media award in the United States. The Emmy award recognizes excellence in television programming. The Academy of Television Arts and Sciences established the award in January 1949.

56. Craig Allen, *Eisenhower and the Mass Media: Peace, Prosperity, and Prime-Time TV* (Chapel Hill: University of North Carolina Press, 1993), 8.

57. It was Rosser Reeves of the Ted Bates Agency in New York who coached Eisenhower on his camera presence and diction.

58. Bernhard, *U.S. Television News,* 143.

59. Evan Thomas, *Ike's Bluff: President Eisenhower's Secret Battle to Save the World* (New York: Back Bay Books, 2012), 16.

60. Walter L. Hixson, *Parting the Curtain: Propaganda, Culture, and the Cold War, 1945–1961* (New York: St. Martin's Press, 1997), 22.

61. The DuMont Television Network was an early rival to NBC and CBS. It began operations in 1946 but succumbed to the costs of broadcasting, FCC regulations that restricted its growth, and competition for viewership. It terminated operations in 1956.

62. Robert P. Keim later served as a campaign manager, then president of the Advertising Council, Inc., New York, after completing his time in the service.

63. For additional information regarding DOD concerns about the programming of the *Armed Forces Hour* see Bernhard, *U.S. Television News*, 140–142.

64. Hostilities commenced when communist forces crossed the border into the South on 25 June 1950.

65. John R. Steelman as quoted in Bernhard, *U.S. Television News*, 117. Steelman served in his position as presidential assistant from 1946 to 1953. After Truman departed office he remained for a short period in his capacity to assist the new president, Dwight Eisenhower. Steelman's position later evolved into that of the White House chief of staff.

66. During the period of the Cold War the "East" referred to those nations generally aligned with the Soviet Union, the People's Republic of China, and communism. The "West" referred to those states aligned with the United States, Western Europe, and democracy.

67. J. Fred MacDonald, *Television and the Red Menace: The Video Road to Vietnam* (New York: Praeger, 1985), 34.

68. NATO is the North Atlantic Treaty Organization. For an excellent summary of the period, see Robert J. McMahon's *The Cold War: A Very Short Introduction* (New York: Oxford University Press, 2003).

69. Karal Ann Marling, *As Seen on TV: The Visual Culture of Everyday Life in the 1950s* (Cambridge, MA: Harvard University Press, 1994), 250. Marling provides a contextual understanding of the importance of this particular event.

70. "Television Facts and Statistics."

71. Salomon conceived the show while serving as a lieutenant commander in the US Navy during World War II. He later gained recognition as a special projects coordinator and producer for NBC Television.

72. Bennett conducted the NBC Symphony Orchestration throughout the

filming. By 1963, the soundtrack had grossed approximately $4 million in album sales. Salomon and Rodgers also received the Distinguished Service Medal from the navy.

73. MacDonald, *Television and the Red Menace*, 112.

74. The series' original title was *Conquest of the Air*.

75. A. William Bluem, *Documentary in American Television: Form, Function, Method* (New York: Hastings House, 1972), 165.

76. Bluem, *Documentary in American Television*, 164.

77. Bernhard, *U.S. Television News*, 147.

78. See "The Interviews: Perry Wolff," Archive of American Television, Television Academy Foundation, accessed 19 October 2020, https://interviews.televisionacademy.com/interviews/perry-wolff?clip=66379#interview-clips.

79. "The Interviews: Perry Wolff."

80. Bernhard, *U.S. Television News*, 145.

81. Bluem, *Documentary in American Television*, 145.

82. See *Big Picture* film "TV in the Army," ARC Identifier 2569535/Local ID 111-TV-265.

83. "TV in the Army."

84. "TV in the Army."

85. "TV in the Army."

86. See *Big Picture* film "Pictorial Report No. 23," Local ID 111-TV-342, accessed 5 February 2021, https://www.youtube.com/watch?v=p1rpJrxM89I. This segment on the TV Mobile Unit was part of a larger episode that also addressed several areas of research and technological advancement in the army.

87. Suid, *Guts and Glory*, 12.

88. Suid, 92.

89. Bernhard, *U.S. Television News*, 142.

90. See *Big Picture* film, "The Big Red One," ARC Identifier 2569480/Local ID 111-TV-210.

91. See *Big Picture* film "A Day in Korea," ARC Identifier 2569466/Local ID 111-TV-196.

92. That pronouncement described the purpose of the show that emphasized the greater struggle against communism and to elicit continued public support in that effort. See *Big Picture* film "Korean Wind-Up," ARC Identifier 2569505/Local ID 111-TV-235.

93. The APC distributed this episode so widely that it was eventually withdrawn from the catalog.

94. See *Big Picture* films "Pictorial Report No. 2," ARC Identifier 2569477/

Local ID 111-TV-207, and "Pictorial Report No. 4," ARC Identifier 2569510/ Local ID 111-TV-240. South Korea officially declared its independence on 17 August 1948.

95. Reference is to a 23 September 1942 *New York Post* article cited in "Early Press Clippings on Army Movie Makers Reviewed," *In Focus* 7, no. 2 (March 1962): 2. The facility would undergo several name changes, evolving from the Signal Corps Photographic Center, to the Signal Corps Pictorial Center (1953), and finally the Army Pictorial Center (1956).

96. Richard Koszarski, "Subway Commandos: Hollywood Filmmakers at the Signal Corps Photographic Center," *Film History* 14, no. 3–4 (2002): 299.

97. "Deadline on Film Site Nears," *New York Times*, 19 December 1971, A19.

98. Thomas M. Pryor, "By Way of Report: Army Film Makers Set-up Cameras Here—A White Elephant Finally Pays Off," *New York Times*, 1 February 1942, X4.

99. Reference is to a 14 January 1942 *Variety* article cited in "Early Press Clippings," 2.

100. See Ladislas Farago, *The Game of the Foxes: The Untold Story of German Espionage in the United States and Great Britain during World War II* (New York: David McKay, 1971), 493.

101. Paul Caster, "Behind the Scenes in Army Film Making," *Army Digest* 22, no. 6 (June 1967): 43.

102. Pryor, "By Way of Report," X4.

103. "Deadline on Film Site Nears," *New York Times*, 19 December 1971, 19.

104. "Deadline on Film Site Nears," 19.

105. Sarah Kershaw, "The Best Years of Their Lives," *New York Times*, 21 September 1996, 21.

106. Arthur Laurents, *Original Story By: A Memoir of Broadway and Hollywood* (New York: Alfred A. Knopf, 2000), 28.

107. Herbert Mitgang, "Big Picture by the Numbers," *New York Times*, 23 October 1960, X13.

108. Peter B. Flint, "John Huston, Film Director, Writer and Actor, Dies at 81," *New York Times*, 29 August 1987, 1. The Legion of Merit is a military award given for exceptionally meritorious conduct and outstanding achievements. It ranks just below the Silver Star and receives high regard.

109. Among his achievements were an Academy Award and a Golden Globe Award for *My Fair Lady* (1964).

110. "Jackson P. Pokress [recollections]," Army Pictorial Center, updated 16 September 2020, http://www.armypictorialcenter.com/jackson_b_pokress .htm.

111. For individual examples see the personnel roster posted at the Army Pictorial Center, Signal Corps Photographic Center, last updated 9 June 2019, http://www.armypictorialcenter.com/personnel_roster.htm.

112. Audie Murphy was America's most decorated hero of World War II, having earned the Medal of Honor among his many awards and citations, including a battlefield commission to lieutenant. After the war he had a presence in Hollywood appearing in a variety of Westerns and action-adventure films.

113. See *Big Picture* film "Challenge of Ideas," ARC Identifier 2569750/Local ID 111-TV-512.

114. Hanson Baldwin authored several military novels, Helen Hayes was an award-winning actress known for her film *My Son John* about the intrusion of communism into the life of an American family, Lowell Thomas was a popular radio broadcaster, and Frank McGee was a well-known television correspondent and news anchor.

115. Uldis Kruze, "Comedy on the Front Lines of the Cold War: Bob Hope's Christmas Specials during the Vietnam War," in *The Cold War and Entertainment Television*, ed. Lori Maguire (Newcastle, UK: Cambridge Scholars, 2016), 231.

116. See Tony Shaw, *Hollywood's Cold War* (Amherst: University of Massachusetts, Press, 2007), 200. Shaw provides an understanding of the enduring links between Hollywood and the Pentagon during the early decades of the Cold War.

117. See *Big Picture* film "A Nation Builds under Fire," ARC Identifier 2569876/Local ID 111-TV-695.

118. "A Nation Builds under Fire."

119. Humphrey would soon distance himself from any stance that supported the war under pressure from the growing antiwar movement and his desire to seek the Democratic nomination for the presidency in 1968.

120. "A Nation Builds under Fire."

121. "A Nation Builds under Fire."

122. Bluem, *Documentary in American Television*, 150.

123. Bluem, 150.

124. Bluem, 147.

125. "The Army's Big Picture," *TV Guide* 10, no. 52 (29 December 1962): 9.

126. Suid, *Guts and Glory*, 302.

127. See *Big Picture* film "Hidden War in Vietnam," ARC Identifier 2569797/Local ID 111-TV-562.

128. Bluem, *Documentary in American Television*, 147.

129. Bluem, 144.

130. "The Army's Big Picture," 9.

131. See "History," Army Pictorial Center, accessed 23 June 2018, http://www.armypictorialcenter.com/what_was_apc_scpc.htm. Although the APC converted to 16 mm, the preferred standard for stage productions remained 35 mm.

132. "The Color Revolution: Television in the Sixties," Television Obscurities, last updated 26 April 2018, https://www.tvobscurities.com/articles/color60s/.

133. The one exception was a short twelve-episode *Big Picture* collection titled "Army in Action" that traced the service's history from World War I to the conclusion of World War II (TV-634 through TV-643).

134. Bluem, *Documentary in American Television*, 168.

135. Bluem, 168. *The Twentieth Century* aired on CBS from October 1957 to January 1970. The narrator was Walter Cronkite. His focus was on news and cultural and historic events.

136. Froula and Takacs, *American Militarism on the Small Screen*, 4.

137. "The First Forty Days in Korea."

138. "A Nation Builds under Fire." It is interesting to note the use of the statement "men and women" of the army at a time when the military was not yet stressing diversity and inclusiveness.

139. The full title of the annex to the Armistice Agreement was "Terms of Reference for Neutral Nations Repatriation Commission."

140. See *Big Picture* film "Military Police Town Patrol," Local ID 111-TV-325, accessed 22 June 2018, https://www.youtube.com/watch?v=w_-UbRxlxCk.

141. "Military Police Patrol."

142. The government issued the last draft call on 7 December 1972, but the process to end conscription began in Congress as early as 1969.

143. See *Big Picture* film "Screaming Eagles in Vietnam," Local ID 111-TV-714, accessed 10 June 2018, https://www.youtube.com/watch?v=fUXxGjCSWIo.

144. Jeffrey Crean, "Something to Compete with 'Gunsmoke': 'The Big Picture' Television Series and Selling a 'Modern, Progressive and Forward Thinking' Army to Cold War America," *War & Society* 35, no. 3 (August 2016): 206. MG G. S. Meloy, chief of information, made the comment as the army struggled with its decision whether to seek commercial endorsement or produce an independent, sponsor-free series.

145. Letter from LTG Charles D. Palmer, Commander, Sixth U.S. Army, to

MG H. P. Storke, CINFO, 21 March 1959, RG 319.4.1-A1 47-20-311.25, General Correspondence, 1959. NARA.

146. Aside from numerous military-themed films, filmstrips, and recordings, *Big Picture* titles were available for selection under a variety of subcategories such as Armor, Atomic Power, World War II, and Public Information.

147. See Chapter 3, "Operations," Paragraph 26, "Film Booking Procedure," Subparagraph e, "Civilian Requests," in US Department of the Army, *Audio-Visual Support Center Operations*, Field Manual 11-41 (Washington, DC: US GPO, 28 November 1966).

148. Memo from COL W. L. Slisher, Chief Information Section, Fifth US Army, to COL W. L. Weaver, Chief, TID, 16 September 1959, RG 319.4.1-A1 47-20-311.25, General Correspondence, 1959, NARA.

149. For description of the area see John B. Wilson, CMH Pub 60–14, *Maneuver and Firepower: The Evolution of Divisions and Separate Brigades*, Army Lineage Series (Washington, DC: Center for Military History, 1998), 218–219.

150. Senator Fulbright, speaking on S. 3217, on 5 December 1969, 91st Cong., 1st sess., 115 Cong. Rec. pt. 28: 37251.

151. 115 Cong. Rec. pt. 28: 37253–5.

152. See the *Richmond Times-Dispatch* for those years.

153. Richard L. Forestall, "Virginia: Population of Counties by Decennial Census: 1900 to 1990," *US Bureau of the Census*, accessed 23 June 2020, https://www.census.gov/population/cencounts/va190090.txt.

154. The census numbers for the Des Moines SMSA for the years 1960 and 1970 were 266,315 and 313,562 respectively. See "Population for Iowa Metropolitan Areas and Geography Components: 1950–2000," State Library of Iowa, State Data Center, accessed 26 June 2020, https://www.iowadata center.org/datatables/MetroArea/metropop19502000.pdf.

155. Gene Plotnik, "TV-Films Reviews: *The Big Picture*," *Billboard*, 11 October 1953, 16.

156. Ziv Television Programs, Inc. (Ziv-TV) was a firm that specialized in distributing first-run television syndication programs through the 1950s. It produced recorded television programs and sold them to television stations. The American Research Bureau (ARB) was an organization that measured and tracked television viewing in all US markets during the 1950s and 1960s. It was the forerunner of the Arbitron system.

157. "TV-Film Industry Leader," *Billboard*, 14 June 1952, 1.

158. "TV-Film Industry Leader," 1

159. "How Stations Rate Non-Network TV Shows," *Billboard*, 6 September 1952, 18.

160. "Billboard 1st Annual TV Film Show Awards," *Billboard*, 21 February 1953, 20.

161. "Victory Pulls Biggest Votes with Documentary Victory," *Billboard*, 31 July 1954, 5.

162. Doug Bailey, "Radio News and Teleoptics," *Maryland News*, 6 November 1952.

163. Bailey, "Radio News and Teleoptics."

164. "Telepix Reviews," *Variety*, 12 November 1952.

165. The ARB based its ratings on the percentage of televisions, in a particular market, watching a particular show at a specified time.

166. Memo from COL George R. Creel, Chief, Civil Liaison Division, to Commander, US Army Exhibit Unit, 16 October 1958, RG 319.4.1-A1 47–18–311.25, General Correspondence, 1958, NARA.

167. Memo from LTC F. K. Tourtellotte, Deputy Chief, TID, to Chief, Army Exhibit Unit, 30 December 1958, RG 319.4.1-A1 47–20–311.25, General Correspondence, 1959, NARA.

168. Letter from LTC Kenneth Lay, Deputy Chief, Information Division, USAREUR, to Office of the CINFO, 4 March 1957, RG 319.4.1-A1 47–18–311.25, General Correspondence, 1957, NARA.

169. Letter from Lay to Office of the CINFO.

170. Memo from COL Daniel Parker, Chief, PID, to COL Morton P. Brooks, Chief, Information Division, USAREUR, 26 November 1957, RG 319.4.1-A1 47–18–311.25, General Correspondence, 1957, NARA.

171. Letter from MG H. P. Storke, CINFO, to MG L. L. "Chubby" Doan, Chief Armor Section, US Continental Army, 24 January 1958, RG 319.4.1-a1 47–18–311.25, General Correspondence, 1958, NARA. The letter acknowledged receipt of the recommendation by the OCINFO.

Chapter 2. Making the Army Relevant Again

1. D. J. Kinney, "Selling Greenland: The Big Picture Television Series and the Army's Bid for Relevance during the Early Cold War," *Centaurus* 55 (2013): 346.

2. Comment made by Maj. Gen. G. S. Meloy, army chief of information, as quoted in Jeffrey Crean, "Something to Compete with 'Gunsmoke': 'The Big Picture' Television Series and Selling a 'Modern, Progressive and Forward Thinking' Army to Cold War America," *War & Society* 35, no. 3 (August 2016): 209.

3. See *Big Picture* film, "The Eyes and Ears of the Army," ARC Identifier 2569462/Local ID 111-TV-192.

4. Kinney, "Selling Greenland," 345.

5. Donald A. Carter, CMH Pub 76–3, *The US Army before Vietnam: 1953–1965* (Washington, DC: Center for Military History, 2015), 10.

6. See Walter G. Hermes, "The Army and the New Look," in *American Military History*, ed. Maurice Matloff (Washington, DC: Center of Military History, 1989), 572.

7. See A. J. Bacevich, *The Pentomic Era: The U.S. Army between Korea and Vietnam* (Washington, DC: National Defense University Press, 1986), and Donald A. Carter, *The U.S. Army before Vietnam: 1953–1965* (Washington, DC: Center of Military History, 2015) for a fuller discussion of the army's resourcing challenges.

8. Kinney, "Selling Greenland," 350.

9. See *Big Picture* film "Tools for a Modern Army," ARC Identifier 2569478/Local ID 111-TV-208.

10. "Tools for a Modern Army."

11. See *Big Picture* film "Guided Missiles," ARC Identifier 2569515/Local ID 111-TV-245.

12. See *Big Picture* films, "The Steel Ring," ARC Identifier 2569526/Local ID 111-TV-256, and "Atomic Battlefield," ARC Identifier 2569664/Local ID 111-TV-396.

13. See *Big Picture* film "Army Satellites," ARC Identifier 2569665/Local ID 111-TV-397.

14. "Army Satellites."

15. The air force established a secret film unit in Laurel Canyon near Hollywood in 1947. Also known as the Lookout Mountain Laboratory, it would evolve into the US government's largest, and by some estimates most comprehensive, film studio during the Cold War. The facility employed numerous Hollywood experts and emerging technologies to produce thousands of hours of film footage and still images recording America's scientific and technological achievements. For a fuller understanding of its contributions, see Kevin Hamilton and Ned O'Gorman, *Lookout America! The Secret Hollywood Studio at the Heart of the Cold War* (Hanover, NH: Dartmouth College Press, 2019).

16. "Army Satellites."

17. Dr. Wernher von Braun pioneered rocket development and space exploration for the United States in the aftermath of World War II. He arrived in America through Operation Paperclip, a program that brought former National Socialist scientists, technicians, and engineers from Germany to the West as competition in the Space Race with the Soviet Union was beginning.

18. Kinney, "Selling Greenland," 347.

19. "BP's Coming Season to Offer Public Look at the 'Modern Army,'" *In Focus* 4, no. 8 (September 1959): 3. *In Focus* was the monthly newspaper released by the Army Pictorial Center. Similar to any military newsletter, it focused on the activities of the personnel serving at the center, from the routine such as promotions and recreational events to providing the progress status of upcoming production releases.

20. "BP's Coming Season," 3.

21. "BP's Coming Season," 3.

22. See *Big Picture* film "Operation Blue Jay," ARC Identifier 2569497/ Local ID 111-TV-227.

23. "Operation Blue Jay."

24. "Operation Blue Jay."

25. Kinney, "Selling Greenland."354.

26. See *Big Picture* film "Research and Development in the Arctic," ARC Identifier 2569635/Local ID 111-TV-366.

27. See *Big Picture* film "Icecap," Local ID 111-TV-664, accessed 8 May 2018, https://www.youtube.com/watch?v=E-io1zZIrRE.

28. See *Big Picture* film "City under the Ice," ARC Identifier 2569752/ Local ID 111-TV-514.

29. See *Big Picture* film "U.S. Army and the Boy Scouts," ARC Identifier 2569758/Local ID 111-TV-520.

30. See *Big Picture* film "Science Moves the Army," ARC Identifier 2569856/Local ID 111-TV-668.

31. See *Big Picture* film "Pioneering for Tomorrow," Local ID 111-TV-815, accessed 5 May 2018, https://www.youtube.com/watch?v=R6qGLuJNovw.

32. See *Big Picture* film "The U.S. Army in Space and under the Sea," Local ID 111-TV-819, accessed 5 May 2018, https://www.youtube.com/watch?v=B2t9I9EBWdA.

33. Ibid.

34. See *Big Picture* film "Top of the World," Local ID 111-TV-543, accessed 5 May 2018, https://www.youtube.com/watch?v=8ToWfwec2os.

35. See "Screen Guild Urges Army Unit Boycott," *New York Times,* 25 October 1967, 41. The SAG protested against the APC rate of pay for actors, which was $60.88 a day versus the industry standard of $100.

36. Lisa M. Mundey, *American Militarism and Anti-Militarism in Popular Media, 1945–1970* (Jefferson, NC: McFarland, 2012), 99. Mundey provides a comprehensive overview of how much of the American popular culture of the early Cold War period reflected antimilitarism.

37. Mundey, *American Militarism*, 100.

38. See *United States Army Recruiting Command*, 16 November 2016, https://ipfs.io/ipfs/QmXoypizjW3WknFiJnKLwHCnL72vedxjQkDDP1mX-Wo6uco/wiki/United_States_Army_Recruiting_Command.html.

39. See *Big Picture* film "Exercise Arctic Night," ARC Identifier 2569606/Local ID 111-TV-337.

40. The Universal Military Training and Service Act of 1951 provided the president with the authority to induct citizens for four years and lowered the draft age to 18. See *United States Army Recruiting Command* website.

41. Crean, "Something to Compete with 'Gunsmoke,'" 208.

42. Mundey, *American Militarism*, 102.

43. Crean, "Something to Compete with 'Gunsmoke,'" 211.

44. Memo, Colonel Robert V. Shinn, Chief PID, to the Assistant Secretary of Defense for Public Affairs, 31 December 1958, RG 319-A1 47–18–311.25, General Correspondence, 1958, National Archives at College Park, Maryland (hereafter NARA).

45. Anna Froula and Stacy Takacs, eds., *American Militarism on the Small Screen* (New York: Routledge, 2016), 5.

46. Froula and Takacs, *American Militarism on the Small Screen*, 142.

47. Froula and Takacs, 143.

48. Froula and Takacs, 143.

49. Lawrence H. Suid, *Guts and Glory: The Making of the American Military Image in Film* (Lexington: University Press of Kentucky, 2002), 144.

50. Suid, *Guts and Glory*, 144.

51. Donald A. Carter, *The U.S. Army before Vietnam: 1953–1965* (Washington, DC: Center of Military History, US Army, 2015), 11.

52. Stanley Field, "The Big Picture." *Journal of Broadcasting* 125 (1962): 126.

53. Nancy Bernhard, *U.S. Television News and Cold War Propaganda, 1947–1960* (Cambridge: Cambridge University Press, 2003), 135.

54. Bernhard, *U.S. Television News*, 135.

55. Letter, MG G. S. Meloy, Chief of Information, to the Army Deputy Chief of Staff for Operations, 18 September 1956, RG 319-A1 47–15–311.25, General Correspondence, 1956, NARA.

56. Crean, "Something to Compete with 'Gunsmoke,'" 211.

57. Memo from COL John O. Weaver, Chief Troop Information Division, to Chief, Motion Picture Branch, APC, 20 October 1959. NARA, RG 319.4.1-A1 47–20–311.25, General Correspondence, 1959.

58. Letter from MG G. S. Meloy, CINO, to Mr. William Grant, President

KOATV-Radio, Denver, Colorado, 6 May 1957, RG 319.4.1-A1 47–18–311.25, General Correspondence, 1957, NARA.

59. Letter from MG H. P. Storke, CINFO, to MG Emerson C. Itschner, Chief of Engineers, 22 December 1958, RG 319.4.1-A1 47–18–311.25, General Correspondence, 1958, NARA.

60. Memo from COL John O. Weaver, Chief, Troop Information Division, to Chief Motion Picture Branch, APC, 7 December 1959, RG 319.4.1-A1 47–20–311.25, General Correspondence, 1959, NARA.

61. *Navy Log* aired on CBS, 1955–1956 at 8:00 p.m. EST, then on ABC, 1956–1958 at 8:30 p.m., then 10:00 p.m. EST.

62. See *Big Picture* film "Atrocities in Korea," ARC Identifier 2569512/ Local ID 111-TV-242.

63. "Atrocities in Korea."

64. At this time the "Big Four" powers consisted of the United States, Great Britain, France, and the Soviet Union. The diplomatic atmosphere was delicate, as the United States and Great Britain were supporting the revitalization of West Germany and did not want to endanger any concessions they sought from the Soviets.

65. "Congressmen Hit Army Film Curb," *New York Times,* 9 January 1954, 2.

66. "Congressmen Hit Army Film Curb."

67. Senator Charles E. Potter speaking on S. Res 178, "Appointment of a Committee by United Nations to Investigate Communist Atrocities in Korea," 11 January 1954, 83rd Cong., 2nd sess. 100 Cong. Rec. pt. 1: 89–128.

68. Rep. R. Thurmond Chatham speaking on "Christian Weapons Can Defeat the Reds," 9 February 1954, 83rd Cong., 2nd sess., 100 Cong. Rec. pt. 2: A1045.

69. The *New York Times* recorded that long-awaited release in its television column that month. "Television in Review: Atrocities in Korea Finally Presented," *New York Times,* 8 February 1954, 30:7.

70. Senator Fulbright, speaking on S. 3217, on 5 December 1969, 91st Cong., 1st sess., 115 Cong, Rec. pt. 28: 37249.

71. Crean, "Something to Compete with 'Gunsmoke,'" 213. Maj. Gen. Harry P. Storke served as army chief of information from 10 September 1957 to 31 May 1959.

72. See *Big Picture* film "Your Defense" ARC Identifier 2569667/Local ID 111-TV-399.

73. Senator Fulbright, speaking on S. 3217, on 5 December 1969, 91st Cong., 1st sess., 115 Cong. Rec. pt. 28: 37250. The cost breakdown was Pro-

duction and Distribution: $881,000.00, Personnel Salaries: $20,466.00, and Flyers-including material: $1,063.34. By comparison, the budget was $971,445 in 1952.

74. Honorable Charles E. Bennett speaking on *Stop Tax-Paid Military Trips for Public Relations Purposes*, 19 November 1970, 91st Cong., 2nd sess., 116 Cong. Rec. pt. 28: 38268.

75. Bennett, on *Stop Tax-Paid Military Trips*.

76. Senator Fulbright speaking on *Department of Defense Appropriations*, 1971, 8 December 1970, 91st Cong., 2nd sess., 116 Cong. Rec. pt. 30: 40428–40430.

77. Fulbright, on *Department of Defense Appropriations*.

78. Fulbright, on *Department of Defense Appropriations*.

79. J. William Fulbright, *The Pentagon Propaganda Machine* (New York: Liveright, 1970), 148. The work represents Fulbright's collected research on the issue. In his acknowledgements the senator gives credit to Edward A. O'Neill for assistance in preparation of the book.

80. See *Big Picture* film "Hidden War in Vietnam," ARC Identifier 2569797/Local ID 111-TV-562.

81. See *Big Picture* film "Why Vietnam?" ARC Identifier 2569861/Local ID 111-TV-674. The reference is to British prime minister Neville Chamberlain's disastrous placation of Adolph Hitler in 1938, which opened the door to further German aggressions.

82. Fulbright, *Pentagon Propaganda Machine*, 70.

83. Fulbright, 70.

84. Fulbright, 71.

85. Fulbright, 152. "V-films" is a reference to Victory Films produced by government or contracted agencies to support the war effort during World War II. They included propaganda and training films.

86. See "William W. Quinn, 92, General and Former Intelligence Officer," *New York Times*, 12 September 2000, https://www.nytimes.com/2000/09/12/us/william-w-quinn-92-general-and-former-intelligence-officer.html.

87. Crean, "Something to Compete with 'Gunsmoke,'" 205.

88. Maj. Gen. Charles G. Dodge, as quoted in Paul Breen Gardner, "The Increasing Gap between Words and Deeds: Teaching Public Affairs at the Colleges of the Army from Academic Year 1947 through Academic Year 1989" (PhD diss., Kansas State University, 2014), 160, https://krex.k-state.edu/dspace/bitstream/handle/2097/17550/PaulGardner2014.pdf?sequence=1.

89. Gardner, "Increasing Gap between Words and Deeds," 161.

90. For a comprehensive understanding of how the American exception-

alist consensus shaped the thinking of the contemporary society see Seymour M. Lipset, *American Exceptionalism: A Double-Edged Sword* (New York: Norton, 1996).

91. "Army's Famed Series Signs Off, 'The Big Picture' Fades from TV Screen," *Stars and Stripes* (Pacific Edition), 16 July 1971, 3.

92. The Freedoms Foundation is a nonprofit educational organization established in 1949 by a duo of advertising executives who sought to reestablish the nation's Christian heritage and believed that the nation was in a battle for the minds of men with the Soviet East.

93. See "Medals for Mettle," *In Focus* 5, no. 2 (March 1960): 6, caption.

94. "Army's Famed Series Signs Off," *Stars and Stripes* (Pacific Edition), 16 July 1971, 3.

Chapter 3. A Big Picture of the Cold War

1. See *Big Picture* film "Korean Wind-Up," ARC Identifier 2569505/Local ID 111-TV-235.

2. See *Big Picture* film "Soldier in Berlin," ARC Identifier 2569502/Local ID 111-TV-232.

3. J. Fred MacDonald, "The Cold War as Entertainment in Fifties Television," *Journal of Popular Film* 7, no. 1 (1978): 3.

4. These included NSC 4 in December 1947, NSC 10/2 in June 1948, NSC 20/4 in November 1948, and NSC 68 in April 1950.

5. Political theorist Joseph S. Nye coined the term "soft power," which referred to the indirect, nonconfrontational manner that nations could exert their influence on one another. See Joseph S. Nye, *Soft Power: The Means to Success in World Politics* (New York: Public Affairs, 2004), 5.

6. Kenneth Osgood, *Total Cold War: Eisenhower's Secret Propaganda Battle at Home and Abroad* (Lawrence: University Press of Kansas, 2008), 48.

7. Kennan was also instrumental in development of the series of NSC documents between 1947 and 1950. See Osgood, *Total Cold War*, 38–40. Also see George F. Kennan, *George F. Kennan: Memoirs, 1925–1950* (New York: Pantheon Books, 1967), 292–295.

8. See *Big Picture* film "Armed Forces Assistance to Korea," ARC Identifier 2569541/Local ID 111-TV-271.

9. See *Big Picture* film "Korea and You," ARC Identifier 2569757/Local ID 111-TV-519.

10. "Expert Asserts 1/3 PWs Yielded to Brainwashing," *Stars and Stripes*, 24 February 1956, 7.

11. "Report GIs in Korea Too Soft," *Chicago Defender*, 10 January 1959, 9.

12. "Report GIs in Korea Too Soft," 9.

13. The military issued the code under Executive Order 10631 on August 17, 1955. See details at Wikipedia, s.v. "Code of the United States Fighting Force," last modified 8 December 2020, 17:12, https://en.wikipedia.org/wiki/Code_of_the_United_States_Fighting_Force.

14. Hollywood took steps in that direction by turning Richard Condon's 1959 novel *The Manchurian Candidate* into a critically acclaimed film in 1961. It relates the uncomfortable story of a politician's son whom the communists capture during the Korean War, hold as prisoner, brainwash, and then release back to the United States.

15. See *Big Picture* film "Escape from a Prisoner of War Camp," ARC Identifier 2569590/Local ID 111-TV-320.

16. See *Big Picture* film "Defense against Enemy Propaganda," ARC Identifier 2569629/Local ID 111-TV-360.

17. "Defense against Enemy Propaganda."

18. See *Big Picture* film "Code of the Fighting Man," ARC Identifier 2569693/Local ID 111-TV-428.

19. "Code of the Fighting Man."

20. See *Big Picture* film "Character Guidance," ARC Identifier 2569694/Local ID 111-TV-429.

21. For additional insight into the use of propaganda by the United States during this time see Osgood, *Total Cold War*, and Lori Lyn Bogle, *The Pentagon's Battle for the American Mind* (College Station: Texas A&M University Press, 2004).

22. See *Big Picture* film "Challenge of Ideas," ARC Identifier 2569750/Local ID 111-TV-512.

23. "Challenge of Ideas."

24. "Challenge of Ideas."

25. See *Big Picture* film "Soldier in Europe," ARC Identifier 2569507/Local ID 111-TV-238.

26. The acronym USAREUR stands for United States Army Europe.

27. One of the engines that drove this fear was the spectacle of the McCarthy HUAC hearings during the 1950s. See John E. Haynes, *Red Scare or Red Menace? American Communism and Anticommunism in the Cold War Era* (Chicago: Ivan R. Dee, 1996).

28. See John W. Lemza, *American Military Communities in West Germany: Life in the Cold War Badlands, 1945–1990* (Jefferson, NC: McFarland, 2016), figure 1.3.

29. USMAAG was the United States Military Assistance Advisory Group. Prior to 1955 in West Germany, its mission was to assist in training the host nation paramilitary police force in the use of conventional weapons and tactics. After 1955 it supported the Bundeswehr (new West German Army).

30. *Gemütlichkeit* is the German term for feelings of cordiality and friendliness.

31. See *Big Picture* film "German Youth Activities," ARC Identifier 2569513/Local ID III-TV-243.

32. "German Youth Activities."

33. See *Big Picture* film "Operation Friendly Hand," ARC Identifier 2569605/Local ID III-TV-336. By 1953, Milcom families participating in Operation Friendly Hand had hosted 150 West German children. That number rose to 600 in 1954.

34. Memo from BG E. A. Brown Jr., Deputy Chief of Information and Education, to Deputy Assistant Secretary of Defense for Public Affairs, 16 April 1956, RG 319.4.1-A1 47-15-311.25, General Correspondence, 1956, National Archives at College Park, Maryland (hereafter NARA).

35. Memo from C. Herschel Schooley, Director, DOD, Office of Public Information, to MG G. S. Meloy, CINFO, 9 April 1956, RG 319.4.1-A1 47-15-311.25, General Correspondence, 1956, NARA.

36. Memo from BG E. A. Brown Jr. to Deputy Assistant Secretary of Defense for Public Affairs.

37. Memo from BG E. A. Brown Jr. to Deputy Assistant Secretary of Defense for Public Affairs.

38. See Osgood, *Total Cold* War, 232–242.

39. See *Big Picture* film "Germany Today," ARC Identifier 2569714/Local ID III-TV-455.

40. See *Big Picture* film "The West Berlin Struggle," ARC Identifier 2569836/Local ID III-TV-628.

41. See *Big Picture* film "The Border Watchers," Local ID III-TV-789, accessed 15 July 2018, https://www.youtube.com/watch?v=pKiE4HKovs8.

42. See *Big Picture* film "Soldier in Austria," ARC Identifier 2569539/Local ID III-TV-269. The United States participated in the partitioning of Austria with the other Western Allies (France and the United Kingdom) and the Soviets beginning in April 1945. That concluded in July 1955, when Austria received full independence after a promise of perpetual neutrality.

43. For political reasons, President Charles De Gaulle withdrew France from NATO in 1966 and demanded the withdrawal of all American troops

from French soil by 1 April 1967. At the time, this was a blow to the integrity of the organization and the American containment strategy.

44. See *Big Picture* film "Ready around the World," Local ID 111-TV-717, accessed 10 August 2018, https://www.youtube.com/watch?v=_Ok6ydHLDOs.

45. "Ready around the World."

46. The US and its Western allies established NATO with the signing of a mutually supportive charter by the original twelve member nations in April 1949.

47. See *Big Picture* film "NATO: Partners in Peace," ARC Identifier 2569537/Local ID 111-TV-267.

48. See *Big Picture* film "NATO Maneuvers," ARC Identifier 2569561/Local ID 111-TV-291.

49. Osgood, 110.

50. Ibid.

51. See *Big Picture* film "Why NATO?" ARC Identifier 2569670/Local ID 111-TV-402.

52. See *Big Picture* film "NATO: The Changed Face of Europe," ARC Identifier 2569840/Local ID 111-TV-632.

53. See *Big Picture* film "Salute to the Canadian Army," Local ID 111-TV-414, accessed 25 September 2018, https://www.youtube.com/watch?v=4uf9WJhvanU.

54. Letter from LTC W. A. Milroy, Director of Public Relations, Canadian Army, to MG H. P. Storke, CINFO, 9 December 1958, RG 319-A1 47-20-311.25, General Correspondence, 1958, NARA.

55. See *Big Picture* film "Southeast Asia Treaty Organization (SEATO) Nations," ARC Identifier 2569671/Local ID 111-TV-403.

56. "1,500 U.S. Troops Sent to Bolster Berlin Force: Johnson Says U.S. Pledges Lives for Berlin," *Stars and Stripes* (European), 20 August 1961, 1.

57. See *Big Picture* film "Road to the Wall," ARC Identifier 2569795/Local ID 111-TV-560.

58. "Road to the Wall."

59. "Road to the Wall."

60. See *Big Picture* film "Pentagon Report," ARC Identifier 2569810/Local ID 111-TV-580.

61. "Pentagon Report, 1963."

62. Under tutelage of Khrushchev, East Germany began construction of the Berlin Wall on 13 August 1961. See Mary Fulbrook, *The Divided Nation: A History of Germany, 1918–1990* (Oxford: Oxford University Press, 1992).

63. "Pentagon Report, 1963."

64. See *Big Picture* film "Hidden War in Vietnam," Local ID 111-TV-562, accessed 9 June 2018, https://www.youtube.com/watch?v=_wgUFXsxtyQ.

65. See *Big Picture* film "The Fight for Vietnam," Local ID 111-TV-574, accessed 9 June 2018, https://www.youtube.com/watch?v=_-lzJq5dKao.

66. Controversy surrounded the incident between North Vietnamese gunboats and the US Navy in August 1964. President Lyndon Johnson used it as a reason to step up American military involvement in the region and generated the Gulf of Tonkin Resolution. See Stanley Karnow, *Vietnam: A History* (New York: Penguin, 1997), 387–392.

67. See *Big Picture* film "Action Vietnam," Local ID 111-TV-654, accessed 9 June 2018, https://www.youtube.com/watch?v=cZo4y43WgaQ.

68. David E. James, "Documenting the Vietnam War," in *From Hollywood to Hanoi: The Vietnam War in American Film*, ed. Linda Dittmar and Gene Michaud (New Brunswick, NJ: Rutgers University Press, 1990), 244–245.

69. The reference is to famed director Frank Capra, who used that technique in creating the World War II film series *Why We Fight*. See Claudia Springer, "Military Propaganda: Defense Department Films from World War II and Vietnam," *Cultural Critique*, no. 3 (Spring 1986): 153.

70. "Action Vietnam."

71. *Big Picture* film "The Unique War," Local ID 111-TV-680.

72. Springer, "Military Propaganda," 156.

73. Tony Shaw, *Hollywood's Cold War* (Amherst: University of Massachusetts Press, 2007), 245.

74. See "The Unique War." See *Big Picture* film "The Fight for Vietnam," Local ID 111-TV-574, accessed 9 June 2018, https://www.youtube.com/watch?v=_-lzJq5dKao.

75. Springer, "Military Propaganda," 161.

76. "The Unique War."

77. See *Big Picture* film "Progress to Peace," Local ID 111-TV-792, accessed 10 July 2018, https://www.youtube.com/watch?v=lEhNJB4enRo.

78. "The 1st Infantry Division in Vietnam (1965–1970)," Local ID 111-TV-807, and "Mission in Action," Local ID 111-TV-809.

79. Scott Laderman, "Small Screen Insurgency: Entertainment Television, the Vietnamese Revolution, and the Cold War, 1953–1967," in *American Militarism on the Small Screen*, ed. Anna Froula and Stacy Takacs (New York: Routledge, 2016), 165.

80. Laderman, "Small Screen Insurgency," 175.

81. See Big Picture film "The First Forty Days in Korea," ARC Identifier 2569439/Local ID 111-TV-169.

82. MacDonald, "Cold War as Entertainment," 14.

Chapter 4. *The Big Picture* through an Exceptionalist Lens

1. See *Big Picture* film "America on the Move," ARC Identifier 2569784/Local ID 111-TV-549. The APC released the episode in 1962.

2. "America on the Move."

3. "America on the Move."

4. Winthrop's words came as he first saw the coastline of Massachusetts and proclaimed the importance of the future colony. See Daniel J. Boorstin, *The Americans: The Colonial Experience* (New York: Random House, 1958), 3.

5. See Alexis de Tocqueville, *Democracy in America*, trans. Gerald Bevan (New York: Penguin, 2003), 336.

6. See Hector St. John Crèvecoeur, *Letters from an American Farmer: Letter III—What Is An American*, The Avalon Project, accessed 12 August 2019, https://avalon.law.yale.edu/18th_century/letter_03.asp.

7. See Michael Kackman, *Citizen Spy: Television, Espionage, and Cold War Culture* (Minneapolis: University of Minnesota Press, 2005), xxxii, and Benedict Anderson, *Imagined Communities* (New York: Verso, 2006). While Anderson's focus is primarily print media, Kackman develops an understanding of the effect of film and the visual media in creating a collective identity.

8. "America on the Move."

9. Edward H. Judge and John W. Langdon, *The Cold War: A History through Documents* (Upper Saddle River, NJ: Prentice Hall), 114.

10. Judge and Langdon, *The Cold War*, 114.

11. See *Big Picture* film "Army in Action—Years of Menace," ARC Identifier 2569843/Local ID 111-TV-645. This 1965 episode highlights numerous global threats to the democratic West and neutral nations posed by communist forces led by the Soviets and the Chinese.

12. "America on the Move."

13. "America on the Move."

14. Thomas Palmer, "Why We Fight: A Study of Indoctrination Activities in the Armed Forces" (PhD diss., University of South Carolina, 1971), 182.

15. See Russell O. Fudge, *Why? The Story of Information in the American Army*, part 2, (Carlisle Barracks: Armed Forces Information School, 1949), 2.

16. Palmer, "Why We Fight," 181.

17. Palmer, "Why We Fight," 8.

18. John A. Hannah, "Doctrine for Information and Education," *Army Information Digest* 8, no. 7 (July 1953): 4. Dr. Hannah served as assistant secretary of defense for manpower and personnel (1953–1954). He was also the first chairman of the US Commission on Civil Rights (1957–1969) and the president of Michigan State University (1941–1969).

19. Hannah, "Doctrine for Information and Education," 5.

20. See Kenneth Osgood, *Total Cold War: Eisenhower's Secret Propaganda Battle at Home and Abroad* (Lawrence: University Press of Kansas, 2008), 253.

21. Osgood, *Total Cold War*, 256. This was a recurring theme in both the USIA programs and many *Big Picture* episodes.

22. Osgood, 254.

23. Elaine Tyler May, *Homeward Bound* (New York: Basic Books, 2008), 9.

24. May, *Homeward Bound*, 91.

25. May, 91.

26. This study examines the way that the *Big Picture* addressed integration, diversity, and the emerging role of women in greater detail in chapter 4.

27. See *Big Picture* film "Preamble to Peace," Local ID 111-TV-373, accessed 14 July 2018, https://www.youtube.com/watch?v=gw9RV-gjo.

28. Shirley Horner, "McCarthy's Purge at Fort Is Recalled," *New York Times*, 3 July 1983, NJ2.

29. See *Big Picture* film "Our Heritage," Local ID 111-TV-684, accessed 23 July 2019, https://www.youtube.com/watch?v=JTiup_LNBwo.

30. "Our Heritage."

31. See *Big Picture* film "Pictorial Report No. 26," ARC Identifier 2569622/ Local ID 111-TV-353.

32. "Pictorial Report No. 26."

33. Memo from MG G. S. Meloy, CINFO, to Assistant Secretary of Defense (Manpower, Personnel and Reserve), 31 October 1956, RG 319.4.1-A1 47–15–311.25, General Correspondence, 1956, National Archives at College Park, Maryland (hereafter NARA).

34. See *Big Picture* film "Ottumwa, U.S.A.," ARC Identifier 2569655/Local ID 111-TV-387.

35. "Ottumwa, U.S.A."

36. "Ottumwa, U.S.A."

37. Letter from MG H. P. Storke, CINFO, to Mr. H. S. Byrum, Manager, Ottumwa Chamber of Commerce, 15 January 1958, RG 319.4.1-A1 47–18–311.25, General Correspondence, 1958, NARA.

38. See *Big Picture* film "U.S. Army and the Boy Scouts," ARC Identifier 2569758/Local ID 111-TV-520.

39. "US Army and the Boy Scouts."

40. "US Army and the Boy Scouts."

41. John Daly was a well-known popular radio and television personality on CBS and ABC. The APC used his presence on this *Big Picture* episode because his familiar face could enhance its message by securing a closer connection with the public.

42. Bruce Cumings, *The Korean War: A History* (Modern Library: New York, 2010), 210.

43. Cumings, *The Korean War*, 217.

44. John W. Lemza, *American Military Communities in West Germany: Life in the Cold War Badlands, 1945–1990* (Jefferson, NC: McFarland, 2016), 14.

45. Cumings, *The Korean War*, 219.

46. Cumings, 219.

47. See Elaine Tyler May's description of the importance of the home in American Cold War society and culture in *Homeward Bound*, 13.

48. See Big Picture episodes "Soldier in Europe" (TV-238), "Why NATO?" (TV-402), "Southeast Asia Treaty Organization (SEATO) Nations" (TV-403), "Decade of NATO" (TV-491), and "Partners in Freedom" (TV-617).

49. May, *Homeward Bound*, 13.

50. May, 95.

51. Presidential Executive Order 10013 was the basis for creation of the committee.

52. Jonathan P. Herzog, *The Spiritual-Industrial Complex: America's Religious Battle against Communism in the Early Cold War* (New York: Oxford University Press, 2011), 117.

53. Herzog, *Spiritual-Industrial Complex*, 121. This training became part of the military's effort to rectify perceptions of the moral laxity and lack of resolve that elites believed were plaguing the armed forces during the early years of the Cold War. This is part of the discussion surrounding the *Big Picture* episode "Character Guidance' (TV-429).

54. In July 1956, Eisenhower approved a Joint Resolution of the 84th Congress (P.L. 84–140) that declared the motto must appear on US currency.

55. J. Fred MacDonald, "The Cold War as Entertainment in Fifties Television," *Journal of Popular Film* 7, no. 1 (1978): 24.

56. See *Big Picture* film "Religious Emphasis Day in Philadelphia," ARC Identifier 2569674/Local ID 111-TV-407.

57. Tony Shaw, *Hollywood's Cold War* (Amherst: University of Massachusetts Press, 2007), 113–115.

58. The show first aired on ABC on 12 February 1952, and the last episode appeared on the DuMont network on 8 April 1957.

59. MacDonald, "Cold War as Entertainment," 22. As MacDonald notes, Sheen's telecasts, as well as other contemporary religious programming, set a tone that was largely "political-religious" in their presentation.

60. See Lori Lyn Bogle, *The Pentagon's Battle for the American Mind* (College Station: Texas A&M University Press, 2004), 50.

61. See *Big Picture* film "The Chaplain and the Commander," ARC Identifier 2569768/Local ID 111-TV-532.

62. Bogle, *Pentagon's Battle*, 50.

63. "Religious Emphasis Day in Philadelphia."

64. Broger served in that position from 1958 to 1984.

65. *Militant Liberty* had a number of advocates in Congress. Among them were Senators Thomas E. Martin (R-IA) and Strom Thurmond (R-SC). Each provided remarks to the *Congressional Record* and participated in hearings regarding its usefulness. See "*Militant Liberty*: Antidote for Communism," *Congressional Record*, 5 January 1956, A25, and U.S. Congress, Senate, Committee on Armed Services, *Military Cold War Education and Speech Review Policies*, 87th Cong., 2d sess. 1962, Part 3, 1035.

66. Osgood, *Total Cold War*, 317, and Lori Bogle's description of the program in *The Pentagon's Battle for the American Mind*, 127.

67. Osgood, *Total Cold War*, 317.

68. See *Big Picture* film "You in Japan," Local ID 111-TV-354, accessed 1 August 2019, https://www.youtube.com/watch?v=4V-T0FrC7zo.

69. From text of speech by Joseph McCarthy at Wheeling, West Virginia, 9 February 1950. See History Matters, GMU, accessed 25 July 2019, http://historymatters.gmu.edu/d/6456/. For a full understanding of Christian anticommunist initiatives and the link with McCarthyism, see also John E. Haynes, *Red Scare or Red Menace? American Communism and Anticommunism in the Cold War Era* (Chicago: Ivan R. Dee, 1996).

70. For a fuller description of the Freedom Foundation's principles and their strong links with President Eisenhower see Bogle, *Pentagon's Battle*, 77–80.

71. In 1967, the Freedoms Foundation presented Broger with their Madison Award in recognition of his efforts as the director of AFI&E to spread the exceptionalist ideals of America.

72. Freedoms Foundation is a nonprofit organization that received grants

from a number of conservative organizations, including Civitan International, during the 1940s and 1950s.

73. That link continued even as successive military leaders retired then went to work on the staff of the foundation. These included Maj. Gen. Harlan N. Hartness, former director of the Armed Forces Information and Education Program; Adm. Felix Stump, former commander of US naval forces in the Pacific; and Admiral Radford. See "Retired General Joins Freedoms Foundation," *New York Times*, 12 February 1956, 85, and "Freedoms Foundation Names Admiral as Aide," *New York Times*, 14 October 1958, 6.

74. See *Big Picture* film "People to People," ARC Identifier 2569695/Local ID 111-TV-430.

75. See *Big Picture* film "The USAREUR Story (Part II)," ARC Identifier 2569777/Local ID 111-TV-542. USAREUR is the acronym for United States Army Europe.

76. CONUS was the military acronym for Continental United States. See *Big Picture* film "Of Soldiers and Altars" (TV-690), US Army Chaplaincy, Office of the Chief of Information, Army Pictorial Center, accessed 19 July 2018, https://www.youtube.com/watch?v=Ez9pwoPMTvg.

77. "Of Soldiers and Altars."

78. See *Big Picture* film "Soldiers' Heritage," ARC Identifier 2569679/Local ID 111-TV-412.

79. "Soldiers' Heritage." "Manifest Destiny" was a popular cultural belief that evolved in the United States during the early 1800s to explain the nation's expansion as a God-given right. Historians often fold it into an understanding of American exceptionalism as a characteristic that sets the United States apart from other nations.

80. Tomb of the Unknowns, or the Tomb of the Unknown Soldier, is located in Arlington National Cemetery in Arlington, Virginia. Opened in 1921, it remains a popular historic tourist attraction.

81. "The *Big Picture* Fades from TV Screen," *Stars and Stripes* (Pacific Edition), 16 July 1971, 3.

82. See *Big Picture* film "The Common Defense," ARC Identifier 2569697/Local ID 111-TV-433.

83. See *Big Picture* film "To Keep and Bear Arms," ARC Identifier 2569792/Local ID 111-TV-557.

84. "To Keep and Bear Arms."

85. "To Keep and Bear Arms."

86. "Report of the National Rifle Association," 114 Cong. Rec. 16506–16507 (1968).

87. See "To Keep and Bear Arms."

88. See "Senator Robert F. Kennedy in Memoriam," 114 Cong. Rec. 16497–16504 (1968). Gaining political momentum after the assassinations of Martin Luther King Jr. and Robert Kennedy, the Gun Control Act of 1968 passed. It limited the mail order purchase of weapons.

Chapter 5. A Big Picture of the Army Way of Life

1. John Labella (former Army officer and 1976 West Point graduate), correspondence with the author, 11 September 2018.

2. Memo to the Secretary of the Army from MG H. P. Storke, CINFO, 14 November 1958, RG 319.4.1-A1 47–18–311.25, General Correspondence, 1958, National Archives at College Park, Maryland (hereafter NARA).

3. Letter to MG H. P. Storke, CINFO from Leslie R. Groves, VP Sperry Rand Corporation, 1 December 1959, RG 319.4.1-A1 47–18–311.25, General Correspondence, 1958, NARA. During World War II, Lt.Gen. Leslie R. Groves supervised the project to construct the Pentagon and oversaw the development of the Manhattan Project.

4. Memorandum for Record, COL S. K. Eaton, Executive, to MG Storke, CINFO, 3 December 1958, RG 319.4.1-A1 47–18–311.25, General Correspondence, 1958, NARA.

5. Memo from MG H. P. Storke, CINFO, to the GEN Maxwell D. Taylor, Army Chief of Staff, 21 May 1959, RG 319.4.1-A1 47–20–311.25, General Correspondence, 1959, NARA.

6. See *Big Picture* film "Famous Generals—Pershing," Local ID 111-TV-588, accessed 26 July 2018, https://www.youtube.com/watch?v=MJjzSZaAjuk.

7. Aaron Blake, "The Long Decline of Veterans in Congress—in 4 Charts," *Washington Post*, 11 November 2013, https://www.washingtonpost.com/news/the-fix/wp/2013/11/11/the-long-decline-of-veterans-in-congress-in-4-charts/?noredirect=on&utm_term=.14b39b8e4d0a .

8. Blake, "The Long Decline of Veterans in Congress."

9. The fact that the episodes "Hawaiian Defense" (TV-237, 1953) and "Soldier in Hawaii" (TV-352, 1956) did air earlier may have influenced that decision.

10. See *Big Picture* film "The Citizen Soldier," ARC Identifier 2569454/Local ID 111-TV-184.

11. See *Big Picture* film "Information and Education Overseas (Part I), Dependent Schools (Part II)" ARC Identifier 2569468/Local ID 111-TV-198.

12. "Information and Education Overseas."

13. See *Big Picture* film "All the Word to All the Troops," Local ID III-TV-810, accessed 30 July 2018, https://www.youtube.com/watch?v=fZFuExqY-ICU. "The Story of American Forces Network" (TV-583) describes the genesis of the military's extensive communications system, established by Generals Eisenhower and Marshall in July 1943, and of its lowly birth in a wartime London basement.

14. See "Information and Education Overseas (Part I), Dependent Schools (Part II)."

15. See "Information and Education Overseas (Part I), Dependent Schools (Part II)." Access to education was central to how Americans viewed themselves as an exceptional people. Overseas schools for service members' families quickly evolved into the extensive network known as Department of Defense Dependent Schools system (DoDDS), with facilities in most of the nations where the US armed forces had troops. During the height of the Cold War this included West Germany, Japan, and South Korea.

16. See *Big Picture* film "Education in the Army," ARC Identifier 2569549/Local ID III-TV-279.

17. "Education in the Army."

18. There was great depth to the types of skills training offered. For example, episodes such as "Pictorial Report No. 4" (TV-240) and "Pictorial Report No. 17" (TV-322) provided insights into training for radio operators, flame-thrower operators, chemical warfare specialists, mechanics, and stevedores.

19. See *Big Picture* film "Education in the Army," ARC Identifier 2569470/Local ID III-TV-200.

20. "Education in the Army."

21. See *Big Picture* film "Graduate: Reserve Officers' Training Corps," ARC Identifier 2569659/Local ID III-TV-391.

22. "Graduate: Reserve Officers' Training Corps."

23. See *Big Picture* film "R.O.T.C.—A Pattern for Progress" ARC Identifier 2569824/Local ID III-TV-609.

24. See *Big Picture* film "Duty, Honor, Country," ARC Identifier 2569456/Local ID III-TV-186.

25. See *Big Picture* film "West Point—Education for Leadership," Local ID III-TV-515, accessed 31 July 2018, https://www.youtube.com/watch?v=asDSATnrr10.

26. See *Big Picture* film "The OCS Story," Local ID III-TV-715, accessed 31 July 2018, https://www.youtube.com/watch?v=N-yMmm8rjKM.

27. Department of Defense, Directorate for Information Operations and

Reports, *Selected Manpower Statistics, FY 1997* (Washington, DC: Washington Headquarters Services, 1997), 68–69.

28. Department of Defense, *Selected Manpower Statistics*, 60.

29. Department of Defense, 71.

30. Department of Defense, 71.

31. See *Big Picture* film "Young American Leaders," Local ID 111-TV-804, accessed 31 July 2018, https://www.youtube.com/watch?v=J9U7aBHpT18.

32. "Young American Leaders."

33. "Young American Leaders."

34. Morris J. MacGregor Jr., *Integration of the Armed Forces, 1940–1965*, Defense Studies Series, Center of Military History, 395, last updated 12 December 2019, https://history.army.mil/html/books/050/50–1-1/index.html, 522.

35. MacGregor, *Integration of the Armed Forces*, 522.

36. MacGregor, 522

37. MacGregor, 522.

38. See "Rolling to the Rhine," U.S. War Department, accessed 2 August 2018, https://www.youtube.com/watch?v=IkphoTLLmqg, a history of the Red Ball Express during World War II. The majority of the vehicle drivers were African American.

39. During the war the unit received eight presidential citations, and its soldiers received 9,486 Purple Hearts, 52 Distinguished Service Crosses, and 21 Medals of Honor.

40. See "U.S. Sixth Corps," Local ID 111-TV-219 at 6:05.

41. See *Big Picture* film "The History of Cavalry," ARC Identifier 2569650/ Local ID 111-TV-382.

42. See *Big Picture* film "OCS Fort Sill," ARC Identifier 2569759/Local ID 111-TV-521.

43. "OCS Fort Sill."

44. See Tony Shaw, *Hollywood's Cold War* (Amherst: University of Massachusetts Press, 2007), 179–181, for how the race issue precipitated a reaction from Hollywood. See also Mary L. Dudziak, *Cold War Civil Rights: Race and the Image of American Democracy* (Princeton, NJ: Princeton University Press, 2000), for a more comprehensive understanding of how America's racial problems cast a negative image abroad.

45. Primetime television shows such as *I Spy* (1965) and *Julia* (1968) dealt with issues that included a racially integrated team of undercover operatives and a single black professional mother.

46. Information about the Baumholder incident comes only from local police reports and personal interviews. According to findings there were hun-

dreds of soldiers involved. There is an absence of information regarding the riot in the *Stars and Stripes*, and US military officials issued no statements. Information about the Berlin incident is in "Army Doing Its Best to Bridge Racial Gap," *Stars and Stripes*, 9 September 1970, 4.

47. See Bettie J. Morden, *The Women's Army Corps, 1945–1978* (Washington, DC: Center of Military History, US Army, Washington, DC, 2000), chapter 2, 41.

48. See *United States Census of Population 1960: Americans Overseas*, vol. 3: *Selected Area Reports* (Washington, DC: U.S. Government Printing Office, 1964), Table B.

49. See "Demographics of the US Military," Council on Foreign Relations, last updated 13 July 2020, https://www.cfr.org/article/demographics-us-military.

50. See "The Role of Nursing in the Military," Carrington College, accessed 3 August 2018, https://carrington.edu/wp-content/uploads/2011/11/role-of-nursinging-military.jpg. During the Korean War 500 nurses served in combat zones, and during the Vietnam conflict over 7,000 served in that theater.

51. See *Big Picture* film "The WAC Is a Soldier, Too," ARC Identifier 2569547/Local ID 111-TV-277.

52. "The WAC Is a Soldier Too."

53. See *Big Picture* film "The Feminine Touch," Local ID 111-TV-780, accessed 14 August 2018, https://www.youtube.com/watch?v=th43sM7P2Fc.

54. "The Feminine Touch."

55. The Army contracted the Battelle Institute, a private nonprofit research and development company, to conduct the study. Its short title was the *Army 75 Study*. United States Department of the Army, Office of the Deputy Chief of Staff for Personnel, Directorate of Personnel Studies and Research, *The Army 75 Personnel Concept Study* (Washington, DC: Office of Deputy Chief of Staff for Personnel, 1969).

56. Beth Bailey, *America's Army: Making the All-Volunteer Force* (Cambridge, MA: Harvard University Press, 2009), 141.

57. Bailey, *America's Army*, 141.

58. Bailey, 154.

59. Bailey, 155.

60. Bailey, 136.

61. It is important to note that the word "Too" in the title "The WAC Is a Soldier Too" implies a male soldier. At the time, men were the presumed universal referent.

62. See *Big Picture* film "Nurses in the Army," ARC Identifier 2569560/Local ID 111-TV-290.

63. In some regards this did appear as timely in the wake of President Kennedy's creation of the Commission on the Status of Women in 1961, together with the approval of the birth control pill, Helen Gurley Brown's publication of *Sex and the Single Girl* in 1962, and Betty Friedan's publication of *The Feminine Mystique* in 1963. See Ruth Rosen, *The World Split Open: How the Modern Women's Movement Changed America* (New York: Penguin Books), 2006.

64. See *Big Picture* film "The Army Nurse," Local ID 111-TV-783, accessed 4 August 2018, https://www.youtube.com/watch?v=H14LqfMFCYI.

65. Sam Lebovic, "'A Breath from Home': Soldier Entertainment and the Nationalist Politics of Pop Culture during World War II," *Journal of Social History* 47, no. 2 (2013): 264.

66. Lebovic, "'A Breath from Home,'" 264.

67. Lebovic, 263.

68. "U.S.O. in the Cold War," *New York Times*, 15 November 1960, 78.

69. "U.S.O. in the Cold War."

70. "U.S.O. in the Cold War."

71. See *Big Picture* film "United Service Organization (USO): Wherever They Go," ARC Identifier 2569724/Local ID 111-TV-467.

72. See *Big Picture* film "USO Wherever They Go," Local ID 111-TV-697, accessed 6 August 2018, https://www.youtube.com/watch?v=XUXA5oAe-eXw.

73. "USO Wherever They Go."

74. "USO Wherever They Go."

75. See *Big Picture* film "Soldiers in Greasepaint," Local ID 111-TV-611, accessed 15 August 2018, https://www.youtube.com/watch?v=Pbw3oUSohhI. Celeste Holm was a popular contemporary Academy Award–winning actress of stage, screen, and television.

76. "Soldiers in Greasepaint."

77. "Soldiers in Greasepaint."

78. James Paashe, "Citizen Bob: Hope's Transmedia Patriotism," paper presented at the Society for Cinema and Media Studies Conference, Atlanta, GA, April 2016, 2.

79. Paashe, "Citizen Bob," 6.

80. Meredith Lair, *Armed with Abundance: Consumerism and Soldiering in the Vietnam War* (Chapel Hill: University of North Carolina Press, 2011), xiii.

Lair's book offers a more comprehensive discussion of the dichotomy that existed for the military in Vietnam, fighting a war and maintaining morale.

81. Bob Hope appeared in seven separate *Big Picture* episodes, more than any other individual.

82. See *Big Picture* film "Army Talent Show," Local ID III-TV-315, accessed 6 August 2018, https://www.youtube.com/watch?v=rWjMZm8AeLk&index=51&list=PL8914666A000F8459.

83. Berry enjoyed a long career as a television sitcom actor and stage performer from the mid-1950s to the early 2000s, appearing in shows such as *F Troop* and *Mayberry, RFD*. Berry also served in the Army Special Services together with Sergeant Leonard Nimoy.

84. See Dwight D. Eisenhower, "Executive Order 10673—Fitness of American Youth, July 16, 1956," *The American Presidency Project*, accessed 8 August 2018, http://www.presidency.ucsb.edu/ws/?pid=106373.

85. See "The Federal Government Takes on Physical Fitness," John F. Kennedy Presidential Library and Museum, accessed 8 August 2018, https://www.jfklibrary.org/JFK/JFK-in-History/Physical-Fitness.aspx.

86. See *Big Picture* film "Sports for All," ARC Identifier 25699518/Local ID III-TV-248.

87. See *Big Picture* film "Helsinki Olympics," ARC Identifier 2569520/Local ID III-TV-250.

88. See *Big Picture* film "Shape of the Nation," ARC Identifier 25699812/Local ID III-TV-582.

89. "Shape of the Nation." Bob Hope's reputation was legend. As Uldis Kruze notes, "By the early 1970s, Hope's popularity was so high that he was ranked third after Jesus as the most admired person in America." See Kruze, "Comedy on the Front Lines of the Cold War: Bob Hope's Christmas Specials during the Vietnam War," in *The Cold War and Entertainment Television*, ed. Lori Maguire (Newcastle, UK: Cambridge Scholars, 2016), 231.

90. "Shape of the Nation."

91. See *Big Picture* film "The Army's All-Americans," ARC Identifier 25699802/Local ID III-TV-568.

92. See *Big Picture* film "Operation Scoreboard," Local ID III-TV-656, accessed 6 August 2018, https://www.youtube.com/watch?v=RJ_nMDpG_C4.

93. On March 4, 1968, Johnson issued Executive Order 11398. See Lyndon B. Johnson, Executive Order 11398—Establishing the President's Council on Physical Fitness and Sports, The American Presidency Project, 04 March 1968, http://www.presidency.ucsb.edu/ws/index.php?pid=106174.

94. See *Big Picture* film "The Army's Civilians," Local ID III-TV-726, accessed 8 August 2018, https://www.youtube.com/watch?v=wi8KnmVz14o.

95. William Gardner, ch. 4: Personnel, "Civilian Personnel," *Department of the Army Historical Summary (DAHSUM) for the Fiscal Year 1969* (Washington, DC: Office of the Chief of Military History, Department of the Army, 1969), 47 [hereafter *DAHSUM, FY 1969*. The DAHSUM series is available through the U.S. Army Center for Military History.

96. Gardner, "Civilian Personnel," 48.

97. See *Big Picture* film "The Army's Civilians."

98. *DAHSUM*, FY 1969, 50.

99. See *Big Picture* film "Tools for a Modern Army," ARC Identifier 25699478/Local ID III-TV-208.

100. "Tools for a Modern Army."

101. See *Big Picture* film "Science Moves the Army," ARC Identifier 2569856/Local ID III-TV-668.

102. "Science Moves the Army."

103. As the Cold War continued to unfold through the 1970s and 1980s, the military-industrial complex continued to grow until that collaboration developed its own power base, overshadowing President Eisenhower's warning about that possibility in January 1961. His concerns also included the potential of Cold War profiteering. See Evan Thomas, *Ike's Bluff: President Eisenhower's Secret Battle to Save the World*. New York: Back Bay Books, 2012, 281.

104. See *Big Picture* film "Foreign Nationals," Local ID III-TV-314, accessed 8 August 2018, https://www.youtube.com/watch?v=1Kb3sEC5yz0.

105. An example of one such labor agreement is at the 1959 NATO SOFA Supplementary Agreement that outlined the conditions and guidelines of local national (LN) employment, not the hiring quotas that were the responsibility of local area military commanders, Article 56, *Labor*, of the "Agreement to Supplement the Agreement between the Parties to the North Atlantic Treaty Regarding the Status of Their Forces with Respect to Foreign Forces Stationed in the Federal Republic of Germany," 3 August 1959. See "NATO SOFA Supplementary Agreement," accessed 3 February 2021, https://www.pref.okinawa.jp/site/chijiko/kichitai/sofa/documents/germany02-2.pdf.

106. See *Big Picture* film "The Army's Civilians," Local ID III-TV-726, accessed 10 July 2018, https://www.youtube.com/watch?v=wi8KnmVz14o.

107. See *Big Picture* film "Your Military Neighbor," Local ID III-TV-675, accessed 18 August 2018, https://www.youtube.com/watch?v=MloNbS1kjtw.

108. See *Big Picture* film "Alexandria: City of Understanding," ARC Iden-

tifier 2569643/Local ID III-TV-375. Alexandria, Virginia, is located just outside the District of Columbia. It is home to many military personnel assigned to one of the nearby military facilities that include the Pentagon, Fort Myer, and Fort Belvoir.

109. "Alexandria—City of Understanding."

110. "Alexandria—City of Understanding."

111. See *Big Picture* film "Citizen Soldier—Community Leader," Local ID III-TV-816, accessed 18 August 2018, https://www.youtube.com/watch?v=D 7mAyjizARo.

112. See *Big Picture* film "The Army's Other Role," Local ID III-TV-812, accessed 18 August 2018, https://www.youtube.com/watch?v=IqAFDrZ_Bis.

113. "The Army's Other Role."

114. "Citizen Soldier—Community Leader."

115. For a fuller understanding of the emergence of the all-volunteer force see Thomas W. Evans, "The All-Volunteer Army after Twenty Years, Recruiting in the Modern Era," *Army History* PB-20–93–4, no. 27 (Summer 1993): 40–46.

116. See *Big Picture* film "Your Military Neighbor," Local ID III-TV-675, accessed 18 August 2018, https://www.youtube.com/watch?v=MloNbS1kjtw.

117. See *Big Picture* film "Boys Town, U.S.A.," ARC Identifier 2569615/ Local ID III-TV-346.

118. Letter from William T. Ellington, Acting Chief, R-T Branch, APC, to Mr. E. C. Gardner, Dean-Registrar, Freed-Hardeman College, Henderson, Tennessee, 10 July 1957, RG 319.4.1-A1 47–18–311.25, General Correspondence, 1957, NARA.

119. Letter Ellington to Gardner.

120. See *Big Picture* film "Army Digest No. 3," Local ID III-TV-479, accessed 1 March 2019, https://www.youtube.com/watch?v=cPHrQ_CKoZw.

121. "Army Digest No. 3."

Conclusion

1. See "Li'l Tigers Star in 'Stripes' Story on U.S. TV," *Stars and Stripes* (Pacific Edition), 19 March 1960, 23.

2. See "Army's Famed Series Signs Off, 'The Big Picture' Fades from TV Screen," *Stars and Stripes* (Pacific Edition), 15 July 1971, 3.

3. "Army's Famed Series Signs Off."

4. See *Big Picture* film "U.S. Army and the Boy Scouts," ARC Identifier 2569758/Local ID III-TV-520.

5. See *Big Picture* film "The History of Cavalry," ARC Identifier 2569650/ Local ID 111-TV-382.

6. See *Big Picture* film "Hidden War in Vietnam," Local ID 111-TV-562, accessed 10 July 2018, https://www.youtube.com/watch?v=_wgUFXsxtyQ.

7. As this study discussed earlier, it is also important to note that collections and archives have notable absences of episodes, which at times offers a challenge to a deeper evaluation of the film series.

8. Kenneth D. Alford (military historian and author), conversation with author, Midlothian, VA, July 2018.

9. "The Big Picture Fades from TV Screen," *Stars and Stripes* (Pacific Edition), 16 July 1971, 3.

10. See *Big Picture* film "Third Division in Korea," Local ID 111-TV-302, accessed 10 May 2018, https://www.youtube.com/watch?v=gjpomvdLEaM. This closing was typical of those used at the conclusion of each episode by the narrators associated with the show. In this case, M.Sgt. Stuart Queen made the comment.

11. "Deadline on Film Site Nears," *New York Times*, 19 December 1971, A19. Following this, the Department of Defense concentrated all audiovisual operations at Norton Air Force Base in San Bernardino, California.

Bibliography

Allen, Craig. *Eisenhower and the Mass Media: Peace, Prosperity, and Prime-Time TV*. Chapel Hill: University of North Carolina Press, 1993.

Anderson, Benedict. *Imagined Communities*. New York: Verso, 2006.

"Army to Issue Video Series of Combat Pix." *Billboard*, 15 December 1951.

Bacevich, A. J. *The Pentomic Era: The U.S. Army between Korea and Vietnam*. Washington, DC: National Defense University Press, 1986.

Bailey, Beth. *America's Army: Making the All-Volunteer Force*. Cambridge, MA: Harvard University Press, 2009.

Bernhard, Nancy. *U.S. Television News and Cold War Propaganda, 1947–1960*. Cambridge: Cambridge University Press, 2003.

Bluem, A. William. *Documentary in American Television: Form, Function, Method*. New York: Hastings House, 1972.

Boddy, William. *Fifties Television: The Industry and Its Critics*. Urbana: University of Illinois Press, 1990.

Bogle, Lori Lyn. *The Pentagon's Battle for the American Mind*. College Station: Texas A&M University Press, 2004.

Boorstin, Daniel J. *The Americans: The Colonial Experience*. New York: Random House, 1958.

"BP's Coming Season to Offer Public Look at the 'Modern Army.'" *In Focus* 4, no. 8 (September 1959).

Carter, Donald A. *The U.S. Army before Vietnam: 1953–1965*. Washington, DC: Center of Military History, US Army, 2015.

Caster, Paul. "Behind the Scenes in Army Film Making." *Army Digest* 22, no. 6 (June 1967): 41–45.

Cohen, Lizabeth. *A Consumer's Republic: The Politics of Mass Consumption in Postwar America*. New York: Vintage Books, 2003.

Crean, Jeffrey. "Something to Compete with 'Gunsmoke': 'The Big Picture' Television Series and Selling a 'Modern, Progressive and Forward Thinking' Army to Cold War America." *War & Society* 35, no. 3 (August 2016): 204–218.

Cumings, Bruce. *The Korean War: A History*. New York: Modern Library, 2010.

Doherty, Thomas. *Cold War, Cool Medium: Television, McCarthyism, and American Culture*. Rev. ed. New York: Columbia University Press, 2005.

———. *Projections of War: Hollywood, American Culture, and World War II*. Rev. ed. New York: Columbia University Press, 1999.

Dudziak, Mary L. *Cold War Civil Rights: Race and the Image of American Democracy*. Princeton, NJ: Princeton University Press, 2000.

"Early Press Clippings on Army Movie Makers Reviewed." *In Focus* 7, no. 2 (March 1962): 2.

Edgerton, Gary R. *The Columbia History of American Television*. New York: Columbia University Press, 2007.

Edwards, Paul M. *A Guide to Films on the Korean War*. Westport, CT: Greenwood Press, 1997.

———. *To Acknowledge a War: The Korean War in American Memory*. Westport, CT: Greenwood Press, 2000.

Evans, Thomas W. "The All-Volunteer Army after Twenty Years: Recruiting in the Modern Era." *Army History* PB-20–93–4, no. 27 (Summer 1993): 40–46.

Farago, Ladislas. *The Game of the Foxes: The Untold Story of German Espionage in the United States and Great Britain during World War II*. New York: David McKay, 1971.

Field, Douglas, ed. *American Cold War Culture*. Edinburgh: Edinburgh University Press, 2005.

Field, Stanley. "The Big Picture." *Journal of Broadcasting* 125 (1962): 125–127.

Froula, Anna, and Stacy Takacs, eds. *American Militarism on the Small Screen*. New York: Routledge, 2016.

Fudge, Russell O. *Why? The Story of Information in the American Army*. Part II. Carlisle Barracks: Armed Forces Information School, 1949.

Fulbright, J. William. *The Pentagon Propaganda Machine*. New York: Liveright, 1970.

Fulbrook, Mary. *The Divided Nation: A History of Germany, 1918–1990*. Oxford: Oxford University Press, 1992.

Gardner, Paul B. "The Increasing Gap between Words and Deeds: Teaching Public Affairs at the Colleges of the Army from Academic Year 1947 through Academic Year 1989." PhD diss., Kansas State University, 2014, https://krex.k-state.edu/dspace/bitstream/handle/2097/17550/Paul Gardner2014.pdf?sequence=1.

Gardner, William. Ch. 4: "Personnel." In *Department of the Army Historical*

Summary (DAHSUM) for the Fiscal Year 1969. Washington, DC: Office of the Chief of Military History, Department of the Army, 1969.

Halberstam, David. *The Fifties*. Reprint. New York: Ballantine Books, 1994.

Hamilton, Kevin, and Ned O'Gorman. *Lookout America! The Secret Hollywood Studio at the Heart of the Cold War*. Hanover, NH: Dartmouth College Press, 2019.

Hannah, John A. "Doctrine for Information and Education." *Army Information Digest* 8, no. 7 (July 1953): 3–7.

Haynes, John E. *Red Scare or Red Menace? American Communism and Anticommunism in the Cold War Era*. Chicago: Ivan R. Dee, 1996.

Hermes, Walter G. "The Army and the New Look." In *American Military History*, edited by Maurice Matloff. Washington, DC: Center of Military History, 1989.

Herzog, Jonathan P. *The Spiritual-Industrial Complex: America's Religious Battle against Communism in the Early Cold War*. New York: Oxford University Press, 2011.

Hixson, Walter L. *Parting the Curtain: Propaganda, Culture, and the Cold War, 1945–1961*. New York: St. Martin's Press, 1997.

James, David E. "Documenting the Vietnam War." In *From Hollywood to Hanoi: The Vietnam War in American Film*, edited by Linda Dittmar and Gene Michaud, 239–254. New Brunswick, NJ: Rutgers University Press, 1990.

Judge, Edward H., and John W. Langdon. *The Cold War: A History through Documents*. Upper Saddle River, NJ: Prentice Hall, 1999.

Kackman, Michael. *Citizen Spy: Television, Espionage, and Cold War Culture*. Minneapolis: University of Minnesota Press, 2005.

Kahana, Jonathan. *Intelligence Work: The Politics of American Documentary*. New York: Columbia University Press, 2008.

Karnow, Stanley. *Vietnam: A History*. New York: Penguin, 1997.

Kennan, George F. *George F. Kennan: Memoirs, 1925–1950*. New York: Pantheon Books, 1967.

Kinney, D. J. "Selling Greenland: The Big Picture Television Series and the Army's Bid for Relevance during the Early Cold War." *Centaurus* 55 (2013): 344–357.

Koszarski, Richard. "Subway Commandos: Hollywood Filmmakers at the Signal Corps Photographic Center." *Film History* 14, no. 3–4 (2002): 296–315.

Kruze, Uldis. "Comedy on the Front Lines of the Cold War: Bob Hope's Christmas Specials during the Vietnam War." In *The Cold War and Entertainment Television*, edited by Lori Maguire, 231–246. Newcastle, UK: Cambridge Scholars, 2016.

Laderman, Scott. "Small Screen Insurgency: Entertainment Television, the Vietnamese Revolution, and the Cold War, 1953–1967." In *American Militarism on the Small Screen*, edited by Anna Froula and Stacy Takacs, 162–177. New York: Routledge, 2016.

Lair, Meredith. *Armed with Abundance: Consumerism and Soldiering in the Vietnam War*. Chapel Hill: University of North Carolina Press, 2011.

Laurents, Arthur. *Original Story By: A Memoir of Broadway and Hollywood*. New York: Alfred A. Knopf, 2000.

Lebovic, Sam. "'A Breath from Home': Solider Entertainment and the Nationalist Politics of Pop Culture during World War II." *Journal of Social History* 47, no. 2 (2013): 263–296.

Lemza, John W. *American Military Communities in West Germany: Life in the Cold War Badlands, 1945–1990*. Jefferson, NC: McFarland, 2016.

Linn, Brian McAllister. *Elvis's Army: Cold War GIs and the Atomic Battlefield*. Cambridge, MA: Harvard University Press, 2016.

Lipset, Seymour M. *American Exceptionalism: A Double-Edged Sword*. New York: Norton, 1996.

MacDonald, J. Fred. "The Cold War as Entertainment in Fifties Television." *Journal of Popular Film* 7, no. 1 (1978): 3–31.

———. *Television and the Red Menace: The Video Road to Vietnam*. Los Angeles: Praeger, 1985.

MacGregor, Morris J. Jr. *Integration of the Armed Forces, 1940–1965*. Defense Studies Series. Center of Military History. Last updated 12 December 2019, https://history.army.mil/html/books/050/50-1-1/index.html.

Maguire, Lori, ed. *The Cold War and Entertainment Television*. Newcastle, UK: Cambridge Scholars, 2016.

Marling, Karal Ann. *As Seen on TV: The Visual Culture of Everyday Life in the 1950s*. Cambridge, MA: Harvard University Press, 1994.

May, Elaine Tyler. *Homeward Bound*. New York: Basic Books, 2008.

McCarthy, Anna. *The Citizen Machine: Governing by Television in 1950s America*. 1st ed. New York: New Press, 2010.

McGregor, Morris J., Jr. *Defense Studies Series: Integration of the Armed Forces, 1940–1965*. Washington, DC: Center of Military History, US Army, 2001.

McMahon, Robert J. *The Cold War: A Very Short Introduction*. New York: Oxford University Press, 2003.

McNeil, Alex. *Total Television*. Rev. ed. New York: Penguin Books, 1996.

"Medals for Mettle." *In Focus* 5, no. 2 (March 1960).

Mickelson, Sig. *The Decade That Shaped Television News: CBS in the 1950s*. Westport, CT: Praeger, 1998.

Morden, Bettie J. *The Women's Army Corps, 1945–1978.* Washington, DC: Center of Military History, US Army, 2000.

Mundey, Lisa M. *American Militarism and Anti-Militarism in Popular Media, 1945–1970.* Jefferson, NC: McFarland, 2012.

Nadel, Alan. "Cold War Television and the Technology of Brainwashing." In *American Cold War Culture,* edited by Douglas Field, 146. Edinburgh: Edinburgh University Press, 2005.

Nye, Joseph S. *Soft Power: The Means to Success in World Politics.* New York: Public Affairs, 2004.

O'Connor, John, ed. *American History-American Television: Interpreting the Video Past.* New York: Unger, 1983.

Osgood, Kenneth. *Total Cold War: Eisenhower's Secret Propaganda Battle at Home and Abroad.* Lawrence: University Press of Kansas, 2008.

Paashe, James. "Citizen Bob: Hope's Transmedia Patriotism." Paper presented at the Society for Cinema and Media Studies Conference, Atlanta, GA, April 2016.

Palmer, Thomas. "Why We Fight: A Study of Indoctrination Activities in the Armed Forces." PhD diss., University of South Carolina, 1971.

Pyle, Ernie. *Here is Your War: The Story of GI Joe.* New York: World Publishing, 1945.

Raines, Rebecca Robbins. *Army Historical Series: Getting the Message Through.* Washington, DC: Center of Military History, US Army, 1996.

Rollins, Peter C. "The Vietnam War: Perceptions through Literature, Film, and Television." *American Quarterly* 36, no. 3 (1984): 419–432.

Rosen, Ruth. *The World Split Open: How the Modern Women's Movement Changed America.* New York: Penguin Books, 2006.

Shaw, Tony. *Hollywood's Cold War.* Amherst: University of Massachusetts Press, 2007.

Springer, Claudia. "Military Propaganda: Defense Department Films from World War II and Vietnam." *Cultural Critique,* no. 3 (Spring 1986): 151–167.

Sterling, Christopher H., and John M. Kittross. *Stay Tuned: A History of American Broadcasting.* Mahwah, NJ: Lawrence Erlbaum, 2002.

St. John de Crèvecoeur, J. Hector. *Letters from an American Farmer: Letter III—What Is An American.* The Avalon Project. Accessed 12 August 2019, https://avalon.law.yale.edu/18th_century/letter_03.asp.

Suid, Lawrence H. *Guts and Glory: The Making of the American Military Image in Film.* Lexington: University Press of Kentucky, 2002.

Suid, Lawrence H., and Dolores A. Haverstick. *Stars and Stripes on Screen.* Lanham, MD: Scarecrow Press, 2005.

Thomas, Evan. *Ike's Bluff: President Eisenhower's Secret Battle to Save the World*. New York: Back Bay Books, 2012.

Thompson, George Raynor, Dixie R. Harris, Pauline M. Oakes, and Dulany Terrett. *The Signal Corps: The Test: December 1941—July 1943*. Washington, DC: Center of Military History, US Army, 2003.

Tocqueville, Alexis de. *Democracy in America*. Translated by Gerald Bevan. New York: Penguin Books, 2003.

US Department of the Army. *Audio-Visual Support Center Operations*. Field Manual 11–41. Washington, DC: US GPO, 28 November 1966.

Whitfield, Stephen J. *The Culture of the Cold War*. Baltimore, MD: Johns Hopkins University Press, 1996.

Wilson, John B. *Maneuver and Firepower: The Evolution of Divisions and Separate Brigades*. Army Lineage Series. Washington, DC: Center of Military History, US Army, 1998.

Index

The initials "TBP" refer to The Big Picture.

10th Cavalry Regiment, 163
100th Infantry Battalion, 164
102nd Armored Cavalry Regiment, 188
353rd Military Police Company, 187
442nd Infantry Regiment, 164, 193, 246n39

ABC, 23, 31, 60, 222n30
Academy of Television Arts and Sciences, 223n55
Adventure Tomorrow, 31
AFI&E (Armed Forces Information and Education Program), 114, 128, 141
AFKN (American Forces Korea Network), 69
AFN (Armed Forces Network), 3
AFN-TV (Armed Forces Network Television), 68–69
African Americans, 130–131, 163, 166. *See also* diversity in the army
AFRTS (Armed Forces Radio and Television), 142, 156, 166, 190
AFV-TV (American Forces Vietnam Television), 69–70
AI&E (Information and Education Program), 3, 4, 10
Air Power, 33, 55, 72
Alcoa Premiere, 121
Alexandria, Virginia, 184–185, 250–251n108
Alford, Kenneth D., 196
AMC (Army Materiel Command, US), 81, 182

American exceptionalism, 10–11, 17, 218n10
   addressing fears of an expanding militarism, 135–136
   adherence to discriminatory expectations for minorities and women, 130–131, 240n26
   anti-communism propaganda and, 129–130
   army's willingness to rethink gender roles, 128
   bolstering of the national resolve in the face of communism, 127–128
   characteristics representing an exceptionalist ideology, 126–128
   concept of a traditional American home and, 136–137
   congressional objections to the military's message about, 95, 194, 233–234n90
   consistency and repetition in messaging about, 146–147, 149
   criticisms of messaging over gun control, 147–148, 193–194
   criticisms of the approach to an exceptional message, 146–147
   depictions of an exceptional lifestyle in America, 132–134
   dramatic proclamations made in TBP, 124, 126, 128
   evolution of the exceptionalist perspective, 125–126

American exceptionalism, *continued*
 exceptional perspective presentation,
  145–146, 148
 featuring of the Boy Scouts, 135, 136
 focus on the nation's founding
  principles, 131–132, 240n28
 geopolitical factors in, 127–128
 glossing over of democratic
  shortcomings, 131
 media's role in messaging about,
  126–127
 message of Americanism during the
  Cold War, 128–129
 religion and (*see* religion and TBP)
 sitcoms about the military, 134–135
American Forces Korea Network
 (AFKN), 69
American Forces Vietnam Television
 (AFVN-TV), 69–70
American Militarism on the Small Screen
 (Froula and Takacs), 5
American National Exhibition, 30
American Red Cross, 185, 191
American Research Bureau (ARB),
 66–67, 227n156
America's New Air Power, 26
AMVETS (American Veterans), 21,
 220n24
Anderson, Benedict, 126, 157, 239n7
Angolan War of Independence, 127
Answer to Stalin, 26
anti-communism messaging. *See* Cold
 War; communism
APC. *See* Army Pictorial Center
Appy, Christian, 218n11
ARB (American Research Bureau),
 66–67, 227n156
Arctic Circle, 78–82, 190
Armed Forces Chaplains Board, 138
Armed Forces Hour, 3, 27–28
Armed Forces Information and
 Education (AFI&E), 114, 128, 141
Armed Forces Network (AFN), 3
Armed Forces Network Television (AFN-
 TV), 68–69

Armed Forces Radio and Television
 (AFRTS), 142, 156, 166, 190
Army, US. *See* US Army
Army 75 Personnel Concept Study, 169,
 245n55
Army Center for Military History, 17
Army Combat Developments Command,
 81
Army Hour, The, 93, 218n1
Army Information Program (AIP), 95
Army Materiel Command, US (AMC),
 81, 182
Army Pictorial Center (APC), 4, 13, 34,
 37, 38, 41 (photo), 42 (photo)
 adherence to the single-episode
  format, 54–55, 226n133
 anti-communism narrative, 100 (*see
  also* Cold War; communism)
 army's attempts to influence fictional
  depictions of the military in films,
  85–86
 army's desire to prove its relevancy
  during the Cold War, 6, 20, 56–57,
  111, 112, 190–191
 army's objections to anti-military
  comedy shows, 84–85
 changes to the opening sequence,
  55–60
 congressional members' criticisms of,
  59–60, 66
 congressional objections to funding
  levels, 90, 232–233n73
 connection to Hollywood, 24–25,
  43–45, 46, 195
 cosmetic changes meant to keep
  viewers engaged, 57, 58 (photo), 59
  (photo)
 decision to switch to syndication, 61,
  226n144
 disaster relief films, 186
 distribution enticements offered to
  secondary markets, 68
 funding challenges in late 1950s, 86–87
 integration of actual combat footage,
  52

integration of musical scores, 53–54, 79, 82
leaders' understanding of the persuasive power of TBP, 93–95
management of TBP, 52
military's transition to television (*see* military and television)
name changes, 224n95
narrator changes, 57–58
number of assigned personnel, 43
postwar mix of military and civilian workers, 45, 225n111
prime-time placement of TBP by the networks, 60
production of informational episodes (*see* informational TBP episodes)
production studio establishment, 40–44
refusal to surrender creative control, 87
standard for production of TBP, 51–52
techniques used to highlight science and technology in films, 81–82
typical duties of assigned personnel, 44
use of actors in some productions, 52–53
video advancements, 54, 226n131
See also *Big Picture, The*
Army Special Services, 177
Army Tank Automotive Center, 80, 165
Arness, James, 49
Arnold, Hap, 152
ASDPA (assistant secretary of defense for public affairs), 25
Asians, 164
Association of the United States Army (AUSA), 77
Audio-Visual Support Center (AVSO), 62
Audio-Visual Support Center Operations, 62
Austria, 109

Bailey, Beth, 169, 170
Baldwin, Hanson, 48, 225n114

Baruch, Donald, 85
Battle of San Pietro, The, 44
Battle Report, 3
Battle Report—Pentagon, 83
Battle Report—Washington, 3, 28, 29, 30
Baumholder in West Germany, 166–167, 246n46
Baxter, Frank C., 132
Bay of Pigs, 127, 162
Beedle, William Franklin, Jr., 45
Belgium, 69
Ben-Hur, 139
Bennett, Charles E., 90
Bennett, Robert Russell, 31, 222n72
Benny, Jack, 176
Berlin Wall, 113–115, 162, 237n62
Bernhard, Nancy, 5
Berry, Ken, 178, 249n83
Big Four Conference, 88, 232n64
Big Picture, The (TBP)
    American exceptionalism messaging (*see* American exceptionalism)
    anti-communism message, 17, 80 (*see also* Cold War; communism)
    APC management of (*see* Army Pictorial Center)
    army heritage stories and, 18–19
    army's embrace of television as technology, 34, 35 (photo), 36 (photo), 36–37, 37 (photo), 223n86
    army's relevancy during the Cold War and, 6, 20, 56–57, 190–191
    association with patriotic consciousness, 21
    attempt to influence congressional decision making, 19–21, 219–220nn23–24
    audience appeal, 3
    awards and recognition, 4, 96–97
    catalog, 63 (photo), 227n146
    chronicling of the army's presence in the Arctic Circle, 78–80
    Cold War messaging (*see* Cold War)
    competition from shows about the navy, 83–84

Big Picture, The (TBP), continued
  competition from sitcoms about the
    military, 84–85, 134–135
  congressional criticisms of, 66
  congressional interest in content
    about Korea, 88–89
  congressional objections to perceived
    political content, 93
  congressional support for, 21, 22
  criticisms of, 2–3
  cultivation of the relationship between
    the army and the public, 18–20,
    218–219nn11–13
  depictions of the army's efforts to
    keep up with societal change,
    192–193
  development of a television presence,
    37–38
  distribution and viewership examples,
    64–65, 65 (table)
  distribution overseas, 68–70
  distribution/syndication, 22, 61–64,
    65–66, 67–68, 190
  documentary style, 4
  East vs. West message, 40, 46–48, 56,
    98, 191–192
  editorial changes made to improve
    on a public relations message,
    107–108
  episodes list (see episodes)
  first-person voices use, 6
  first thirteen episodes, 14–17
  highlighting of army technological
    innovation, 74–77
  Hollywood's involvement in (see
    Hollywood)
  integration of musical scores, 53–54,
    79, 82
  Korean War focus of first episodes, 14,
    16–17
  layout of first episodes, 14
  leaders' understanding of the
    persuasive power of, 93–95
  legacy of, 123, 196, 252n11
  limits to its influence on audiences,
    66
  major themes, 2, 46, 55
  narrator in first episodes, 14
  number of episodes, 17, 190
  objections over perceived pro-war
    content in, 89–91, 93, 194
  objections to contents of some
    episodes, 87–89
  original production team, 13
  origin of, 2
  pace of production in late 1950s, 74
  primacy over other shows, 3
  public relations involving the Boy
    Scouts, 80, 135, 136, 187
  quality and availability of author's
    source material, 6–8
  regional distribution model, 9
  shift away from anti-communism
    message, 122–123
  shift toward depicting the modern
    army, 19
  shortcomings in references to
    marginalized groups, 193
  sources of ideas for episodes, 19,
    70–71
  standard for production, 51–52
  television ratings after syndication,
    66–67, 228n165
  termination of production, 95–96,
    189–190, 195–196
  topics featured, 4
  use as propaganda and policy, 3, 4–5,
    217n4
  use of dialogue in first episodes, 15
  value as a record of the Korean War, 17
  Vietnam War messaging (see Vietnam
    War)
Billboard, 66
Binger, Lester, 43
Birmingham, Alabama, 166
Blue Badge series, 37–38, 51, 58, 150
Bluem, A. William, 5, 33, 53, 55
Bogle, Lori, 140
Boy Scouts, 80, 135, 136, 187
Boys Town School, 187
Bradley, Omar, 161
Broger, John C., 141, 142, 242n71

Brown, Helen Gurley, 248n63
Brown, Joe E., 176
Brown, William Jr., 13, 218n2
Brown v. Board of Education, 130, 163
Bruton, Carl, 1, 2, 13, 14, 36, 60
Burkey, David, 1, 2, 13
Burr, Raymond, 121

Caine Mutiny, The (Wouk), 85
Camp Century, Greenland, 79, 80, 187
Canada, 111–112
Canadian Broadcast Network, 112
Capra, Frank, 33, 44, 129, 238n69
CBS, 23, 29, 31, 60, 220n30
Central Film and Equipment Exchange Office, 61
Chamberlain, Neville, 233n81
Chicago Fire (1871), 185
China, 112, 123
CIB (Combat Infantryman Badge), 37
Civilian Marksmanship Program (CMP), 147
Civil Rights Act (1964), 166
Clark, Benjamin, 164
Clarke, Bruce C., 143
code of conduct, 101–103, 235n13
Cold War, 10
    America's commitment to Europe and, 104–105
    America's commitment to West Germany and, 105–108
    anti-communism propaganda production role of TBP, 105–108, 129–130
    army's desire to prove its relevancy during, 6, 20, 111, 112, 190–191
    Berlin Wall and, 113–115
    code of conduct development, 101–103, 235n13
    Cuban Missile Crisis and, 115
    East vs. West message, 29, 40, 98, 100, 102–103, 105, 110, 191, 222n66, 235n21
    educating of Americans about NATO, 109–112, 237n46
    educating of Americans about SEATO, 112
    embracing of soft power to confront communism, 99–100, 112–113, 234n5
    focus on the nation's founding principles, 103–104, 131–132
    geopolitical landscape in the late 1950s, 30
    HUAC hearings, 24, 221n45, 235n27
    legacy of TBP during, 2, 3, 4, 123, 128–129
    message of Americanism during, 128–129
    military-industrial complex and, 182, 250n103
    propaganda and policy promoted through television, 23, 24, 221n46
    shift away from anti-communism message, 122–123
    TBP episodes about the military around the globe, 109, 236nn42–43
    Vietnam War messaging and (*see* Vietnam War)
    See also communism
Cold War, Cool Medium: Television, McCarthyism, and American Culture (Doherty), 5
Cold War, The: Act I, II and III, 26
"Cold War as Entertainment in Fifties Television, The" (MacDonald), 5
Collins, Joseph Lawton, 155
Colonna, Jerry, 48
Combat Infantryman Badge (CIB), 37
Commission on the Status of Women, 248n63
communism
    anti-communism messaging, 17, 80, 100
    anti-communism messaging and religion, 138
    anti-communism propaganda, 129–130
    anti-communism television programming, 28–29, 56

communism, *continued*
    bolstering of the national resolve in the face of, 127–128
    embracing of soft power to confront, 99–100, 112–113, 234n5
    HUAC hearings, 24, 221n45
    shift away from anti-communism message by TBP, 122–123
    See also Cold War
Congo Crisis, 127
Congress
    congressional support for TBP, 21, 22
    criticisms of APC, 59–60, 66
    informational TBP episodes on members of Congress, 154
    interest in content about Korea, 88–89
    objections over perceived pro-war content in TBP, 89–91, 194
    objections to APC funding levels, 90, 232–233n73
    objections to perceived political content in TBP, 93
    objections to the military's message about exceptionalism, 95, 194, 233–234n90
    TBP's attempt to influence, 19–21, 219–220nn23–24
Congressional Record, 20–21, 21, 22
conscription (draft), 57, 83, 169, 186–187, 226n142, 231n40
consumerism, 23, 30
CONUS, 143, 243n76
Crean, Jeffrey, 5
Crisis in Korea, 29
Cronkite, Walter, 29, 33, 48, 226n135
Crusade in Europe, 4, 26, 51, 67
Crusade in the Pacific, 31, 51, 55, 67, 72, 152
Cuban Missile Crisis (1962), 115, 162, 219n23
Cuban Revolution (1959), 30, 127
Cukor, George, 45, 224n109
Cumings, Bruce, 135

Daly, John, 135, 241n41
Dean, William, 88

Defense Language Institute (DLI), 159
De Gaulle, Charles, 236n43
Democratic National Convention, 1948, 24
Denmark, 80, 111
Department of Defense (DOD), 25
Department of Defense Dependent Schools system (DoDDS), 245n15
Des Moines, Iowa, 64–65, 65 (table), 227n154
de Tocqueville, Alexis, 125
Diller, Phyllis, 50
Dillon, Charles, 26, 28
diversity in the army
    army's embracing of integration, 166–167
    changes in the proportion of blacks in the military, 163
    missing mention of minority groups in some TBP episodes, 163–164
    racial tensions and progress, 165–167, 246n46
    shortcomings in TBP references to marginalized groups, 193
    TBP depictions of integration in the military in the 1960s, 165
    TBP's advocacy of women's rights and racial integration, 171–172
DLI (Defense Language Institute), 159
Documentary in American Television (Bluem), 5
DOD (Department of Defense), 25
Dodd, Thomas J., 148
Dodge, Charles G., 94
Doherty, Thomas, 5
Dominican Civil War, 127
draft (conscription), 57, 83, 169, 186–187, 226n142, 231n40
DuMont Television Network, 23, 27–28, 29, 220n30, 222n61

Eisenhower, Dwight D.
    Bob Hope and, 177
    code of conduct development and, 101
    concerns about over-producing military documentaries, 53

concerns over an expanding
militarism, 136, 250n103
Crusade in Europe and, 26
East vs. West strategy, 99
embrace of television, 26–27, 221n57
encouragement of physical fitness,
178–179
"New Look" focus of the army and, 73
racial tensions and, 165
support of a civil-military religious
connection, 139, 142
TBP episode about, 152, 153, 161
Ellington, William, 52
Emmys, 4, 26, 31, 97, 139, 221n55
England, 69
episodes
"3rd Armored Division, The—
Spearhead," 104
"8th Infantry Division," 104
"Action Vietnam," 117, 118
"Aid to Nationalist China," 112
"Alaskan Earthquake," 185
"Alaska—The Outpost State," 155–156
"Alexandria: City of Understanding,"
184–185, 250–251n108
"All the Word to All the Troops," 156
"Americal Division, The," 120
"American Soldier," 145, 146
"American Way of Life, The," 137
"America on the Move," 11, 124, 126,
128, 217n8
"Armed Forces Assistance to Korea,"
100
"Armored Combat Power," 70
"Army Aviation," 73
"Army Ballistic Missile Agency," 190
"Army Chaplain, The—Yesterday and
Today," 140, 195
"Army Chaplains, The," 138, 195
"Army Combat Team, The," 37
"Army Digest No. 3," 188
"Army in Action," 55, 151
"Army in Action—Years of Menace,"
127, 239n11
"Army Language School," 158–159
"Army Medical Corps, The," 73

"Army Moves, An," 163, 192
"Army Nurse, The," 171, 172 (photo)
"Army Nurse, The: Soldier of Mercy,"
171
"Army Nurse Story, The," 171
"Army's All-Americans, The," 179, 180
"Army Satellites," 75, 190
"Army's Civilians, The," 12, 180–181,
184
"Army's Helping Hand, The," 113
"Army's Music Men, The," 159
"Army's Other Role, The," 185, 191
"Army Talent Show," 178
"Army Technical Schools in Europe,"
157
"Army Transportation Corps," 163
"Assignment Iran," 109
"Atomic Battlefield," 57
"Atrocities in Korea," 6, 7, 56, 87–89,
89, 232n69
"Battle of Manila," 152
"Battle of Salerno," 151
"Battle of San Pietro," 4, 151
"Battle of the Bulge," 151
"Beyond the Call," 154
"Big Red One, The," 58, 150
"Blue Badge Series," 37–38
"Border Watchers, The," 108, 191
"Boys Town, U.S.A.," 187
"Bridge, The," 140
"Broken Bridge," 46
"Call Me Mister," 159
"Challenge of Ideas," 46, 103, 129,
132, 195
"Chaplain and the Commander, The,"
140, 195
"Character Guidance," 102
"Christmas in Korea," 6, 39, 138, 144,
223n93
"Citizen Soldier, The," 37, 156
"Citizen Soldier—Community
Leader," 185, 192
"Civil Assistance, Korea," 38
"Code of Conduct," 129
"Code of the Fighting Man," 102,
102–103

episodes, *continued*

"Combat Soldier, The," 37
"Common Defense, The," 147
"Day in America, A," 123, 137
"Day in Korea, A," 38
"D-Day Anniversary," 154
"D-Day Convoy to Normandy," 151
"Decade of NATO," 110, 191
"Defense against Enemy
   Propaganda," 129
"Defense of Japan," 109
"Division in Europe," 104
"Drill Sergeant," 95
"Duty, Honor, Country," 37, 160
"Education in the Army," 157
"Eisenhower Story, The," 153
"Escape from a Prisoner of War
   Camp," 101, 102
"Exercise Arctic Night," 56, 190
"Eyes and Ears of the Army, The," 73
"Feminine Touch, The," 168, 170, 192
"Fight for Vietnam, The," 116, 119, 145
"Foreign Nationals," 182
"General Bradley Story, The," 152
"General MacArthur Story, The," 152
"General Marshall Story, The," 152,
   153
"German Youth Activities," 105, 106,
   191
"Germany Today," 108
"Graduate: Reserve Officers' Training
   Corps," 159
"Guided Missiles," 75, 190
"Hall of Heroes," 153 (photo)
"Helsinki Olympics," 179
"Hidden War in Vietnam," 49, 52, 53,
   91, 94, 116, 122, 145, 194
"History of Aviation, The," 154
"History of Cavalry, The," 18, 19, 70,
   163, 164, 193, 219n17
"Ice Cap," 60, 81
"Information and Education
   Overseas," 156
"Invasion of Southern France," 151
"Japan—Our Far East Partner," 112
"Korea and You," 100

"Korean Wind-Up," 38, 58, 60
"Korea Today," 39
"Language Power for Peach," 159
"Largest School House in the World,
   The," 157, 158
"Making of a West Pointer, The," 160
"Meeting Tomorrow's Challenge," 20,
   81, 123
"Military Justice," 53
"Military Police Town Patrol," 52
"Missile Man," 190
"Missile on Target," 190
"Mission of the Army, The," 37
"Mister Army," 86
"Mouth-to-Mouth Resuscitation," 159
"Nation Builds under Fire, A," 50,
   226n138
"NATO Maneuvers," 110
"NATO: Partners in Peace," 110
"NATO: The Changed Face of
   Europe," 110, 111
"Ninth Infantry Division, The," 120,
   167
"Nurses in the Army," 170, 192
"OCS Fort Sill," 161, 164, 165
"OCS Story, The," 161, 165, 192
"Of Soldiers and Altars," 143, 196
"Old Glory," 18
"One Week in October," 115
"Operation Blue Jay," 60, 78, 122, 190
"Operation Friendly Hand," 105, 106,
   107, 191
"Operation Lead Dog," 19, 56, 190
"Operation Montagnard," 116, 119
"Operation Noah," 184, 191
"Operation Scoreboard," 179, 180
"Opportunity to Learn," 157
"Ottumwa, U.S.A.," 65, 133, 137
"Our Heritage," 18, 132
"Partners in Freedom," 191
"Partners in Progress," 19
"Patterns of History," 18
"Pay Off in the Pacific," 152
"Pentagon Report," 115
"Pentomic 101st," 74
"Pentomic Army," 74

"Pentomic Seventh Army," 74
"People to People," 105, 106, 108, 143, 191
"Pictorial History of the U.S. Cavalry, A," 163
"Pictorial Report No. 17," 245n18
"Pictorial Report No. 23," 34
"Pictorial Report No. 26," 133, 137
"Pictorial Report No. 4," 245n18
"Pioneering for Tomorrow," 20, 81, 181–182
"Prelude to Taps," 146
"Progress to Peace," 121
"Ready around the World," 109
"Red Diamond, The," 96–97
"Religious Emphasis Day in Philadelphia," 138–139, 140, 195
"Road to the Wall," 114
"R.O.T.C.—A Pattern for Progress," 160, 165
"ROTC Summer Training," 159
"Salute to the Canadian Army," 111
"Science Moves the Army," 54, 80, 165, 181–182
"Screaming Eagles in Vietnam," 49, 120, 177
"Shape of the Nation," 48, 179
"Sharper Sword and Stronger Shield, A," 74
"Soldier in Austria," 109, 236n42
"Soldier in Berlin," 58, 98, 191
"Soldier in Europe," 104, 191
"Soldier in France," 109, 191
"Soldier in Panama," 109, 141, 191
"Soldiers at Law," 159
"Soldier's Christmas, The," 137, 144
"Soldiers' Heritage, The," 145
"Song of the Soldier, The," 4, 97, 178
"Southeast Asian Treaty Organization (SEATO) Nations," 191
"Special Forces," 57
"Sports for All," 179
"Story of American Forces Network, The," 156, 245n13
"Story of Stars and Stripes, The," 156
"Thayer of West Point," 87

"There Is a Way," 57
"Third Division in Korea," 46
"Third Korean Winter," 38
"To Keep and Bear Arms," 21, 147, 193
"Tools for a Modern Army," 60, 74, 181
"Tools for Learning," 157
"Top of the World," 81, 122
"To Serve a Soldier," 177
"Toward a Better Environment," 123
"Turning of the Tide, The," 6
"TV in the Army," 34
"Unique War, The," 117, 118, 119, 194
"United Nations Offensive, The," 46
"United Services Organization (USO)," 87
"United Services Organization (USO): Wherever They Go," 174
"United States Army Europe," 191
"UN Line Is Stabilized While Truce Talks Continue, The," 6, 36–37
"USAREUR Story, Parts I and II," 104, 143
"U.S. Army Advisor in Vietnam," 116, 194
"U.S. Army and the Boy Scouts," 80, 111, 135, 187
"U.S. Army in Berlin: Checkpoint Charlie," 105, 114
"U.S. Army in Berlin: Timetable for Crisis," 105, 114
"U.S. Army in Space and under the Sea, The," 81
"U.S. Army in the Andes," 141
"U.S. Army Language School," 158–159
"USMAAG Germany," 105
"USO—30 Years of Service," 174
"U.S. Sixth Corps," 44, 151, 164
"Vietnam Crucible," 122
"Vietnam Village Reborn," 119
"Visit to Mars, A," 123
"WAC Is a Soldier, Too, The," 168, 170
"West Berlin Struggle, The," 108

episodes, *continued*
  "West Point—Education for
     Leadership," 160, 192
  "When the Chips are Down," 49
  "Why NATO?," 110
  "Why Vietnam?," 91, 117, 118
  "Women in the Army," 168
  "You in Japan," 113, 141
  "Young American Leaders," 162
  "Your Army Reports Number 17," 7,
     91
  "Your Defense," 89
  "Your Military Neighbor," 185, 192
Europe, 30, 80, 104–105, 109–112,
     222n68, 237n46
Explorer I, 75

Facts We Face, The, 3, 29, 30, 83
Far East Broadcasting Company (FEBC),
     141
Far East Network (FEN), 69
Federal Communications Commission
     (FCC), 22–23, 220n34
Firestone, Harvey, Jr., 174
Flight, 31
Flint, Carl, 13, 220n2
France, 69, 236n43
Freedoms Foundation, 4, 31, 96,
     96 (photo), 139, 142, 234n92,
     242–243nn71–73
Friedan, Betty, 248n63
Froehlke, Robert F., 169
From Here to Eternity (Jones), 85, 86
Froula, Anna, 5
Fulbright, J. William, 51, 60, 66, 89,
     90–91, 93, 95, 121, 122, 194, 195,
     217n4, 238n75

Galax, Virginia, 133
Gemütlichkeit, 106, 107, 236n30
Germany, 183
German Youth Activities (GYA), 105–106
Get Smart, 70
Greenberg, Benjamin S., 27
Greene, Lorne, 48
Greenland, 78–80, 81–82, 187

Groves, Leslie R., 244n3
Gruenther, Alfred M., 185
Gulf of Tonkin (1964), 116, 118, 238n66
Gun Control Act (1968), 244n88
gun control messaging, 21, 147–148,
     193–194
*Guts and Glory: The Making of the
     American Military Image in Film*
     (Suid), 5, 85
GYA (German Youth Activities), 105–106

Hall, William E., 173
Hannah, John A., 129, 240n18
Harkins, Paul D., 91, 194
Harry Diamond Laboratories, 182
Hartness, Harlan N., 243n73
Hayes, Helen, 48, 225n114
Hennock, Frieda Barkin, 220n34
Hispanics, 164
Hodges, Courtney H., 155
Holden, John R., 21
Holden, William, 45
Hollywood
     APC's connection to, 24–25, 43–45,
        46, 195
     contributions to TBP from celebrity
        figures, 44–45, 46–50, 120
     television and the military and, 24–25
Hollywood's Cold War (Shaw), 5, 119
Holm, Celeste, 176, 248n75
Honest John missile, 56, 74
Hope, Bob, 48, 49–50, 120, 174, 175
     (photo), 176, 177, 180, 249n89
House Un-American Activities
     Committee (HUAC), 24, 221n45,
     235n27
Humphrey, Hubert H., 50, 225n119
Hungarian Revolution (1956), 30, 111,
     127
Huston, John, 4, 44

IGY (International Geophysical Year), 79
*Index of Army Motion Pictures and
     Related Audio-Visual Aids,* 62
Industry on Parade, 66
In Focus, 230n19

informational TBP episodes
  on acts of valor, 154–155
  on educational opportunities for
    soldiers, 156–158, 188–189, 245n15
  on language training, 158–159
  on members of Congress, 154
  on military leadership development,
    159–161, 162
  non-controversial nature of, 155–156
  on the Pacific Theater, 152
  popularity of episodes on military
    history, 151
  on senior military leaders, 152–154
  on specialized training, 159
  in support of recruitment, 161–162
  TBP's position in the military
    community, 157
  on World War II, 151
Information Officer's Guide, 3
International Film Festival, 97
International Geophysical Year (IGY), 79
I Spy, 246n45
Italy, 69

James, David E., 118
Japan, 69, 112, 183
Japanese Americans, 164, 193
Johnson, Lyndon B., 118, 177, 180, 184
Jolson, Al, 46
Jones, James, 85
Julia, 246n45
Junior Essex Troop, 188

Kackman, Michael, 126, 239n7
Kahana, Jonathan, 23
Kefauver, Estes, 221n45
Keim, Robert P., 27, 222n62
Kennan, George F., 99, 136, 234n7
Kennedy, John F., 26, 48, 127, 135, 177,
    178, 179
Kennedy, Robert, 148, 193
Khrushchev, Nikita, 30, 115
King, Martin Luther, Jr., 148, 193
Kirby, Edward M., 13, 218n3
Kitchen Debate, 30
Koedel, Simon Emil, 42

Korean War, 7, 127
  anti-communism television
    programming, 28–29, 56
  concern over the fortitude of POWs,
    101–102, 235n14
  congressional interest in TBP content
    about, 88–89
  depictions of in TBP, 87–88
  East vs. West message, 29, 40, 100,
    102–103, 222n66
  focus on in TBP, 14, 17
  military's partnership with TV
    networks during, 26
  military TV's return to the subject of,
    38–40, 223n92
  postwar manpower drawdown, 73
  production techniques used to
    explain, 16–17
  television distribution of TBP
    following, 69
  TV network's offerings during, 29–30
Kyes, Roger M., 88

Labella, John, 151
Laderman, Scott, 121
La Guardia, Fiorello H., 40
Laurents, Arthur, 44, 45
Lebovic, Sam, 173
Legion of Merit, 44, 224n108
Let There Be Light, 44
Life Is Worth Living, 139, 242n58
Little Rock, Arkansas, 165
Lookout Mountain Laboratory, 76,
    229n15

MacArthur, Douglas, 16, 161
MacDonald, J. Fred, 5
Mailer, Norman, 85
Manifest Destiny, 145, 243n79
Mansfield, James, 58
Mansfield, Mike, 148
March of Time, 26, 31, 34
March on Washington (1963), 166
Martin, Thomas E., 242n65
M*A*S*H, 134–135
Massey, Raymond, 48, 154

Matthau, Walter, 48, 49 (photo), 154

May, Elaine Tyler, 130, 136, 137

McCarthy, Joseph "Tail Gunner Joe," 24, 131, 142, 221n46, 235n27, 240n28, 242n69

McGee, Frank, 48, 225n114

McNair Barracks in Berlin, 166–167, 246n46

Meloy, G. S., 86, 226n144, 228n2

Meredith, James, 165

Middleton, Harry, 133–134

Militant Liberty, 131, 141, 242n65

military and television
  anti-communism programming, 28–29
  anti-communist, American exceptionalism message, 30
  army's embrace of television as technology, 34, 35 (photo), 36 (photo), 36–37, 37 (photo), 223n86
  cancellation of *Battle Report*, 29
  criticisms of a network-air force documentary, 33
  disagreements over content of *Armed Forces Hour*, 27–28
  Eisenhower's embrace of television, 26–27
  establishment of the military documentary as a genre, 33–34
  first documentary series produced, 26–27
  Korean War focus, 28–30, 38–40, 223n92
  military shows from 1949–1959, 32 (table)
  network partnerships with military branches, 26, 31
  OPI mission and, 25
  praise for network-navy documentaries, 31
  relationship with Hollywood and, 24–25
  TBP's development of a television presence, 37–38
  value and reach of airtime provided by the networks, 25–26, 221nn52–53
  See also Army Pictorial Center

Mitchum, Robert, 49

Morale Branch, 128

Mundey, Lisa, 83, 230n36

Murphy, Audie, 46, 225n112

Murrow, Edward R., 33, 47, 48, 103, 110

Naked and the Dead, The (Mailer), 85

Natick Laboratory, 182

National Academy of Television Arts and Sciences, 4, 97

National Aeronautics and Space Administration (NASA), 77

National Archives and Records Administration (NARA), 5–6, 6–7

National Rifle Association (NRA), 21, 147–148, 193

National Security Bill, 25

National Security Council (NSC), 98

Native Americans, 164

NATO (North Atlantic Treaty Organization), 30, 80, 109–112, 222n68, 234n43, 237n46

Navy Log, 3, 31, 53, 72, 83, 87, 121, 152

NBC, 23, 24, 27–28, 29, 31, 220n30

New Jersey Army National Guard, 188

New York Times, 42, 44, 232n69

Nimitz, Admiral, 152

Nisei, 164, 193

Nixon, Richard, 30, 123, 177

North Atlantic Treaty Organization (NATO), 30, 80, 109–112, 222n68, 234n43, 237n46

Norton Air Force Base, 43

NRA (National Rifle Association), 21, 147–148, 193

NSC (National Security Council), 98

Nye, Joseph S., 234n5

Office of Public Information (OPI), 25, 37

Office of the Chief of Information (OCINFO), 59–60

Officer Candidate School (OCS), 159, 161, 164, 165

Olympic Games, 179

O'Neill, Edward A., 233n79

On Guard, 3, 31
Operation Paperclip, 229n17
Osgood, Kenneth, 130, 141

Palmer, Thomas, 128
Paramount, 41
Parker, Quanah, 164
Paskarbis, Gudrun, 107
Patton, George, 152, 161
Peabody Award, 26, 31, 221n55
Pentagon, 29
Pentagon Propaganda Machine, The
    (Fulbright), 90–91, 233n79
Phil Silvers Show, 84, 135
Porter, Charles O., 21, 88
President's Committee on Religion and
    Welfare in the Armed Forces, 137
President's Council on Youth Fitness,
    179
Public Information Division (PID), 61,
    84
Pyle, Ernie, 1, 15, 16, 36, 217n1

Queen, Stuart, 58, 98, 101
Quinn, William W. "Buffalo Bill," 37–38,
    58, 93, 94 (photo), 96 (photo), 150

Radford, Arthur W., 141, 243n73
Radio-Television Branch, US Army, 13
Rally Round the Flag, 136
Reagan, Ronald, 48, 154
Red Ball Express, 164, 246n38
Red Buttons Show, 60
Redstone Arsenal, 43, 43 (photo)
Reeves, Rosser, 221n57
religion and TBP
    anti-communism messaging and, 138,
        139, 241n59
    effort to create a Christian ideological
        framework for the military, 141–142
    messaging about faith and freedom,
        140–141
    messaging in support of Christian
        evangelism, 195
    messaging partnership with a
        conservative Christian group, 142

presidential level encouragement of
    religious activities, 125, 137–138,
    241n51, 241n54
propagation of a civil-religious
    connection, 139–140
religion's place in the exceptional
    expression, 125, 138–139, 143–144
spiritual worship presented as
    common cultural ground, 143
troop training centering on religious
    values, 138, 241n53
Report from the Aleutians, 44
Republican National Convention, 1948,
    24
Reserve Officer Training Corps (ROTC),
    159–160, 165
Reuss, Henry, 90
Richmond, Virginia, 64
Ridgway, Matthew, 168
Robe, The, 139
Rodgers, Richard, 31, 223n72

Salomon, Henry "Pete," 31, 222n71
Scott, Robert Lee, Sr., 33
Screen Actors Guild (SAG), 82, 230n35
SEATO (Southeast Asian Treaty
    Organization), 109, 112, 136, 191
Sergeant Bilko, 84
Shadel, Willard F., 29
Shaw, Tony, 5, 119
Sheen, Fulton J., 139
Shinn, Robert, 84
Signal Corps, US Army, 2, 7, 14, 18, 36,
    42, 43, 44, 73, 131, 151, 179
Signal Corps Photographic Center
    (SCPC), 16 (photo), 40, 224n95.
    See also Army Pictorial Center
Slisher, W. E., 19
Smith, Walter Bedell, 88
"Something to Compete with
    Gunsmoke" (Crean), 5
Southeast Asian Treaty Organization
    (SEATO), 109, 112, 136, 191
South Korea, 183. *See also* Korean War
Soviet Union, 30, 123
Special Services Division, 128

Sperry Rand Corporation, 152
Springer, Claudia, 118
Sputnik I, 30, 75
Stars and Stripes, 69, 95, 100, 113–115, 140, 143, 156
Steelman, John R., 28, 222n65
St. John Crèvecoeur, Hector, 125
Storke, Harry P., 87, 89, 112
Stump, Felix, 245n73
Suid, Lawrence, 5, 20, 36, 52, 85, 219n20
Sullivan, Ed, 60

Takacs, Stacy, 5
Taylor, Maxwell, 74
TBP. See *Big Picture, The*
television
    broadcast reach by 1948, 22, 220n30
    connection between viewers and world news, 23–24
    coverage of political events, 24
    factors fueling its growth, 23
    geopolitical landscape in the late 1950s, 30
    limitations imposed on by the FCC, 22–23, 220n34
    military's transition to (*see* military and television)
    number of households with color TVs, 54
    number of sets in the US by 1959, 30
    popularity of by mid-1950s, 23
    promotion of propaganda and policy, 24, 221n46
Ten Commandments, The, 139
"Terms of Reference," 56, 226n139
Tet Offensive (1968), 120, 121
Thayer, Sylvanus, 87
Thomas, Lowell, 48, 225n114
Thurmond, Strom, 242n65
TID (Troop Information Division), 19, 61, 68
Time, Inc., 26, 31
Toast of the Town, 60
Tomb of the Unknowns, 146, 243n80
Tonight Show, 69
Towne, Clair, 85

Troop Information and Education (TI&E), 140, 157
Troop Information Division (TID), 19, 61, 68
Truman, Henry S, 78, 98, 137, 162
Truman administration, 28
Twentieth Century, The, 55, 226n135

Uncommon Valor, 31, 72
Underwood, George V., 95
United Services Organization (USO), 175 (photo)
    Bob Hope and, 174, 175 (photo), 177
    history of, 173
    relationship with the military, 173–174
    representation of women, 176
    TBP episodes about, 174–177
United States Army Europe (USAREUR), 70
US Army, 9, 11–12, 188
    attempts to influence fictional depictions of the military in films, 85–86
    civilian employment numbers, 181
    civilian partnerships, 191–192
    civilians' role in, 180–181, 184
    communities and, 184–187
    competition from navy propaganda, 31, 83–84
    connection with young men, 187–188
    desire to prove its relevancy, 6, 20, 56–57, 72, 74, 79–81, 111, 112, 190–191
    foreign nationals employment, 182–183, 250n105
    highlighting of an Arctic Circle presence, 78–82
    highlighting of army technological innovation through TBP, 74–77, 80–81
    impact of creation of NASA on, 77
    leaders' understanding of the persuasive power of TBP, 93–95
    manpower levels, 161–162
    morale in (*see* United Services Organization)

"New Look" restructuring focus, 73, 75

new Pentomic configuration, 73–74

objections to anti-military comedy shows, 84–85

post-Korean War manpower drawdown, 73

presidential initiatives on fitness, 178–179

production of TBP (see Army Pictorial Center)

promotion of "The Modern Army" theme, 77

public relations and recruitment role of community service films, 186–187

racial integration and (see diversity in the army)

Radio-Television Branch, 13

TBP depictions of integration in the military in the 1960s, 165

TBP episodes about interaction of army units with communities, 184–186

TBP episodes about troop recreation, 177–178

TBP episodes advocating physical fitness, 179–180

TBP episodes highlighting civilian essential roles, 181–182, 184

TBP episodes on military leadership development, 159–161, 162

TBP episodes supporting recruitment, 161–162, 188

use of TBP as propaganda and policy, 3, 4–5, 72, 89–93, 217n4

women and (see women in the army)

US Army Materiel Command (AMC), 81, 182

US Army Motion Picture/Television Production Division, 43

US Army Signal Corps, 2, 7, 14, 18, 36, 42, 43, 44, 73, 131, 151, 179

US Information Agency (USIA), 110, 129, 141, 166

USMAAG (United States Military Assistance Advisory Group), 236n29

US Military Academy at West Point, 37, 159, 160–161, 161

US Military Academy Preparatory School, 57

US Military Assistance Advisory Group (USMAAG), 236n29

US Naval Academy, 161

USO. See United Services Organization

U.S. Television News and Cold War Propaganda (Bernhard), 5

Variety, 42, 67

Victory at Sea, 4, 5, 31, 51, 52, 53, 55, 67, 72, 152

Victory Films, 93, 233n85

Vietnam War
 celebrities' contribution to TBP during, 49–51
 disconnect between reality and the TBP message, 118, 238n69
 efforts to counterbalance negative opinions about, 116–118, 117 (photo)
 final policy message from TBP, 121
 messaging around, 50–51, 118–119
 patronizing tone of TBP's ethnographic treatment of Vietnam, 119–120
 policy themes in TBP episodes, 91, 92 (table), 93
 purpose of TBP episodes about, 116
 TBP's adherence to a message of support for military involvement, 120–122, 194
 TBP's use of manipulated imagery, 119
 television distribution of TBP following, 69–70

Von Braun, Wernher, 76, 229n17

Voting Rights Act (1965), 166

WAC (Women's Air Corps), 167, 170, 247n61

Wallace, Mike, 48

Wall Street Journal, 90

Warner Brothers, 41

Warsaw Pact, 30, 111
Wayne, John, 47 (photo), 48, 49, 50, 104, 120
Weaver, John O., 19, 61, 86, 155
Weaver, Sylvester "Pat," 23
Wells, Reginald, 133–134
West Germany, 69, 113
West Point. *See* US Military Academy at West Point
White House Committee on Health and Fitness, 179
Why We Fight, 34, 44, 129, 238n69
Wilson, Charles, 101
Winthrop, John, 125, 239n4
Wolff, Perry, 33
women in the army
    acceptance into the ranks, 167–168, 247n50
    army's willingness to rethink gender roles, 128

    patronizing depictions of WAC women in TBP, 170, 247n61
    TBP episodes highlighting, 9
    TBP's advocacy of women's rights and racial integration, 171–172
    tone of TBP episodes about the Nurse Corps, 170–171
    value of TBP episodes as a recruiting tool, 169–170
Women's Army Corps (WAC), 167, 170, 247n61
Woronstsoff, Nicholas Jr., 18
Wouk, Herman, 85
WTOP, 60

Zimmermann, Carl, 6, 13, 14, 15 (photo), 16, 16 (photo), 17, 34, 36, 38, 55, 57–58, 73, 74, 157, 218n1, 218n4
Ziv Television Programs, Inc. (ZIV-TV), 66, 227n156